Researching Children's Popular Culture

Despite the
lasting imp
largely ove
Culture: The
children's c

Claudia
graphic and
culture. Ex
dolls, toys,
children's p
the child's
in contemp
challenges
new approa

Claudia M
McGill Un
Don't Look
Teachers (R
studies at
University.
ture, dance
contempora
dolls.

Media, Education and Culture

Series Editors:
David Buckingham, Institute of Education, University of London, U.K., and Julian Sefton-Green, WAC Performing Arts and Media College, U.K.

Cultural Studies has developed rigorous and exciting approaches to pedagogy. The **Media, Education and Culture** series extends the research and debate that is developing in this interface between cultural studies and education.

Digital Diversions: Youth Culture in the Age of Multimedia
Edited by Julian Sefton-Green

Teaching Popular Culture: Beyond Radical Pedagogy
Edited by David Buckingham

Wired Up: Young People and the Electronic Media
Edited by Sue Howard

Teen Spirits: Music and Identity in Media Education
Chris Richards

Fans, Feminism and "Quality" Media
Lyn Thomas

The Making of Citizens: Young People, News and Politics
David Buckingham

Researching Children's Popular Culture: The Cultural Spaces of Childhood
Claudia Mitchell and Jacqueline Reid-Walsh

Researching Children's Popular Culture

The cultural spaces of childhood

Claudia Mitchell and
Jacqueline Reid-Walsh

London and New York

First published 2002
by Routledge
11 New Fetter Lane, London EC4P 4EE

Simultaneously published in the USA and Canada
by Routledge
29 West 35th Street, New York, NY 10001

Routledge is an imprint of the Taylor & Francis Group

Typeset in Garamond by Florence Production Ltd, Stoodleigh, Devon
Printed and bound in Great Britain by The Cromwell Press, Trowbridge, Wiltshire

British Library Cataloguing in Publication Data
A catalogue record for this book is available from the British Library

Library of Congress Cataloging in Publication Data
A catalog record for this book has been requested

ISBN 0–415–23968–0 (hbk)
ISBN 0–415–23969–9 (pbk)

(*Claudia Mitchell*) To Jakob Mitchell Peterli who came into the world just in time to newly inspire us on the significance of childhood as a cultural space.

(*Jacqui Reid-Walsh*) To my father Don Reid who initiated me into the genre of the television western and let me ask questions all the way through.

Contents

Figures

Figures

Acknowledgments

We would like to acknowledge a number of people who inspired and supported us in the writing of *Researching Children's Popular Culture.*

We must begin by acknowledging our series editor David Buckingham, of the Youth and Media Studies Centre at the Institute of Education, University of London. Works like this have to have a "space" in the first place, something David was able to see in encouraging us to conceptualize the book the way we have.

To our many undergraduate and graduate students who over the years have participated in our classes and seminars on children's culture at McGill University and the University of the Witwatersrand, we offer our thanks for their contributions to our thinking and for providing us with specific examples of popular culture that we might have otherwise missed. At McGill these students have been enrolled in the Multicultured Classroom, Childhood as a Cultural Space, the Meanings of Literacy, and the Women's Studies Seminar, and at the University of the Witwatersrand (1999 and 2000) in the Department of English in the Masters in English Education course on Media Studies, and in the module on popular culture within the Centres and Margins course.

To our colleagues, and most especially to Sandra Weber of Concordia University, we say a sincere thanks for their ongoing enthusiasm for our work. We would like to say thank you too to the many friends, graduate students and colleagues with children who have willingly shared photographs and anecdotes of children's culture in action. Barbara Pyontka, in particular, has always come through.

We would also like to acknowledge the participation of those who attended the various conference presentations we have given over the years and which have led into the development of several of the chapters: "Nine going on Seventeen" at the American Educational Research Association (Montreal, 1999); "*Toy Story 2*, Whose story too" at the National and Cultural Identities conference on children's literature (University of Reading, 2001), and "Girls, digital technology and popular culture" at the Girlhood – A New Feminist Order Conference (King's College, November, 2001).

We are greatly indebted to Farah Malik, our Research Assistant at McGill University whose dedication, interest and enthusiasm, insights, and hard work have been crucial in getting the manuscript finished. We would also like to thank Andrea Borrelli for her work in the early stages of this book, and Honore Kerwin-Borrelli for her ongoing assistance in looking after the "business" side of writing and publishing.

Our children have had no small role in the writing of this book. Dorian Mitchell and Krista Walsh and their friends who have been "passing through childhood" as we have been working on the book have, as informants, provided us with endless contemporary data. Krista has also been helpful in sharing her digital literacy.

We would also like to acknowledge the contributions of Sarah and Rebecca Mitchell, Zac Campbell, and Marcus Peterli for the various family anecdotes, memory pieces, and photographs that have now found their way into the chapters of this book.

Finally, we would like to acknowledge the central role of our partners, Ann Smith and Michael Walsh. At various points, Ann encouraged us to rethink both the content and organization of the book, offered her own insights on childhood culture, provided excellent suggestions for revision, and generally played a key editing role. Both guided us in our work on "the cyber frontier" of Chapter 5: Michael as a specialist in the field of digital technology, especially the Web, and Ann as a specialist in literary theory.

Introduction

A Fairy Tale Beginning

As an entry point to this book, we use a personal recollection, a childhood memory of watching Disney's *Snow White and the Seven Dwarfs*. Jacqui recalls, as a child, being terrified by the scene in the film where the evil stepmother stands on a cliff shrieking and gesticulating her anger against the young woman who, according to the magic mirror, is the "most beautiful of all." As a near-sighted child, frozen in her seat in the darkened movie theater, the impact of the Gothic image of the witch on her overrode any possible pleasure in any conventional "happy ending" Disney could produce in his demonstration of the triumph of good over evil. Jacqui recalls enduring nightmares for several days after this experience, and she remembers being haunted by images of an apparently omnipotent evil bearing down on her. Afterwards, as she remembers it, she preferred to read fairy tales, especially the "original" versions, or to watch Disney fairy tales on the small television screen, where she was in control of her mobility, so different from being unable to move around in the cinema, and where she had the power to close the book or turn off the television set. While this memory of watching *Snow White and the Seven Dwarfs* could be interpreted in many ways, ranging from one based on Jungian psychoanalysis to one rooted in a feminist analysis of stereotypes, what interests us is the contrast between the size, mobility and potency of the popular image of evil and the fixity and powerlessness of the small (naive) child. The contrast in size is such that the individual child seems pitted against a witch=feminine ogre=masculine ogre of such proportions that it has the power of a collective force.

It has often seemed to us that in the popular literature on children and popular culture as well as in some of the critical literature, variations of this Gothic image similarly haunt adults concerned about childhood culture. Popular culture, especially mass media culture, is often constructed as a monolithic giant, while the child is depicted as a powerless object who is about to be consumed. The researchers seem to see themselves as the off-screen saviors, rushing in to save the child who is unable to save himself or herself: the researchers, battling and conquering evil, play the role of the prince in fairy tales. Or perhaps they see themselves as the hero of the western – riding in on a white horse and saving the day!

Other cultural critics, notably John Fiske (1987, 1993), argue for a more potent position for the viewer of popular culture, one that allows agency: the "user" of popular culture can construct meanings that are in opposition to, or which resist, the status quo. Although Fiske's work does not specifically address children, this line of reasoning provides a much-needed counter argument, in that a more optimistic account is presented, one which liberates the user of popular culture from being seen to be in the position of cultural dupe. In their attempts to create an alternative, more optimistic view of the relation between children (as disenfranchised members of society) and the popular mass media, these critics seek to empower the individual child. In terms of the initial image, this view could be seen as superimposing a David and Goliath story on top of the fairy tale: through subversive readings the individual child can overcome the power of the media, and despite the odds, win the battle.

Occupying a position that combines a cultural studies approach with ethnographic studies of children and their use of popular media, other critics, notably David Buckingham, have posited the idea of children existing as a "situated audience" vis-à-vis the television, or a film. In being considered to be members of an audience, and for this to be seen to be a social practice, not a fixed state, children as viewers are recognized as possessing the ability to make meaning. Accordingly, children possess limited power within social, economic, and developmental age-delineated constraints (Buckingham 1993: 13–15). Working within a similar rubric, Henry Jenkins adapts de Certeau's notion of a "nomadic poaching" based on critical distance to argue that, on the contrary, the close emotional relationship between popular culture (television) fans and their material enables them to feel free to criticize, consume and remake texts (Jenkins 1992: 61–3). Thus, if we were to superimpose a fairy tale onto these kinds of theoretical readings, we could draw upon Grimm's version of "Hansel and Gretel" where the children work together and use their knowledge strategically in order to turn the tables on the witch. The image of the witch burning within a small, confined oven, while the children escape into the open space to return home, enacts an "eye for an eye" justice, while encouraging an image of children and childhood that combines notions of limited agency, companionship, and the possibility of collective action.

Each of these readings suggests to us that the study of children's popular culture has a great deal to say about childhood, and the relationship of adults to childhood. More specifically, they highlight the possibilities for seeing popular culture as an "entry point" in and of itself for studying childhood as an area that is informed by such features as the age, status, and insider-knowledge of children themselves, the ephemerality – and long-lastingness – of the material culture under study, as well as the centrality of childhood (and memories and experiences of childhood) in adulthood. Such a perspective, however, is one that brings with it a number of key challenges in terms of methodology. How, for example, can adults engage the child-as-expert in the study of a form of material culture that is of low status and often outside the boundaries of what is accepted as "quality" children's play? What credibility does the adult "outsider" bring to the research site? How might we legitimize (or at least make transparent) the role of parent-researchers in childhood research? And where do we engage in such studies, if, for example, Barbies or Pokemon cards are in circulation only outside of such "official" research sites as classrooms? How might we conduct fieldwork in the spaces where popular culture is more naturally encountered – movie theaters, shopping malls and children's bedrooms? Does the study of childhood within the social sciences only involve doing fieldwork with child-participants, and where do we make a space for childhood-in-memory as a primary data source? To what extent can social-science researchers begin to engage more directly in working with material culture as text-based field sites? Finally, how do we blend and adapt methodologies from a variety of areas such as visual studies, biographical studies through memory and autobiography, studies in material culture and historical studies – all areas that are not necessarily associated with researching children's popular culture and contemporary childhood?

At the heart of this book is the idea of children's popular culture as a rich research site, one made up of a number of spaces for "*doing research*." As Alison James, Chris Jenks, and Alan Prout write:

> It is timely, not to say urgent, that a discussion about methods of researching childhood takes place. In the first place there is a need to pay heed to methodology lest the upsurge of research activity about children and childhood fails to reap a proper and considered benefit. Furthermore, given the particular character of childhood as a phenomenon, the reconstruction of children as social actors and the consequent view of children as the new subjects, rather than objects of research, we should pause to ask whether our standard research techniques, which as social scientists we so readily employ, are indeed the most appropriate. Although, in our view, studying children need not of itself necessitate the adoption of new or exotic techniques, time to reflect may allow us to be more *adventurous* and more *critical* of the standard methodological array (emphasis added, 1998: 191).

While we make no claims to being exhaustive in our approach, we do pay attention to the need to reflect on the appropriateness of standard research techniques in the study of a cultural space that is infused with boundary issues about commodification, marketing and the sanctity of childhood, boundary debates about "high" and "low" culture and the ensuing moral panics, boundaries between pleasure and taste, and, as we explore in the "Mind the Gap" section that follows, the blurring of boundaries within contemporary popular culture itself in relation to childhood and adulthood.

Mind the Gap

> There we are in the flea market stall, in Rosebank, which features temporary tattoos – my partner and I, two women who are in our 50s, and Monique and Estelle, two girls who are all of 9. As two pairs, awaiting our respective turns to be treated by the tattoo artist, we establish a bond in each other's designs. Monique and Estelle have opted for matching butterflies. My partner and I go for a more medieval-type of design to be painted on to our wrists. Some might regard my partner and me as the "odd women out" – after all, what do women of our age want with tattoos, and as our adult children might wonder "whatever will happen when you are put into nursing homes – tattoos and all?" We, on the other hand, look at Monique and Estelle as babes in a post-Spice Girls age dressed in scant tops, fully apparent belly buttons, hip-hugger bell bottoms and 3-inch sandals and wonder why, at age nine, they aren't at home playing hopscotch or house? (Claudia's fieldnotes).

The concerns that adults might have for the two young girls Monique and Estelle, and their foray into the tattoo parlor, however temporary the tattoos may be, could be read in the context of a number of issues related to popular culture and childhood. These issues range from concerns about the eroticization of young girls, to some "hurried girlhood" version of David Elkind's "hurried childhood" (1982), to a sense that somehow childhood innocence as a period of life separate from the world of adults has been disturbed, to the idea of the actual death of childhood. But the tattoos also invite a number of readings related to the fluidity of boundaries between childhood, adolescence, and adulthood so that someone might ask what either of the two pairs – the little girls or the fifty-something women – is doing in the tattoo parlor since neither seems to be appropriately acting their ages: two middle-aged women appearing to act out a youth fantasy, and two little girls appearing to act like "wannabes" in relation to their big sisters. There is here a sense of what Joe Kincheloe (1998) calls the "adultified" child (Estelle or Monique) and the "childified" adult (Claudia or Ann). This is something that can now be seen in a visit to any outlet of The Gap clothing store found in many shopping malls and downtown areas of the U.K., North America, Germany, France, and Japan. Indeed, contrary to the provocative 1991 Gap ad "Every generation has its Gap," there is no obvious generation gap when it comes to buying at The Gap but rather an invitation to "mind the Gap" – to pay attention to the one style (rather than the one size) that fits all. The several different floors of The Gap outlet in Montreal, for example – two devoted to Gap "regular" and the other devoted to Gap Kids and babies – are virtually indistinguishable at a distance in relation to most of the product lines. (The main exceptions, of course, have to do with the dome fasteners on overalls in the baby section of Gap Kids for ease of diapering, and similarly with the size and features of Gap Kids mannequins.) This indistinguishability then could perhaps suggest a one-age-fits-all approach to fashion – or even an infantilization of fashion! The Gap television ads, too, pick up on this marketed indistinguishability and blurring of boundaries by incorporating into the text of the advertisement multi-aged music to accompany the images: swing music from the 1940s is recast as contemporary, or "Mellow Yellow" from the 1960s is remixed to sound as "with-it" to five-year-olds as to their Boomer grandparents.[1]

Another aspect of what we call "minding the gap" was evident at a session on "girling popular culture" at the annual conference of the Modern Languages Association held in Chicago (December 1999). There, one of the speakers – Cynthia J. Fuchs – noting the range of meanings associated with "girl power" or "girrrrl power" made the observation that there are at least five generations of females who might classify themselves or who might be classified as girls! She was speaking, of course, of how different generations are represented in such phenomena as girl-group rock bands from Generation X, 55-year-old women as Gap shoppers along with their five-year-old Gap Kid granddaughters, little girls playing Barbie or My Little Pony, representations of Monica Lewinsky as "just a girl," American Girlhood viewed as a commodity in the form of the American Girlhood dolls, books, trading cards and stores, as well as the pre-teen group of "tween girls" who now wield so much shopping power that they have their own catalogs, stores, and fashions.

But fashion style and girl-texts are not the only sites for intergenerational interrogation. Prime-time animated television programs are no longer the "just cartoons" of *Bugs Bunny* or *Yogi Bear* directed towards children but also include *The Simpsons*, *Bob and Margaret*, *Beavis and Butthead* and *South Park*, shows which have a mature rating. Given the X-rated content of *South Park*, however, it is not surprising that this program raises questions regarding the suitability of its content for children. Indeed, in the movie *South Park* it is this very issue that is explored. Should Kenny and company, foul-mouthed as they already are, be allowed into an X-rated film that is full of off-color language? The flip side of this question, though, raises the issue about what is suitable for adults. Claudia recalls that when *The Flintstones* television series was first aired in the 1960s, scheduled during prime time on a Monday night, her father would often join her and her brothers in watching it. Her mother, not a television viewer and in any case always tied to doing the weekly ironing on a Monday night, only heard the television dialogue from the kitchen, and regarded it as a regular "father knows best" type of show. Imagine her shock years later when, by accident, she discovered that all those years her husband had been watching a show that was just a child's cartoon series! Related to this issue of who may look at what, in terms of age and suitability, we find it significant that there are now websites on the Internet not only rated, as movies are in terms of "adult" or "general" subject matter, but also even "policed," under the category of "for children only!"

At the same time, it is not always easy to distinguish between who counts as the adult and who counts as the child in terms of being a consumer of popular culture, as we saw in the tattoo episode noted above. An incident told to us by one of our research colleagues Leigh, a parent in his early forties, serves as a strong reminder of both the marketing and research significance of this notion of "minding the gap." Leigh talks of taking his two sons, aged six and nine, to the movie *Toy Story*, the high-tech computer-animated Pixar–Disney film, when it was first released. For the boys it was, as Leigh described it, "one huge toy catalog." As each new toy appeared on the screen they exclaimed, "Cool. . . . Hey, look at Mr. Potato Head! . . . I want that . . . and that . . . and that!" But what mattered for Leigh, the adult, was the apparent "custody battle" going on around these toys, many of which were toys from his childhood (for instance, Mr. Potato Head and Etch A Sketch). He observes that he felt like saying to his sons, in response to their "I want" enthusiasm, "You can't have the Mr. Potato Head – I've already had it!" Based on this anecdote, we feel compelled to ask: "Whose childhood is it anyway?"

Thus, we locate this book within other recent work in the area of age studies more generally where, as Kathleen Woodward (1999: x) observes, "old age and middle age are part of the larger continuum of a discourse on age itself, a system of age that includes infancy, childhood, adolescence and young adulthood." As might be expected, each age is addressed within an emerging body of literature, ranging from titles such as *Constructing and Reconstructing Childhood* (James and Prout 1997); *Pictures of Innocence: The History and Crisis of Ideal Childhood* (Higonnet 1998); *Children's Childhoods Observed and Experienced* (Mayall 1994); *Theorizing Childhood* (James et al. 1998); to *Growing Up and Growing Old* (Hockey and James 1993); *Figuring Age: Women, Bodies, Generations* (Woodward 1999); and *Aging and its Discontents: Freud and Other Fictions* (Woodward 1991). While thus far there has been relatively little cross-over from one area to the other (a notable exception is to be found in the work of Jenny Hockey and Allison James in *Growing Up and Growing Old* (1993) which includes a deconstruction of the notion of old age and "second childhood"), we propose that research which is meant to contest purely biological and essentialist meanings of age must first and foremost seek out methodologies which serve to decolonize particular age forms as monolithic categories (such as the child, the elderly, and so on).

Like Berry Mayall, Allison James, Alan Prout, Chris Jenks, Judith Ennew, and others – who contest the fixed category of "child" – we see our work fitting into the new social studies of childhood. Speaking of the notion of childhood in the U.K., Allison James writes:

> when is a child not a child depends upon what it is doing. For example, at five, children can legally drink alcohol in private but they cannot buy drinks in public places until eighteen years old. At sixteen, on the other hand, they can be bought beer, cider, wine or sherry to be drunk in public as an accompaniment to a meal. At seven a child may withdraw money from his or her Post Office account but cannot earn money until thirteen and he or she can work for two hours a

> day and one on a Sunday. From birth a child may have a Premium Bond in his or her name but cannot buy one until sixteen.
>
> Moreover these classifications vary according to gender. A girl is legally permitted to consent to sexual intercourse at sixteen but a boy can be charged with rape at fourteen years old. A girl can join the armed forces with parental consent at seventeen; a boy can do so at sixteen. . . . The age at which childhood ends and adolescence begins, when adolescence turns to adulthood is both fluid and context specific, despite attempts to bind it legally (1986: 157).

These contradictions are being investigated in a variety of settings. Lise Bird (1994), for example, in her study of the "after school" domestic work that eleven-year-old children carry out in working- and middle-class families where parents are at work, raises questions about the significance to the child of solitude and responsibility. Indeed, as some of the recent work within the politics of childhood suggests, even very young children can and do participate in decisions about themselves that seem to call into question the idea that by definition as children, they are innocent and unknowing. This is also something that is acknowledged when it comes to the actions and experiences of children during extreme conditions of poverty or war, say in terms of the children who marched in the 1976 riots against apartheid in South Africa, the bravery of Anne Frank, and the labors today of children, especially girls, in sub-Saharan Africa to contribute to the family income, by working on the streets, and so on. Ennew (1994), for example, studies street children within the urban spaces of poverty, and contributes to an understanding of childhood by contesting the idea that children are not capable of caring for themselves. She discusses issues related to situations in which, when street children are offered places in shelters, they find they have much less freedom and fewer opportunities to participate in decision-making. Pamela Reynold's work as a psychologist studying townships in South Africa and tribal areas of Zimbabwe (1996) contests the notion of a universalized childhood. Ironically, children may appear to lose certain rights – or are made to "regain" their innocence when the conditions have changed, not unlike the situation of women during World War II whose femininity was not in question as long as their services were required in munitions factories, but whose "essence" came into question when their services were no longer required.

These concerns, of course, are not unrelated to the context within which children's popular culture is encountered and experienced, located at the beginning of the twenty-first century primarily as a Western phenomenon. It is true, of course, as Mattel, the makers of Barbie, contend, that "Barbie is everywhere" and indeed Barbie can be found in 135 countries (as confirmed by the 1–800 Barbie Information Request line). At the same time, Barbie as she is known, loved or reviled in North America and other Western contexts does not exist in most developing countries as a commodity encountered in quite the same way. Yes, she is "everywhere" – but she is nowhere in the lives of the majority of girls around the world, something that can be read in the context of Helen Penn's (1999) notion of "minority childhood" (First World) as compared to the "majority childhood" lived in developing countries. While many critics of Barbie might cheer the fact that millions of seven-year-old girls will never experience Barbie, this is not because of any ideological rejection of Barbie per se. Seven-year-old girls are not caring for baby dolls or Barbie dolls because they are the principal care-givers in HIV- and AIDS-affected families. Western popular culture artifacts may end up in some countries not as play objects but as part of a production line staffed by the very children who will never get to own one. These children are not unlike those of poor families in eighteenth-century England who were employed to "color in" by hand the illustrations in books produced for children of the well-to-do – the sorts of children we regularly encounter in paintings by Hogarth.

An Orientation to Researching Children's Popular Culture

Throughout this book we use the concept of spaces literally, metaphorically, and in different disciplinary contexts. In a literal way, the concept might be regarded as being analogous to the "small spaces" occupied by many artifacts of children's culture, ranging from the Polly Pocket Plastic Worlds that fit into the palm of your hand, to Matchbox cars and Pokemon cards. We wonder about how these artifacts exist in the space of a child's collection. But the concept of spaces also refers to the physical spaces occupied by children themselves: bedrooms, hide-outs, forts, and so on. At the same time, as we often find in our own households, there is often an unclear demarcation between child and adult spaces: the spilling over of items of material culture into the common and even the so-called adult areas of a house or apartment. This spilling over and taking over might be indicative of children and their objects as being space invaders, for, as with the low-tech video-arcade game of the late 1970s, one by one the little space creatures manage to take over all the space of Earth!

Within a disciplinary context, the concept of spaces refers to a discussion, say, of the historical space around some of these objects, for example, of Barbie as a manifestation of the fashion doll. Going beyond the materiality of the objects, or studying them as phenomena, how can we construct methodologies for studying popular culture? Our approach is not limited to the examination of one or two cultural artifacts or texts – say, Cabbage Patch Dolls, or Spice Girls, or Ninja Turtles, or R. L. Stine horror fiction. This is because we think that if an analysis is tied specifically to a particular product or text, then when the product is no longer produced or when it loses popularity with the child user/reader/viewer, the value of the commentary might become lessened or even lost. It is as if the observations become as transitory as the object or text under analysis.

Our approach is to consider examples of popular culture as case studies for analysis: both as objects that exist in their own right, in their own period and context, and as texts which provide us with a way to examine the space of children in society. We select examples that are both dated and current. For instance, we study popular culture motifs such as the cowboy and cowgirl that had become obsolete but then reappear. At the same time, we examine the relative long-lastingness of certain artifacts such as those "over forty" (Barbie, Nancy Drew, Disney's Winnie-the-Pooh). They are inviting instances of paradox since being "new" is an important part of the appeal of popular culture. Is there a difference between "old" cultural artifacts that continue to reinvent themselves over several generations, and recent ones? What about multigenerational use? In terms of casting time into a spatial metaphor, is there a difference in the temporal space "consumed" by Barbie for over forty years as opposed to the space occupied by a baby doll?

In this book we are interested in domestic environments as play spaces or spaces of leisure in consideration of the notion of what geographers call "spatiality" as a dialectical process whereby the spatial becomes the social and the social becomes the spatial (Soja 1985, cited in Aitken 1998: 22). Neither is value free or neutral. Geographers of childhood such as Aitken draw upon the work of Henri Lefebvre (1991) and his notion of "trial by space" whereby groups are considered "subjects" only if they succeed in producing an identifiable space (in Aitken 1998: 99–100). By this logic then, in urban environments there are fewer public spaces relegated to children and youth, and even fewer where they are not supervised. In a world of apparently shrinking "free" or open space, what does this mean to a child? How might this have an impact on a child who has little physical freedom and is under adult surveillance or control much of the time (Jenkins 1998b)? How children may manage this limited physical space has different dimensions. Children may transform their bedrooms literally into a creative domain; or they may use the family computer to create unique domains in cyberspace; or they may engage with different types of popular culture at different times of day, such as a young adolescent staying up so late at night listening to the radio or playing on the Internet that he or she seems to turn night into day, to create a kind of private space in a crowded apartment (White 1993).

Each of these spaces that we explore in this book – political spaces, memory spaces, visual spaces, physical spaces, virtual spaces, and historical spaces – locates the adult researcher within a particularized place with respect to researching children and childhood through popular culture. In some ways, as we discuss throughout the book, we recognize that children possess an expertise about their own popular culture that is theirs by virtue of their being the intended audience and/or customer, but is also theirs by their willing and sometimes passionate engagement with the show, book, or toy. Only a seven-year-old girl who is a Barbie aficionado can fully experience the complexities of being a Barbie player, a Barbie owner, one who is subjected to Barbie-bashing and so on. Similarly, only a nine-year-old boy who is a Hardy Boys fan can completely understand the difficulties of talking about a story when there are two different versions of the same story in many of the early books.

These children are experts based on their experiential knowledge and their zeal. The idea, however, that children can be experts at anything when pitted against the experience and expertise of adults is troubling, and is, in itself, a feature of age studies worthy of interrogation.

At the same time, as we take up in our analysis of the popular children's movie *Toy Story 2,* we acknowledge that childhood-in-memory is a feature of researching children's popular culture. This has two aspects: on the one hand, for adults engaging in memory work about child play and engagement with popular culture it is a fascinating way to study their own identity and childhood of a certain era. On the other hand, producers of popular culture may use this type of knowledge to "re-create" for a new age group what children play with, in their projection of what it is that children will be likely to consume. As we observe in our consideration of the politics of researching childhood, the "valuing" of children's likes and dislikes has a direct commercial application. It is the successful toy designer and the astute marketer who, in a sense, have the most effective take on childhood, as evidenced by sales.

In the academic world, by contrast, studying children and childhood is not generally held in much esteem outside of important subspecialities in medicine and education. This is evidenced in the transparent attitude behind the critical tone sometimes taken by observers. This may be seen in responses such as "Cabbage Patch dolls or pogs, why would you want to research that?" The low status of the topic in terms of critical reception can also be seen in the dearth of publicly accessible and well-documented collections of children's popular culture, so it may be difficult for a researcher to obtain basic information about the date of a book or toy. This lack is mitigated somewhat in relation to older items, for as artifacts age, they gain a patina of value. For example, the New York Public Library, like many other libraries, did not carry the Hardy Boys or Nancy Drew mystery series, or any other series produced by the Stratemeyer Syndicate, because they were not considered to be good children's literature. Nonetheless, in 1993 the new owners of the Syndicate, Simon & Schuster, donated all the original papers to the rare books division, where they are now housed!

The low value accorded to researching children's popular culture in the research community is simply a reflection of the low status accorded to popular culture generally. Despite the rise and fall in popularity of certain objects or texts, as Kirsten Drotner observes (1992), there has been a continuing association in the critical reception of children's and youth popular culture with a reaction of "moral panic" (Cohen 1972). In the modern period – since the chapmen peddled cheap paper-covered volumes of sensational stories and ballads, but specifically ever since the rise in popularity of the sensational and sentimental novel in the eighteenth century – there has been an accompanying concern by moralists about the dangers of stimulating and corrupting impressionable young minds (Brewer 1997; Buckingham 2000:125). In the contemporary period, these fears tend to be gendered as well, in that most worries around boys and young men concern violence and antisocial behavior

(Cohen 1972), while with girls and young women the concerns revolve around (hetero-)sexuality and unconventional behavior (Christian-Smith 1990).

Finally, the notion of space and spatiality also serves as an organizational feature, so that each of the chapters is configured as particular research space. In Chapter 1, "Political Spaces: Contexts for Researching Children's Popular Culture," we look at the interplay of the age of the players, the status of their popular culture, and the (supposed) ephemerality of the objects in the context of power relations in conducting research. Following from this, the book moves on to examine various ethnographic and textual approaches to researching children, childhood, and popular culture. Thus, in Chapter 2, "Memory Spaces: Exploring the Afterlife of Children's Popular Culture," we consider the place of children's popular culture in adult memory, and in Chapter 3, "Visual Spaces: The Gaze of the Child," we explore the participation of children as visual ethnographers. We go on in Chapter 4, "Physical Spaces: Children's Bedrooms as Cultural Texts," to read children's bedrooms as archival sites in the landscape of childhood. In Chapter 5, "Virtual Spaces: Children on the Cyber Frontier," we look at children's websites and the Internet as a new space within which to explore childhood. Finally, in Chapter 6, "Historical Spaces: Barbie Looks Back," we provide a retrospective view of the fashion doll and doll play as a context for deciphering Barbie's place in present-day girls' popular culture. At the same time, however, in configuring this final chapter in the context of "Barbie Looks Back" we go beyond Barbie to consider the ways in which researching children's popular culture serves to tweak a sociohistorical nerve in the space of childhood more generally.

The six research spaces that we look at, of course, are by no means discrete; there are many overlaps, for example, between visual spaces and the gaze of the child, and physical spaces or play areas that children occupy. Indeed, in reviewing the many references in the book we realize that the child's bedroom within the context of Western childhood occupies a central position in conducting research related to popular culture and play. The whole book is about children's bedrooms! At the same time we want to point out that the six spaces we have chosen to focus on in the book are by no means the only spaces that could be discussed in the context of children's popular culture, and we say very little, for example, about literary spaces or musical spaces, and offer here only a limited analysis of issues pertaining to globalization and the responses to popular culture outside of a Western context. Even within the context of Western society, there is a great deal more to be written about the social conditions within which children's contemporary popular culture is encountered. In writing this book, our overall purpose has been really only to open up the space of childhood and children's popular culture by demonstrating its richness as a field site.

Chapter One

Political Spaces: Contexts for Researching Children's Popular Culture

> We were ten years old when she came into existence, just Barbie, there was no Skipper, no Midge, no fancy cars and dream house or the other mountains of plastic junk created for her in the intervening years. Barbie was a solo act – a doll that was a woman and not a baby. Sitting on Kathy's upper bunk bed, we invented lives and situations for our Barbies. We did not focus on her glamorous body shape. What we cared about was that Barbie could get dressed up and go some place. Kathy could draw, design, and sew, and she made elaborate outfits for our Barbies, as we could not afford the regular Mattel-issue Barbie clothes. When we decided what we wanted our Barbies to be, and to do, and where they were to go, Kathy would lay out the appropriate wardrobes for their independent lives. She said she was going to be a fashion designer; I thought she was brilliant. (She went to graduate school and became a public health professional.) Despite the political incorrectness of the statement, I cannot help but believe our Barbies saved us. No, I don't believe it; I know it. Barbie was our liberator (Brill 1995: 20).

Barbie a liberator? The words of feminist activist Anita Brill go strongly against the grain of most discussions about Barbie. They also go against the grain of most discussions about children's popular culture, regardless of whether the talk is in university classrooms, at academic conferences, critique in the general press, or in the day-to-day commentary that takes place in stores, living rooms, on buses or sidewalks, or anywhere that adults are likely to come into contact with children's popular culture. Indeed, while Barbie might be taken as the ultimate in what's wrong with girls' popular culture, she is by no means the only popular culture artifact that is trashed. The computer game *Mortal Kombat*, for example, is often regarded as encouraging violence. Cabbage Patch dolls at the height of their popularity in the mid-1980s were said to give children the idea that childhood has a price tag. It is also believed that series fiction spoils children for good books. And even if it turns out that children's popular culture is taken to be quite benign, there is still often the sense that it is of no apparent value and hardly something that is worth talking about. Like the imaginary reader the narrator evokes in Jane Austen's *Northanger Abbey* (1818) who apologizes for reading fiction with "oh! it is only a novel," the users of Barbie, even those who are as young as four or five, are likely to be fully aware of the fact that the doll does not have high status among adults in general. And while it is true that researching any aspect of childhood may carry with it the stigma of low status, the particular status of carrying out research on *Peter Rabbit* or *Anne of Green Gables* (1908) (even *Anne of Green Gables,* the television series) as opposed to Barbie or Mickey Mouse must be noted.

We are interested in the relationship between the status of children's popular culture and the status of childhood. It is a relationship, as we argue throughout the book, that is at one and the same time both vexing as well as rich in terms of what it can illuminate about childhood itself. And while we hope its richness will become evident throughout this book, here it is our intention to critique the conditions and circumstances within which to consider research related to children's popular culture. Who researches children's popular culture, anyway? How might we begin to refigure research on children's popular culture? As Dan Fleming observes:

> What can toys tell us about culture and vice versa? Toys tell us something about demand. In a colloquial sense first: parents know too well the insistent tug of "I want". There is more than individual desire here. Or rather, as individual desire is always articulated with socially constructed objects – the desirable – and with equally socially constructed ways of wanting – the routines of consumption – so there is, as the very engine of "I want", an unmistakable "massification" of demand. The child's demand is really a chorus, orchestrated but none the less breathed and felt as an individual desire by this child, at this particular moment. In fact, toys are a wonderful place to look at the complex interactions between the desiring individual and the massified demand. It's all so visible here – the child appealing for satisfaction and the market providing the very vocabulary of appeal. Both are visibly and audibly present in the toyshop – neither can be reduced to a pale reflection of the other, without some deeply troublesome sense of having simplified what's going on (1996: 8).

In entitling this chapter "Political Spaces" our intention is to set an agenda for the remaining chapters that operates to create a decolonizing space for engaging in research on children's popular culture. Like Linda Tuhiwai Smith we are interested in the idea of "decolonizing methodologies." Speaking of her interest in indigenous research she writes:

> Some methodologies regard the values and beliefs, practices and customs of communities as "barriers" to research or as exotic customs with which researchers need to be familiar in order to carry out their

> work without causing offence. Indigenous methodologies tend to approach cultural protocols, values and behaviours as an integral part of methodology. They are "factors" to be built in to research explicitly, to be thought about reflexively (1999: 15).

In the context of childhood studies, this need for decolonizing methodologies is no less significant. The status of children's culture, the relations between adult researchers and child consumers, and so on, are all integral to the project – and are to be regarded as factors not barriers.

Thus in this first chapter we are interested in questions that arise out of the decision to see this space as political instead of merely neutral. We start by mapping out what we regard as the critical space of children's popular culture, noting both the critical reception to children's popular culture as well as the underpinnings of what we see as a perception of children's popular culture as "junk food." In the second section we focus on the dynamic of the relationship between adults and children within the political spaces of researching children's popular culture. In the third section we ask the question "Who cares about children's popular culture, anyway?" noting the significance of the blurring of the boundaries – academic/commercial, professional/personal – within the research community, and the ways in which these boundary blurrings contribute to the political space. How, for example, does the methodology of those working within the toy industry or the world of collecting and collectibles differ from those working in academic settings?

Mapping the Critical Spaces of Popular Culture

Although popular culture is usually considered in opposition to high culture, we suggest that the relationship between them is more complex: that popular culture exists also within or inside high culture. If this complexity is recast into a spatial metaphor, perhaps high culture and popular culture do not exist in two separate spaces, but one inside the other. The relationship may be thought of as resembling nested folk dolls which contain one within the other. A child's engagement with popular culture is often determined by the child not the adult, so the space of popular culture may exist as a pocket of resistance, within and against a larger space of quality culture. For example, at many daycare centers, popular culture toys such as Barbie or Action Man figures are not allowed, since the centers prefer to control the play culture through offering educational and quality toys. A pre-school child may conceal an action figure in his backpack, knowing full well that such toys are prohibited. The act of hiding the figure in the backpack is an act of secrecy, like a doll being hidden inside another. It may also be an assertion of individual identity against the regime of the daycare center. In a similar way, a pre-adolescent may be asserting individuality when he insists on doing an oral book report on Hardy Boys mysteries. Although he is considered scholastically a poor reader, his assertion of a literary taste in popular mysteries that are not valued culturally may be a way to assert individual identity through resisting what is considered "good" reading. Although this is an open act, not a secretive one, his space of resistance exists within and against high culture. Since engaging with popular culture is a space which is relatively unregulated by adults, the act of selection in itself is important to the child. It may reveal a group identity such as that established by using Bart Simpson's gestures, the wearing of certain T-shirts, or eating certain candy, and it may also serve as a space to assert oneself against adult regulation. The notion of "nested" space also suggests a kind of secret or internal space relatively free from adult intervention – indeed, a type of forbidden space similar to that associated with reading secretly with a flashlight after the lights have been turned out.

These forbidden spaces exist, we propose, because of the critical reception to children's popular culture generally. Our focus on the notion of examining critical reception as part of researching children's popular culture dates back to work on studying images of teachers in children's popular culture (Weber and Mitchell, *That's Funny, You Don't Look Like a Teacher*, 1995). Amidst images of Miss Grundy in *Archie* or Miss Stacey in *Anne of Green Gables* are images of Barbie: as student teacher in a *Barbie* comic, and a year or two later Barbie as Teacher Barbie. The idea of discussing Barbie, who is banned regularly from classrooms by teachers, as associated with teachers and teaching provides a certain irony, but it has also raised a number of issues for us about the status of children's culture:

> To mention the name "Barbie" at almost any adult gathering is to invite derision or interrogation – a chorus of unbelieving "oh no's." Our families wonder what could possibly be "academic" about Barbie, and ask how we could devote so much time, energy, and even research funds to this seemingly frivolous subject. A few of our university colleagues express similar concerns, and some of our undergraduate students squirm and look embarrassed when we bring up Barbie, only to reveal that it wasn't so long ago that they stopped playing with Barbie themselves! Even colleagues in Cultural Studies or Communications, who themselves study texts such as feminist detective fiction, Madonna, *Dallas*, *Y and R* (*The Young and the Restless*) or *Star Wars*, disparage this text of girlhood, this *doll* (Weber and Mitchell 1995: 115).

Following on from this work, we began to pay more attention to what colleagues and friends would say in response to our research on teen romances – Nancy Drew and the Hardy Boys as well as other popular culture texts – and of course we encouraged our graduate students to do the same. By systematically noting down the responses to work on children's popular culture over several years, we have begun to construct a cultural map of childhood that speaks to the status of the researched, the status of the objects, and certainly the status of the researcher. Consider, for example, the following comment made by one of Claudia's graduate students after she embarked upon a cultural studies project on children's popular culture:

> "I thought about status – about how some books 'have it' like *Charlotte's Web* and some books like *Nancy Drew* you have to fight for it. Perhaps that's not a fair comparison. But how about the whole idea of how we view 'the scholar.' I know if I walked around and said I was studying *Nancy Drew* or *Beauty and the Beast* as I worked toward my Masters Degree in Education, I'd raise a few eyebrows. It brings me back to that notion of how we consider our time – and what constitutes valuable or important 'research.' I could spend the next ten years studying people's reactions to what I'm studying!"

Another participant in the class who was engaging in research on romance reading observes:

> "I feel that the knowledge I already have about these texts as well as the great number of colleagues and friends who have read these novels makes it easy to do interviewing. I must say, though, that I feel that analyzing the significance of doing meaningful research on something important to an audience that is outside of academia would seem worthless to others. I know that I would enjoy this type of project but I feel that I should research good-quality children's literature. Sure, within our class the other students would not say anything but I would feel that I wasn't doing a professional 'study' simply because I would be interviewing romance readers. I could imagine what the men in my family would say if word would get out . . . I remember telling a couple of my colleagues that I watched *Mr. Dressup* because I was looking for a program that involved literacy. Their response was 'Oh! what other useless things are those McGill professors going to have you do next!' I felt a need to explain my interest in the project and the value it carries."

The comments of critical reception that students heard from friends and colleagues in relation to the texts they were studying rivaled the very comments that are sometimes made by those who are users of the particular popular culture text in the first place, as in the case of Barbie survivors: "Hi, my name is _____ and I had a Barbie" (Peabody and Ebersole 1993: xvi).

In a similar vein, we recall attending a panel session at a conference on popular culture devoted to locating specific archives of material collections. Discussions abounded about where to find the best collection of sound recordings of music from the Vietnam War era, or particular artifacts related to 1950s television shows such as the *Honeymooners*. At one point we asked about how to track down particular collections of children's popular culture artifacts. The response from the chair of the panel was emphatic: "There can't be collections of *everything*. It would be like having museums of hubcaps." While this response sounds like intellectual arrogance, in fact it is not unlike what a number of researchers working in the area of child studies have already observed about responses to childhood research generally, and popular culture research specifically. Ann Oakley, for example, in speaking of the status of "child," notes: "What does it mean to criticize someone for being childlike? Certainly in English the terms 'adultlike' and 'adultish' are not uttered as condemnations in the ways 'childlike' and 'childish' are" (Oakley 1994: 15). In reality, of course, it is possible that a museum of hubcaps might be subject to a greater degree of systematization than some collections of children's material culture. We have noted, for example, that when it comes to children's popular culture scholars are not always as careful as they would be with other academic discourse. This lack of care ranges from cataloging and organizing material culture to actual arguments and conclusions that are made about childhood. Scholars, for example, who would otherwise be scrupulous about dates or identifying editions when it comes to other texts (including adult popular culture texts) may be less so when it comes to children's culture.

What is significant, we offer, is the fact that cultural studies itself, focused as it is on the subject of exclusion, marginality, and the critical divide between the canonical and noncanonical, has had little to say about young children and popular culture, something that, as Henry Jenkins and others suggest, might have its own form of exclusivity. Jenkins notes that the acts of children are rarely interpreted within the discourse of resistance the way the acts of adolescents are:

> Like everyone else, we have a lot invested in seeing childhood as banal and transparent, as without any concealed meanings of the sort that ideological critics might excavate, as without any political agency of the kinds that ethnographers of subcultures document, as without any sexuality that queer and feminist critics might investigate. Carey Bazalgette and David Buckingham identify a "division of labor" within academic research that subjects youth culture to intense sociological scrutiny while seeing childhood as a fit subject only for developmental psychology. . . . Sociological critics focus on the "deviance" and "destructiveness" of youth cultures, their "irresponsibility" or the "rituals" of their subcultural "resistance." While we often celebrate the "resistant" behaviours of youth cultures as subversive, the "misbehaviour" of children is almost never understood in similar terms (1998a: 2).

In a similar way, Valerie Walkerdine comments that "tiny tots certainly come low in the resistance stakes!" (1998b: 255).

Notwithstanding the exclusion of children's popular culture from much of the work in cultural studies, we have observed that, even when children's popular culture is included, the responses to it may be quite different from other work within popular culture. For example, we noted the ways that academic research on children's popular culture invites a type of response that seems to go directly to the everyday lives of the audience, often bypassing, in a sense, the academic critique. Consider the following examples: Claudia has just given a paper at an academic conference on Nancy Drew and the ways in which Nancy has now become enshrined as a feminist role model – "the girl who can do anything." Immediately after she finishes speaking, a woman in the audience asks her if she thinks it would be wise to try to get her ten-year-old daughter to read some of these books, since to date the girl has insisted on reading childhood classics such as *Charlotte's Web*. She wonders if her daughter is perhaps missing something. At another time, we are speaking at a conference on women and popular culture in which we focus on the idea that Barbie serves as an interesting contradiction in that she stands for both her emancipating "dressed up and going out" image as well as her image of conventional femininity. The upshot of the paper is that Barbie cannot be treated as simple text (Mitchell and Reid-Walsh 1993). Following our presentation, one of the members of the audience comes up to us and asks whether we think it was perhaps inappropriate to have been so censorious of her daughter playing with Barbie. Should she be encouraging her to play with Barbie? We see the same response to the work of a peer from another university: a visiting professor at McGill is speaking on the topic of girls' popular literature. One of the first comments following her paper is, "Where can we buy these books? I have twin daughters and I'd love to have them read these books."

On the one hand, we ought to laud the fact that the academic community can become engaged personally in research, so that it is not detached or absorbed in a totally objective world that has nothing to do with the everyday. On the other hand, we have sometimes been taken aback by the absence of critique, where someone will become so excited as a fan or foe of the topic under investigation, that the issue is not accorded the same kind of rigor as are other areas of research. Where, as academics, we might listen to a paper on other topics with critical distance, commenting, for example, on the method or the theoretical underpinnings or on the nature of the analysis, somehow when we encounter children's texts – and especially, popular texts – we seem to be more inclined to become first and foremost former children or parents (or aunts and uncles). Perhaps the notion of "kitchen research," the term used to describe the kind of research that toy executives carry out in their own homes, also describes the tendency of adults generally to relate to children's culture, as opposed to other phenomena at a personal level. It may also speak, though, to the fact that there is a particular political context to research on children's popular culture which suggests a complexity that is never quite separate from the personal, the everyday – "What about my children?" or "What about my childhood?" Far from dismissing it, or rejecting it, we would suggest that perhaps we need to acknowledge the significance of these comments in a more self-conscious and self-reflexive way. In other words, what is the significance of these responses to the research area itself?

Popular Culture as Junk Food

"Promotional toys," as Stern and Schoenhaus (1990) write, "could be considered the junk food of the toy world. . . . They are not usually the toys parents would choose for their children. They are the toys children choose for themselves" (1991: 29). This is something that Claudia Kishi, one of the characters in an episode of Ann M. Martin's Babysitter's Club series, also points out:

> I also love to read *Nancy Drew* mysteries and I adore junk food. Doritos, M&M's, Twinkies – I never say no to any of it. My parents, however, don't like me to read *Nancy Drew* books (they would prefer that I read "classics") and they *really* don't like me to eat junk food. "Proper nutrition is *important* . . ." You know the line. So I've learned to hide my secret vices. The *Nancy Drew* books get stuck under my mattress, or on the top shelf of my closet under a pile of dirty clothes. The junk food gets stashed anywhere and everywhere – it's always turning up where I least expect it (1991: 3–4).

There is a certain amount of irony contained in this observation by a fictional character who is herself a character in what is regarded as a "junk food" series! As we observed in the Introduction, we believe the regular disparaging of children's popular culture is something that has to be addressed within the research space of children's culture. As we noted there, the point about "moral panics" and "media panics" conveys something of the diagnosis. However, in this section we are interested in some of the features of children's popular culture which contribute to the overall disparaging, with the idea that by laying bare the various tensions and contradictions within the research space we can contribute to mapping out revised agendas within the study of children's culture. The issues, as we discuss them here, are diverse in that they vary from a consideration of kids' culture as something that is meant to be deliberately distinct from the culture of grownups, to the nature of the objects and paraphernalia of the material culture itself, to the unease that adults often have with the possibility that there is something not totally innocent about children.

Junk food as resistance

We start with the idea of children's agency and the ways children themselves might choose to enact the notion of junk food as resistance. This is taken up by Allison James in her analysis of "kets" or the "penny candy" cheap sweets that belong exclusively to the world of childhood. In her study, which took place in a northern community in Britain, these kets included such concoctions as "Syco Discs, Fizzy Bullets, Supersonic Flyers, Robots, Traffic Lights, Coconut Bongos, Diddy Bags" (1979 (1998): 397–8). In our own quick survey of Canadian informants, we managed to come up with an equally rich list of kets: Warheads, Jaw Breakers, Slimy Snakes, Peach Fizzies, Twizzlers, Nerds, Tots, and so on. The point James makes is that buying and eating these confections over which children have maximum control – including financial – as opposed to regular adult food (over which they have no control) – is an aspect of defining the self:

> This ability to consume metaphoric rubbish is an integral part of the child's culture. Children, by the very nature of their position as a group outside adult society, have sought out an alternative system of meanings through which they can establish their own integrity. Adult order is manipulated so that what adults esteem is made to appear ridiculous; what adults despise is invested with prestige. By disordering and confusing the conceptual categories of the adult world, children erect a new boundary over which adults have no authority (1979: 94 (1998: 404)).

Alongside this form of resistance is the in-built "I want ness" which we referred to in the Introduction, in relation to Leigh and his two sons at the movie *Toy Story*. The marketing strategies of the toy industry, as many researchers have observed, include a built-in acquisitiveness. The circumstances for many parents is that their children whine and badger, and then as parents they "cave in." There is something about the physical presence of the objects, so acquired, that reminds adults that they have so little control over their children that they must give in to the whims of children, lining up for hours, for example, to ensure that their child gets an Elmo or a Cabbage Patch doll. Tangential to this is James Kincaid's observation in his book *Child-Loving: The Erotic Child and Victorian Culture* (1994) that as adults we may like the idea of children's play – in theory enjoying it at a distance in a description, for example, of child's play in a novel or a painting – but not in reality. In reality, children's play seldom resembles some version of Hogarth's *The Children's Party* (1730) or *Two Children of the Nollekens Family Playing With a Top and Playing Cards* (1745)! Play is mostly messy and disorganized, at least from the point of view of the adult.

Of no apparent value

An additional tension within the whole area of children's popular culture is the sense that it is of no apparent value. The toy industry is huge, and relies heavily on new generations of children, new fads, and the idea that children will want new things. While we do discuss elsewhere (Mitchell and Reid-Walsh 1996) the knowledge children have as a result of their contact with popular culture,[1] the point is that it is often seen to be junk because it is not "educational." Perhaps there is something in what Nick Gillespie of the *New*

York Times service has to say about "the educational TV trap" (July 6, 1999). Commenting on a recent study conducted by the Annenburg Public Policy Center at the University of Pennsylvania which has concluded that "there's little of value in children's television," he observes that perhaps we are too "hell bent" on finding something educational in television. And countering, in a sense, the spurt of literature that suggests that childhood – infancy – is the time to learn, he asks why we think television for children should be educational in the first place:

> Don't we already have schools and parents for that? Children are spending more time than ever before in educational settings, whether it's pre-school, year-round schools or after-school tutoring programs. Children today are every bit as busy as their parents. Must we deny them a few moments of ostensibly mindless entertainment between Hooked On Phonics tapes? . . . Forget about openly educational programming like The Magic School Bus and Street Cents. What these shows tell children about the human body or counting their change can be picked up easily enough elsewhere, whether on a playground, in the library, or at the mall.

Class and popular culture

There are a number of class distinctions operating when it comes to critiquing popular culture. A critique of the highly sexualized examples of popular culture associated with Barbie – on the surface at least – is that girls grow up too fast. However, if Barbie hurries girls, then there is something of an irony since there seems to be no similar concern about hurrying girls into housework through the Fisher Price play oven or kitchen set, or products such as Little Sweepers. Similarly there is no great concern about hurrying children into education, as we noted above. We mention girls' work toys and educational toys as examples of children's toys in order to draw attention to what we perceive to be class-related tensions, and which support the notion of children's popular culture as junk food. As Valerie Walkerdine observes in her analysis of class in *Daddy's Girl* (1997), there is often an association between the hyper-sexual girls' culture of Barbie, Britney Spears, the Spice Girls, and the MiniPops – and working-class culture. Somehow it is *those* girls who play with Barbie or *those* parents who lack taste and sensibility. The recent success of American Girl inserts an interesting class marker into girls' play. In the high-end American Girl shops, the costs of the dolls and paraphernalia along with the exclusivity of the shops ensure that many parents who are not middle class cannot afford to buy their daughters these toys. Indeed, as Ellen Seiter writes, this exclusiveness extends into school itself in relation to what children have already been exposed to in their play and school success:

> The promotional, mass-market toys sold in Toys"R"Us and most available to and popular with working-class children are the toys most likely to be excluded from the culture of the classroom. So-called quality toys, the materials that conscientious affluent parents will have provided for the kids when they have taken expert advice to heart (and had the time to follow through on it by providing recommended toys), will be precisely the kinds of things the child will encounter in preschool and kindergarten. The familiarity of the school materials – including toys – will be just one of the many advantages that will bear on the child's future success in the classroom. Promotional toys, on the other hand, are likely to meet a cool reception by teachers. No Barbies or Ninja Turtles will be among the toys supplied by the school, and some evidence suggests many children will rapidly learn not to talk about their favorite toys with teachers, or about what they have seen on TV (1993: 226).

Ephemerality

A separate but related issue in relation to children's popular culture as junk food pertains to the ephemerality of the individual objects, as well as the perceived ephemerality of the various fads within children's popular culture. Unlike in the Hogarth paintings, the objects that children are playing with are seldom the girls' porcelain doll or the boys' wholesome-looking hoop or blocks. Rather, the artifacts themselves often have a tawdriness about them, manufactured as they are in bright, often gawdy metal and plastic, and are not meant to last – even though, of course, they do! Garage sales are full of popular culture items that last.

Indeed, many so-called fads within popular culture last. *Sesame Street*, first broadcast in 1968, is already in its thirties. G.I. Joe is "pushing forty." Barbie has been around since 1959. Paddington Bear was "bearing up well at forty in 1998," Mr. Potato Head dates back to 1952; *Seventeen* magazine dates back to the 1940s; Nancy Drew has been around since 1929, the Hardy Boys since 1927. Winnie-the-Pooh first appeared in 1924. Indeed, when we compiled the above list of children's popular culture "milestones" for a conference presentation, we were as surprised as most of the participants with the realization that many of these texts of popular culture had been around for so long: "*Seventeen* magazine from the forties? You've got to be kidding! I thought it was a sixties (or seventies or eighties – depending on the age of the respondents) magazine." Or "You mean my mother (or grandmother) read *Seventeen*? I'll have to ask her. I wonder what she thought." But equally, many of the participants – especially those without children or grandchildren – were even more surprised that these artifacts were still around, not just as "relics" but as new episodes: "*Nancy Drew*, are they still writing those? I read those as a girl." A phenomenon we have noted in our interviews with many former

Nancy Drew and Hardy Boys readers is that they not only claim to have "read them all," but they also believe that once they have "done with them" the books cease to exist and the publishers close down. Many popular culture texts, of course, do immediately disappear – often after one season. Pound Puppies from 1978 are probably now only items in someone's Christmas photographs from that year. Some items, such as Cabbage Patch Kids, while "hot" for one year, still exist but with a greatly reduced following, with appearances on the Internet, however, offering a new lease on life! Some of these texts no longer exist in quite the same form as the "originals." Nancy Drew and the Hardy Boys, for example, have expanded to include new lines altogether – the "case files" series which are marketed against other popular series such as Sweet Valley High, a line that combines the young sleuths working together in Hardy Boys and Nancy Drew – as well as extensions to the readership upward and downward so that there is a junior Nancy Drew as well as Nancy Drew at university. At the same time, however, we have uncovered many nostalgia Internet sites that keep the memories going. The point is that the ephemerality associated with the "junk food" quality of popular culture has its own contradictions built into it.

We regard the criticism of Barbie, in particular, as emblematic of the tensions and contradictions associated with the ephemerality argument. As one Barbie supporter observes:

> "I really don't see anything wrong with Barbie. She's just a doll for God's sake. I grew up loving her despite her exaggerated proportions and I resent the person who said she leads to eating disorders. Perhaps these people should take a deep look within themselves and quit blaming everything else for their shortcomings. People believe what's right and wrong and if they are unable to discriminate between the two then maybe they should look at how they're being brought up and the values they're being taught in the home. Stop being so damn critical and pointing the finger at everyone else, especially a doll" (Chase in Boston – homearts conversation, <http://www.homearts.com/instpost/instacc.html> December 20, 1997). (File no longer available on website.)

On the one hand, there are arguments that Barbie is more than just a doll since to understand the Barbie phenomenon, one must also understand the various artifacts of material culture which surround Barbie – comic books, magazines, trading cards, and so on. In that work we have tried to demonstrate that Barbie and the tie-in products carry diverse and oppositional messages, and that Barbie-as-a-text is deserving of as measured and nuanced an investigation as other commodities of play and popular culture. On the other hand, the expression "She is just a doll – mom" suggests that adults may read far more into children's play artifacts than is warranted. Play is play – children grow into and grow out of toys while adults are still trying to figure out their social significance. Barbie, for example, has a relatively short shelf life for most girls. They may get their first Barbie at age three but by seven or eight may be mostly into something else. We might well take heed of Arthur Daigon's statement about Nancy Drew readers – "Like the measles or the chicken pox, Nancy Drew must run her course" (1964: 669) – to consider that the reading of Nancy Drew or the Hardy Boys series, Baby-Sitters Club, Sweet Valley High, and so on usually represents no more than a season or a school term.

The arguments noted above highlight the unease that we as adults have about children's popular culture. The tensions, as we point out, have as much to do with what we think we ought to be doing as parents or teachers, than necessarily anything indigenous to the artifacts themselves. Elsewhere Claudia has written about the idea of Toys"R"Us as a vehicle for teachers' self-study, particularly in the context of school-related paraphernalia such as the Little Professor, Teacher Barbie, and so on (Mitchell and Weber 1999). While we have not set out to frame these issues in a self-study context, we would suggest that the tensions and contradictions inherent in the junk food argument are ones that help to shed light on issues related to the social construction of "adult" and "child."

On Working Directly with Children

Ann Oakley (1994) in her work on the role of the child as researcher concludes that engaging in research with children should be no different from engaging in research with adults. As she writes:

> The consensus that emerges from studies exploring children's perspectives is that the major issues of the researcher–researched relationship are *essentially the same* with children as they are with adults. These issues include the need to be aware of and respect the imbalanced *power relations* of the researcher vis-à-vis the researched, the importance of distinguishing "*private*" from "*public*" accounts, and the need to handle controversial and or personal topics with *sensitivity* (1994: 26). . . . Most supposed differences between children and adults as research subjects disappear on close inspection. Even as regards size and age disparities, the issues that are highlighted in thinking about the research in the area of children's studies are not a particular class of issues: they are questions to which all good researchers will attend in conducting their research in both a scientific and a moral manner (1994: 27).

While in principle we concur with Oakley, in practice we see that there are several constraints in terms of the relationship of adults to children – as informants, co-participants, co-researchers, or as experts in their own right –

in engaging in research related to popular culture. After all, children's culture is their culture! Thus, we have been interested in the approaches that various researchers have taken to "gaining entry" to children's culture in ways that take account of the dynamics of adult–child relationships, the fact that the culture is "theirs" and it is about pleasure, and the fact that children may be used to having their play devalued by adults. While we focus in Chapter 3 on the role of children as researchers themselves, here we are interested in those approaches which serve to minimize the inherent tensions of adults (with all the power and outsider status) studying children (with none of the power and all the insider status). We acknowledge, however, that the dynamics of adult–child relationships in relation to children's popular culture raise a number of social and ethical issues, ranging from "gaining access" to children's culture to a consideration of the moral and political implications.

While there are, of course, a number of issues about how adult researchers negotiate with other adults – parents and teachers (the gatekeepers to any research on children) – our particular interest is in relation to the children themselves, the ultimate gatekeepers in deciding what they are going to say or do. We believe this is particularly important, in view of the fact that many of the popular culture artifacts being investigated – from Bart Simpson to Barbie – are regarded as the "ket" of children's material culture, and they are often meant to subvert the very adult world that is represented by the adult researcher. Frequently, as we noted above, popular culture texts such as *Archie* comics, Power Ranger figurines, or Bart Simpson "I'm an underachiever and proud of it" T-shirts are officially or unofficially banned from daycare centers, kindergartens, and schools. Considering that a great deal of child research is conducted in kindergartens and schools, what are the implications for conducting research about these texts in such an environment?

Is it possible to embark upon studies of these texts with children in ways that are seen to be neutral? While, as David Buckingham has pointed out, this might have something to do with convincing children that one is not there to trash their interests, it also has something to do with convincing the gatekeepers in the research study that one is not out to pollute or corrupt children. Is an apparently neutral stance taken to be a pro-stance? Alison Lurie (1990) notes in her book on children's reading *Don't Tell the Grown-Ups: Why Kids Love the Books They Do*, that there are certain "rules" which govern how children and adults are supposed to interact, and who is supposed to know what about the other. The question, of course, of "Who's asking?" is an important one along with "What is it that adults want to know?", "Why are they asking?", or "Is this some sort of trick so that as soon as we admit we like something, the adults will try to talk us out of it?" Buckingham notes that children are so used to having adults "trash" their play that there is a built-in antenna which goes up when they appear to be taken seriously around popular culture (1993). In this respect the insidiousness of the "moral panic" about Barbie, Power Rangers, Cabbage Patch dolls or whatever else is currently popular is not wasted on children. Moreover, there are often boundaries, things that kids will tell an adult who is not identified as being a real adult. Erica Rand, for example, talks of children who recall dismembering Barbie (1995). It is not as though we distrust such accounts, having witnessed first hand some dismemberings of Barbie in our own homes, but more the need to be cautious about the shock value of certain accounts. And while any research might be subjected to this shock value, our concern is in relation to the ways popular culture is often linked to the violent, the sexual, and so on. We are thinking, for example, of an episode of working with a group of ten-year-old girls who were describing their early Barbie play. While they made comments about Barbie and Ken together, we were not in a position to question them too directly about exactly what it was that Barbie and Ken did together. One of the child participants, a relative, later revealed that it was the sexual nature of the relationship between Barbie and Ken to which they were referring but that they did not want to mention sex in front of the adults!

Frances Chaput Waksler makes a similar point in her study of "the hard times of childhood" where she chose to focus on the remembered stories of the harsh realities of childhood, by college freshmen rather than children. As she observes: "the kinds of experiences in which I am interested are those that children may well find politically unwise to disclose to adults. Indeed, to my surprise, these experiences proved somewhat problematic for college students to tell their own parents" (1996: 218).

Children's Voices

The idea of working directly with children raises a number of questions about respecting children's voices – a version of Spivak's "Can the subaltern speak?" (1988) which raises the question of whether the subaltern can be heard and listened to, as well. On the one hand, there is often a tendency to either sentimentalize the voice of the child, or to accord it a greater truth value simply because it comes from a child. On the other hand, in at least some of the work with children-as-informants they are regarded as cultural dupes, totally taken in by whatever advertising campaign or ideology is at hand. For this reason, children are often regarded as less trustworthy – "what can *they* know since after all, they are *only* children?" – in their role as informants. It is important to point out that the debates themselves are ones which sometimes transcend "child culture" so that in some ways they apply to popular culture more generally. John Fiske, for example, notes the possibility that each user of popular culture can make his or her own meaning: "despite the power of ideology to reproduce itself in its subjects, despite the hegemonic force of the dominant classes, the people still manage to make their own meanings and to construct their own culture within, and often against that which the industry provides for them" (1987: 286). At the same time, Farber et al. offer the cautionary note that "it is possible to romanticize the open capacity of readers to invent fresh meanings for texts and create their own culture" (1994: 11).

On the sentimental side, we think of a popular syndicated radio show in North America *Art Linkletter and the Kids*, in which Art Linkletter would conduct face-to-face interviews with children around such topics as "Who works harder, your mom or your dad?" or "What does your mommy say when she's mad at your dad?" The adult audience would find hilarious the "from the mouths of babes" answers which would amount to such things as "My dad works hard, 'coz my mom stays in bed all day painting her toe-nails" or "My mom gets mad at my dad when he has lipstick on his collar." We see a Hollywood version of this phenomenon in a scene in the movie *Kindergarten Cop* where Mr. Kimble (Arnold Schwarzenegger), an undercover policeman impersonating a kindergarten teacher, has to work out a strategy for determining which child in the class is the one who is about to be kidnapped by his father. Because he knows it is a child whose parents are separated, he comes up with an "Art Linkletter-type" protocol for getting each child to talk about what his or her daddy does for a living, hoping to find out whose daddy does not live with the child.

In a related vein, albeit in a less innocent view of childhood, Joe Kincheloe in his analysis of *Home Alone* and similar movies uses the term "pre-pubescent wise ass" to describe the "kiddie-noir hero" or "smart kid with an attitude" character of Kevin. Kincheloe writes:

> Almost every child depicted on TV in the contemporary era – Alex Keaton on *Family Ties*, Michele in *Full House*, Lisa and Bart Simpson on *The Simpsons*, Rudi on the *Cosby Show* – is worldly and wise. Bart Simpson may be an underachiever, but only in school – a place he finds boring, confining and based on a childhood that no longer exists. Bart is not childish, the school is. The smart ass kid à la Culkin and Bart Simpson is the symbol for contemporary childhood (1998: 174).

While on the surface there may appear to be little relationship between the apparently innocent "darnest things" voices and the "wise ass" voices, we conjecture that there is at the root of both an "uncontesting" or "overprivileging" of the voice of the child. Michelle Fine in her study on negotiations of power within feminist research draws on the work of Joan Scott to problematize this idea of "voice," observing that relying on "the presumption that we can take at face value the voices of experience as if they were the events per se, rather than stories about the events, is to de-historicize and decontextualize the very experiences being reported" (1994: 21). Relying on these "unadulterated voices," as she calls them, is simply another form of ventriloquy or speaking for the other (ibid.). While this criticism can be leveled against much of the work with adult participants too, we think there is a special case to be made for work with children. We are not suggesting that children are inherent liars or even that they say only what they think adults want to hear, although both of these are possible in some research situations (as is also the case with research involving adults). Erica Rand (1995), for example, points to the fact that some of the child participants in her study of Barbie play seemed to be hedging their bets that they might be able to get a Barbie doll out of the researcher, causing her to begin to question the authenticity of their responses.

The converse of the privileging of the voice of the child is, of course, to pay no attention to what children say or, worse, to regard children as being untrustworthy, saying whatever they think adults want them to say. While this may be true, as we noted above, we are also interested in the question: Why do we think adults are any more trustworthy? Adults have as much at stake (and often more sometimes) when they respond to questions about their television or reading habits – and are perhaps even more likely to respond in socially desirable ways – telling researchers what they think they should hear. Buckingham cites the example of parents who, not wanting to be seen as bad parents, minimize, in their reporting on their children's viewing habits, the amount of television they or their children watch. They might also exaggerate the amount of time given over to watching good-quality television shows such as *National Geographic* specials or to viewing public broadcasting channels (1996: 258).

Aside from the idea that children might be seen as in some way untrustworthy, there is a related topic around whether children are simply cultural dupes who passively absorb all the evil that popular culture emits so that there is no likelihood that they might offer some enlightened commentary about these texts anyway. As we noted above, this view is not offered only in relation to the use of popular culture by children and adolescents; a similar point of view is put forward generally about women who are romance readers, viewers of soap operas, readers of the *National Inquirer*, and so on. In writing about adolescent girls and their reading of such magazines as *Jackie*, for example, McRobbie (citing Paul Johnson) writes that there is often the view that

> Cheap, superficial, exploitive and debasing, mass culture reduces its audience to a mass of mindless morons: the open sagging mouths and glazed eyes, the hands mindlessly drumming in time to the music, the broken stiletto heels, the shoddy, stereotyped "with it" clothes: here apparently, is a collective portrait of a generation enslaved by a commercial machine (1991: 84).

She goes on to show how adolescent girls in their reading of fashion magazines are actively engaged in making meaning. Similarly, David Buckingham (1996) in his analysis of the responses of children to television reveals the ways in which children are far from passive in their use of popular culture, and that furthermore, placed in a context of actually working with the texts, they are able to produce quite sophisticated readings of popular culture. While age/developmental issues cannot be disregarded – obviously a three-year-old will normally have access to less sophisticated language than say an eight-year-old – this should not be taken to mean that children are simply passive consumers.

Achieving "Least Adult" Status

Mandell (1988) has been successful, through her research, in working to minimize the distance between adults and children. Her efforts to involve children directly and meaningfully in research on popular culture research serve to exemplify what she terms "least adult" status, where researchers are less like "us" (adults) and more like "them" (children). In some work, notably that of Llewellyn (1980), there is the idea of actually "passing" as a child. Lynn Davies (1984) refers to being "adopted" by the children. And Vivienne Griffiths, in her study of girls' friendships, chronicles the process of moving "in": "The girls began to show a certain possessiveness and pride in having me around. They enjoyed showing me off, introducing me to their other friends, sometimes dragging people up to meet me. Was I becoming the class pet?" (1995: 16). This work is challenging in terms of ethical issues. Aside from the obvious ethical concerns about "passing," there is the danger, as Griffiths points out, of becoming too "in" and she cites the work of Peter Woods in terms of "according primacy to the views of a particular group," that is, identifying so strongly with the members that defending their values comes to take precedence over actually studying them (1995: 34).

Aside from the conflicts that might arise from having access to information that is of a confidential nature or which should be passed on to other adults (such as school authorities or parents), there is also criticism that adults might take on an insider role that is not quite genuine. While, to a certain extent, this might be a criticism of many ethnographic relationships, we regard childhood participants as being particularly vulnerable. We think of our own early experiences as beginning teachers and the idea of wanting to be "on the side of the kids" – as opposed to the other adults in the system. As an outsider to the school system, it may be tempting for an adult researcher to also position herself in a "we" (with the kids) versus "they" (against the adults) relationship. In addition, at the risk of appearing to elevate the role of the adult researcher to some sort of Messiah status, it is important to draw attention to what a number of researchers have observed in their work with girls and women. Angela McRobbie (1991), for example, observes that there are few feminist scholars who have gained access to the world of girls and women who have not noted something of the savior role. As she writes:

> Sociology does not prepare us for the humility of powerless women, for their often totally deferential attitude to the researcher. "Why are *you* interested in *me*. I'm only a housewife?" Or else the surprise on the part of girls that any adults could be really interested in what *they* had to say, or indeed that adult women outside their immediate environment could be "normal," might swear, be quite nice or interesting and lead exciting lives. Almost all feminist researchers have reported this sense of flattery on the part of women subjects, as though so rarely in their lives have they ever been singled out for attention by anybody (1991: 77).

This position may carry with it particular responsibilities that go beyond the limitations of working with consenting adults. What is the responsibility of the researcher to the researched? Does the success of such approaches lead to a type of violation of children's rights to privacy – or to a "gray area" in relation to an abuse of the position? Blackman (1998), a male researcher, for example, discusses his apparently successful "negotiation" into the out-of-school world of girls who are in their early adolescence. He notes the "success" of actually being invited into the homes of the girls for sleep-overs. In his analysis he refers to the challenges for a male researcher to enter into/interpret the world of girls and women, and indeed offers possibilities for how the girls themselves might be involved in the interpretive process; we are interested in the ethical issues of "gaining entry" in the first place. On the one hand, we need ways of working with children that are not limited by their school life which is often "off limits" to popular culture. On the other hand, these approaches should not invade their privacy or present any risks to children. While research institutions such as universities, policy units, and the like all have procedures in place for conducting research involving minors, procedures which in a sense ensure that the researcher makes explicit a plan that takes all reasonable steps to minimize dangers and risks to participants, we nonetheless highlight research in children's popular culture as being a special case – one which might suggest seeking approaches that are less invasive or intrusive and more collaborative from the very beginning.

Tampering with Children's Culture

Ethically, of course, there are concerns about the idea of tampering with children's culture in the first place. What does it mean to study the culture of childhood by working directly with children? As with other research involving adults' participation in children's culture we are referring to what might be described as "researching sensitive topics." While the idea of sensitive subjects is usually taken to mean research related to child abuse, say, or studying sociability in the classroom by interviewing children about their friends or favorite teachers, we can also question the role of adults in querying children about popular culture texts – potentially "blowing" the myth of the Tooth Fairy, Easter Bunny and Santa Claus. Consider, for example, an episode with Matthew, an eleven-year-old boy who participates in an interview about the Hardy Boys and the prolific output of the author, Franklin W. Dixon. In the course of the interview Matthew talks about which version of the series he prefers – the earlier books written in the 1930s or the more recent Case Files which have been published only in the late 1980s and onward. In the middle of a sentence in which he questions the ways that the books have changed over time, he begins to falter: "Dixon's certainly been writing for a long – er – uh time uh. . . . He must be really old." And then suddenly, he asks, "There really is a Franklin W. Dixon, isn't there?" As two responsible adults, we look at each other and our eyes ask, "Who's going to tell him that all these books are produced by a stable of ghostwriters?" "Are we going to tell him at all?" "How can we not tell him?" We are saved when Matthew suddenly declares, "Oh, well, maybe they were written by different people."

Equally though in working directly with children is the fact that researching what is deemed "cool" at any one point might compromise the social status of the child researcher. The authority of the child in terms of what's "in" may be so fragile that children themselves may not want to proclaim on a particular trend, especially in groups, for fear of revealing something that is "not cool." Consider, for example, the interview noted earlier where we discussed with four ten-year-old girls their reading and television interests. They were often hesitant in revealing what they really liked for fear that it would no longer be popular. In mid-1998, the Spice Girls, for example, occupied a curious position. Marketed vigorously towards the under-eight crowd, the group could not so easily be embraced by older fans. Thus it might have been "OK" if you were ten or eleven to listen to their music, but not to admit that you really liked it. Interestingly, in the course of that interview it became easier to rephrase questions so that the girls were commenting on their own tastes from an earlier age. The girls became visibly more relaxed when talking about *then* – i.e. their interest in Barbie whom they have all more or less left behind several years ago – than they were in talking about *now*: their current interests. The present is not quite safe enough; they reveal some unsureness about whether it is "OK" to express a preference for one musical group over another, or for a certain reading series over some other one. We find ourselves rephrasing questions to consider the past rather than the present: "Can you remember what you were like when you were seven?" or "What do you think seven-year-olds think about this?" as opposed to "What do you like about Spice Girls or Blur?" In this example, Penny, the initial "informant" in terms of identifying other girls in her class who might be interested in participating, is in the awkward situation of being closer to the center of the research team than to being one of the interview participants. There is no easy way for her to be "just one of the participants." She says very little during the interview, something that cannot be very satisfying for her. And while nothing obvious happens in the interview setting that would warrant some sort of social ostracism, we learn later that she is treated at least for a brief time as an outcast by the other participants. We consider, as well, that there are ethical concerns about asking children to comment on or analyze self-consciously the very culture within which their identity is being formed. We would ask whether we should be asking questions, which on the surface might seem benign, but which could be quite harmful. Here we are thinking, for example, of peer rejection and bullying and the ways in which access to material goods – including popular culture artifacts – is often a reason or an excuse for children to exclude one another from a social group, something we take up in the next chapter by exploring women's memories of childhood play.

Childhood Knowing/Adult Innocence

The issue of childhood sexuality is particularly fraught in terms of the ethics of studying with children their popular culture, given that many of the said artifacts are reviled precisely because of their sexual connotations. As adults, we cannot ethically ask a six-year-old how she feels when she dresses up her Barbie in what would to an adult appear to be a sexually provocative way, or when she does a Britney Spears "living-room performance" complete with bare midriff. A university research ethics board, for example, would have some concern about a researcher sending home a letter to parents requesting that he or she be allowed to interview girls about sexual activity and Barbie play, even though, as Erica Rand points out (as would many parents), that the narratives which children come up with in their Barbie play are often very explicit sexually. In order to get permission, the researcher might have to couch the request for informed consent from the parents in terms that mask the real focus, or decide that the only way the study could be carried out would be by declaring up front to an ethics committee the need for deception. Neither should be acceptable. Thus at present much of the work on "moral panics" has to be done in a way that is *about* children. For example, in the well-known case in the U.K. involving Tory MP Peter Luff, where there was a concern that his thirteen-year-old daughter was reading *Sugar* magazine, the follow-up media coverage drew on the reactions and responses primarily of adults.

> Luff was worried about the fact that this aggressively promoted material was being read by much younger girls than the publishers were willing to admit. Actually teenage magazines are always read by an age range below the target readership the editors officially aim at, for the simple reason that they perform the teasing role of guides to girls as to what is in store for them at the next stage of growing up. So magazines like *More!* are indeed consumed most avidly by fourteen-year-olds. What the moral guardians found inside the pages of these publications were features like the now-notorious "position of the fortnight" showing a line drawing of a couple experimenting with different ways of having sex (McRobbie 1999: 51–3).

While for McRobbie an important issue in this case was the fact that the division line was between men and women respondents, as opposed to, say, feminists and nonfeminists, it is still a debate that does not centrally include young girls themselves.

Similarly, Higonnet (1998) and Hirsch (1997) discuss the very controversial photographs of Sally Mann who photographed her own children in poses that were sexually suggestive. In Mann's photograph "The New Mothers," for example, her two young daughters are wheeling their doll strollers, wearing sunglasses, each holding a cigarette in her hand, and looking back at the photographer, their mother, in a flirtatious pose. The younger daughter is holding a Cabbage Patch doll in her arms at a casual angle that suggests something of "Yeah, well, it's my kid and I can do what I want." As Marianne Hirsch writes:

> The children seem completely self-absorbed in childhood fantasy and a play-world to which viewers have only limited access, and, at the same time, they appear overly self-conscious and knowledgeable, available as mediators of unsettling and sensational cultural representations, fears, and fantasies. What we have before us is not a childhood glimpsed but a childhood invented – one that is performed and theatricalized with makeup, costumes, and props (1997: 152).

The public was uneasy with many of these images, even – or especially – because they were taken by the mother. Hirsch goes on to observe:

> Sally Mann's photography is, in the terms of the *New York Times*, "disturbing" precisely because it brings together two equally intense cultural obsessions: the vulnerability of childhood, on the one hand, and the idealization and fears of maternity, the fantasy of maternal omnipotence, on the other (1997: 153).

Similarly, Henry Giroux (1998) in his recent work on childhood beauty pageants draws attention to the taboos that surround explicit references to child sexuality.

In summary, we have tried to show in this section the ways in which a consideration of adults working directly with children and popular culture is fraught. At the same time we would argue that the very issues being raised are ones that contribute to an understanding of the politics of childhood. In the next section we turn to a consideration of the various research communities who are concerned about children's popular culture. In so doing, we offer that these various communities operate in ways that address, at least in part, some of the questions raised in this section.

Who Cares About Children's Popular Culture, Anyway? Boundary Crossings and Political Spaces

It may seem odd to pose the question of "who" with regard to researching children's popular culture. Why do we need to question who carries out the research? Unlike questions about who can write of women or race or class where there is almost assuredly an adult who is doing the research, the "inside track" on childhood studies might be regarded as a space to contest "whose adulthood?" In other words, how should adults be positioned to work "on the inside track" and alongside children? Here we are interested in the question of "who," not in relation to age but rather in relation to boundary crossings between the academic and nonacademic status of the research, between commercial research and "pure" research, and in relation to who is on the inside of children's culture. Which adults can ethically and legitimately have access to children and their culture?

At a three-day conference on Nancy Drew held in Iowa City in 1993, there was an important convergence of research worlds related to childhood and popular culture: former readers-now-adults giving testimony to the significance of Nancy Drew in their girlhood, academics (some also fans) offering analyses on various components of the books, ranging from the state of sex-based, racial stereotyping in the early versions of novels, to a consideration of whether George was a lesbian, representatives from the publishing industry talking about the production side of the texts, ghost writers, feminist detective writers, collectors – and real girl readers! Similarly at a one-day symposium held at MIT in 1997, there was a corresponding convergence of research worlds related to childhood and popular culture: there were representatives from the video game industry – people working for Mattel and so on, those working primarily within the academic world, some, such as Marsha Kinder who are involved in a "cross-over" of the industry and the academy. In addition, some youthful popular culture enthusiasts attended the conference, and samples of their responses are included in the edited volume that resulted: *From Barbie to Mortal Kombat* (Cassell and Jenkins 1998). We mention conferences such as these because they provide examples of alternative spaces for deliberation on the "insider" research community interested in children's popular culture: research within the toy industry, adult collectors, and "kitchen research" in the homes of researchers.

Research Within the Toy Industry

> "You've got three months to have those toys coming off the assembly line."
> "Three months! Impossible, we have to do focus groups and . . . and . . ."
> "Three months or your jobs are on the line!" (From *Small Soldiers*).

Thanks to Hollywood and the kinds of explicit "toy-talk" scenes we see in movies like *Small Soldiers*, cinematic representations of "made-for-children" childhood might be regarded as ethnographic studies of the research space of children's popular culture. Indeed, as Ian Wojcik-Andrews observes, some children's movies such as *Toy Story* are self-conscious in their references to ethnography, explicit, for example, in the scene where Buzz Lightyear comments to the other toys on the fact that Andy has inscribed his name on his shoe: "It looks as though I've been accepted into your culture" (2000: 192). Within this "popular" space we are thinking in particular of all those movies which self-consciously interrogate the creation, marketing, and procuring of children's popular culture toys – usually in the form of "the ultimate toy" or some version of "what do children want?" or "what do marketers want children to want?" These toy movies – ranging from *Babes in Toyland*, to *Toy Story 1* and *2*, *Toys*, *Jack*, *Small Soldiers*, *Jingle Bells*, *Big* – might be regarded as a subgenre of the "state of childhood" movies made for children.

These made-for-children toy movies can have a variety of functions within the research space of children's popular culture, ranging from offering the "raw material" for interrogating particular themes of childhood culture, to serving as a memory or recognition/interview prompt, as researchers such as Hallam and Marshment (1995) have explored. *Big*, for example, offers an interesting exploration of the "eight-year-old child" mentality that the toy industry must be ever mindful of in its toy invention and marketing strategies. As Stern and Schoenhaus observe:

> The secret of success lies inside the head of an eight-year-old child. That is the eternal paradox of the toy industry. Adults running multi-million-dollar toy companies are always trying to climb back inside that eight-year-old head. Creative people in the business like to boast that they have not grown up, that they have retained enough youthful enthusiasm to know what children will consider fun (1990: 23).

The story is based on a twelve-year-old's wish to be big; when his wish is fulfilled he finds himself in the body of a man who lands a job working for a toy company. He becomes successful, rising quickly to become the "boy wonder" of the company because he knows so much about what children want. Stories of intrigue, spying, theft, copying, closely guarded secrets around distribution and sales, accidental inventions, legal battles – these are the tales of the toy industry that Stern and Schoenhaus describe in *Toyland: The High-Stakes Game of the Toy Industry* (1990), and which are also taken up in Wayne Miller's (1998) *Toy Wars: The Epic Struggle Between G.I. Joe, Barbie and the Companies that Make Them.*

The movie *Toys* which provides the raw material for examining the conflict between an exploitative war-toy mentality and a sense of childhood innocence provides a reading on the links between commodification ("at any cost") and social responsibility. *Toy Story 2* sheds light on the world of adult collectors, and *Small Soldiers*, as noted above, provides some insight into product development within the toy industry. The CEO of the toy company demands that the toys be able to do exactly what they are depicted doing in the ad. "Does that action figure really punch his way out of the box?" he asks the designers, and when they say "no," his response is that we owe it to children not to trick them! While there is of course a questionable morality here in terms of producing toys that actually kill, the position of the CEO is that we should stop treating children as cultural dupes through false advertising. The film also deals with the theme of "give 'em what they want" in another way. Alan, the protagonist of the movie, is looking after his father's very unsuccessful toy store called "Inner Child." His father refuses to stock any war toys and relies upon the nostalgia factor of wooden blocks, train sets, teddy bears, and so on for stocking his store. However, this is clearly not much of a selling feature with contemporary children. As one of the disgruntled child customers observes: "There's nothing in there a kid would want."

As opposed to real life, of course, Stephen Kline observes, toy manufacturers, if they are not about to go out of business, have clearly done their research. He writes:

> The merchants and marketers of children's goods have always paid more diligent attention than educationists to children's active imaginations and incidental cultural interests. These researchers don't bother to observe comatose children in the classroom being battered with literacy; they study them at play, at home watching television or in groups on the streets and in shops. They have talked to kids about why they like playing Nintendo or trading sports cards. In their research they have used much more discursive methods that provide more insight into children's emotional and social perceptions. And they are not discouraged when they discover that peer perceptions, the love of stories, strong attachments to goods, vivid imaginations and a lively fantasy life lie at the heart of children's conversations and leisure preoccupations. Marketing's ethnography of childhood has validated children's emotional and fantasy experience, which the educational researchers have by and large avoided and derided. The marketers did not have to assume that children's daydreams, hero worship, absurdist humour and keen sense of group identity were meaningless distractions or artefacts of immaturity. . . . Identifying the basis of children's daily experience provided the means for transforming them into a market segment (1993: 18–19).

Kline goes on to observe that there has been relatively little research on what it is that collections and possessions mean to children so that there is a limited appreciation on the part of psychologists with regard to "the part that mental processes associated with shopping, toys, televison, stories, music, clothing or the economy have in children's development" (ibid.: 14). In full agreement with Kline's view of the careful research carried out within the commodified world, we recall an interview we had with Anne Greenberg, then editor-in-chief of Simon & Schuster, and producer of the Nancy Drew and Hardy Boys series. In that interview we were struck by the careful analysis that the editor herself has made of what Frank and Joe ought to look like on the covers of the Case Files, personally choosing, as she revealed, the models.[2] In essence, then, the toy industry, normally the subject of critique with media and within popular culture studies (which company has merged with another, the questionable marketing practices of a particular company, and so on) is one that could also be recognized within the research community more explicitly. While we recognize that the "space" between private sector research and academic research is one that is not without its complexity, we are simply arguing in this section that as researchers interested in children's popular culture, we should take account of the research that takes place in this community.

Collectors as Researchers

If the toy industry itself, through its approach to studying children and their toys is the closest to tapping into what children want, it is the collectors as researchers who are most likely to tap into the value of the artifacts of popular culture. Indeed, the basic plot of the movie *Toy Story 2* plays on this phenomenon by having Chicken Al, a collector of the Woody's Roundup series characters depicted as being positively gleeful (and somewhat unethical) in his desire to buy and sell the whole set. Barbie collectors are probably the best known in the collecting world of children's culture. With the various Barbie collector journals and magazines (*Barbie Collector*, *Barbie's Accessories*, and so on), regular conferences, websites, and the like, Barbie collections are big business. A mint-condition vintage 1959 original Barbie, as advertised over eBay, a virtual auction site, could fetch at least $2500. But Barbie is certainly not the only childhood artifact collectible, as the account of Jim Hambrick – in Jim Lehrer's "And now, a word of praise for the pack rats among us" – noted below attests:

> When Jim Hambrick was 6 years old he spent several weeks in the hospital. To cheer him up, his mother bought him a Superman lunch box. But little Jimmy never used that lunch box for lunch. Instead he took it home and put it on the shelf. Thirty years later it is touring the country as part of a special exhibit celebrating the 50th anniversary of the "Man of Steel." Little Jimmy now has the largest assemblage of Superman comic books, toys, coffee mugs, clocks and such this side of the planet Krypton – 40,000 items all told, valued at about $2 million. Hambrick (at right) is joined here by a small following from his collection, including a life-size figure of George Reeves, TV's first Superman. Jim's goal is to "take the collection to the ultimate. But you have to be careful," he contends. "Collecting can take control of you. I can't stop looking for Superman" (Lehrer 1990: 59).

As we noted above, the Nancy Drew Conference included in its participants various collectors who have made it their business to be able to tell the difference between a Nancy Drew episode from the first series – "Nancy classics" – as opposed to the stories that were rewritten from the 1960s onwards. Karen Plunkett-Powell in her book lists, for example, a number of speciality organizations and publications for the Nancy Drew collector: the *Whispered Watchword*, *Yellowback Library*, and *Martha's Kidlit* newsletter. She also lists several collector guides: *Farah's Price Guide to Nancy Drew Books and Collectibles*, and *Girls' Series Companion*, along with a chapter devoted to clues for "dating and rating your *Drew* books and memorabilia" (1993: 149–67). On any newsstand in North America it is possible to find a range of magazines given over to collectibles, some of which are devoted entirely to nostalgia artifacts of childhood culture. The summer 1999 issue of *Collectibles: Flea Market Finds*, for example, includes articles on vintage coloring books (a 1971 uncaptioned *Flintstones Coloring Book*, for example, can go for anywhere between $5 and $15; a 1950s *Gene Autry* coloring book between $30 and $60), and metal sand pails, ranging from a 1940s Mickey and Donald "Disney pail" (for $125–$175) to pails with cowboy themes and space designs. What is interesting about these collecting magazines is that they are clearly not just about "buy, sell, or trade," although there are some publications on toys that exist solely as a set of classified ads as in *Toy Shop: The Toy Collector's Marketplace*, along with websites on the Internet. Collector magazines often, for example, include articles about the history of the artifacts themselves. They often point out the pleasures of collecting too, something that resonates with the comments made by several academics who also acknowledge their consumer-fan status. Shirley Steinberg, for example, speaks of the ways in which Barbie artifacts became part of her personal collection in the course of doing the research:

> Four years ago I became fascinated with the effect that Barbie had on little girls. I started to pick up Barbies, Barbie furniture, Barbie comics, Barbie books, Barbie jewelry, and Barbie toys wherever I went. I was even able to find the Benettib Barbie in Istanbul's airport (under the sign featuring the Marlboro man). In order to do thorough textual analyses of Barbie and Barbie accoutrements, I needed to purchase my artefacts. I sit now, with great embarrassment, in an office with no less than 40 Barbies, ten Kens, several Skippers (including a beauty princess and a cheerleading skipper) and a plethora of "ethnic" and "special-edition" Barbies. . . . My ownership of Barbies and related paraphernalia qualifies me as an expert. I am a consumer and a scholar – no better combination (1997: 210).

Likewise, Henry Jenkins writes about the fact that he is both a fan and an academic in his treatment of *Star Trek*:

> Most of what I write originates from the same types of passions and pleasures that draw me to the fan community, but it is these feelings which often seem to be most difficult to communicate within academic discourse. Every word speaks of my own pleasures, my own experiences, but I have trouble finding a space to acknowledge my own involvement with the structure of the scholarly essay. Admittedly, this type of ethnographic project always entails a slippery move between objective analysis and subjective involvement. As a participant in this culture,

> I cannot help but map my own meanings and desires onto the community which I seek to document. Still this type of participatory observation allows us to create a dialogue between media scholarship and audiences that not only illuminates popular practices, but also at times reflects back on the meaning of our own academic pursuits (1992: 17).

What interests us about these statements, sometimes offered as confessions, sometimes as background, is that they are rarely offered as self-conscious acknowledgments that we "start with ourselves," although in many other areas of qualitative research methodology the notion of self-reflexiveness in terms of the role of researcher is one that is clearly established. The fact that children's culture is so inflected by issues of ephemerality, memory work, and nostalgia means that it is all the more significant that we understand the position of the researcher – and our own childhood experiences.

"Family Ties" and Kitchen Research

Dorian: Mum, what are you writing about?

Claudia: Researchers of children's popular culture who write about their own children.

To be asked what you are writing about by your own child just as you are writing about "kitchen research" may seem like the height of reflexivity! In this section, we are interested in the ways that researchers of children's popular culture, like our counterparts in the toy industry, tend to draw on their families as part of the research. Our interest here is not so much about convenient samples, although that of course could be part of it. (For example, when we needed a list of comparable "kets" in Canada we simply asked one of our children and her friends the names of some of the junk candy on the market.) Rather, what concerns us is the question of what it is that adults can know about the personal desires and pleasures of children, particularly since much of what children desire is often regarded as being outside of the acceptable in relation to schools and daycare centers. At the same time, there is also the sense that "you had to be there" to understand fully the meaning of certain acts and behaviors – so that what might be regarded as transgressive by an outsider-adult would have a more practical explanation by an insider-adult. In other words, if our goal is to understand behavior, it may not be possible to easily do so as outsiders. For example, one of Claudia's daughters, desperate for a Ken doll to go with her Barbie dolls, shaved the hair and cut off the breasts of a Barbie so that there would be a stand-in for Ken. Should this be read as a violent mutilation, as an example of a queering (Rand 1995), or just a practical solution to a problem? As the parent, Claudia knew that it was probably the latter; it is simply the kind of knowing that adults will have by virtue of being witness to spare plastic body parts lying around the house.

"Kitchen research" is thus more than just about convenience. The fact that so much of the naturalistic play of children takes place at home means that the homes of researchers of children's popular culture become logical field sites.

It has seemed to us, as we have reflected on our own work (and in particular the presence of our own children Rebecca, Sarah, Dorian, and Krista in our work), as well as having scanned the research studies of children's popular culture, that many of those writing in the area seem to write as parents and as former children. Thus we are interested in a "family ties" research space, something we have rarely seen discussed in the research literature on childhood, outside of the work of Patricia and Peter Adler (1998) who discuss the role of parents as researchers in their book, *Peer Power: Preadolescent Culture and Identity*, although it is worth noting that the research literature in childhood studies more broadly is replete with examples of parents researching their own children, ranging from the academic work of Jean Piaget, B. F. Skinner, Jean-Jacques Rousseau, and so on, to the more popular writings about raising children.[3] While we make no claim to have reviewed all existing literature on popular culture within childhood studies with a statistical breakdown on personal family references in this literature as compared with all other childhood research, we have nonetheless begun to scrutinize various studies, looking at the kinds of narrative accounts researchers include which might speak to either the childhood experiences of their children or their own childhood experiences. In particular, we have posed questions such as the following: To what extent do researchers refer to the childhood of their children and their own childhood? Were researchers of children's popular culture involved in popular culture studies of childhood before they had children? Do their interests/foci change as their children age? How do parent academics insert themselves into the debates – pro and con – of Barbie, *Sesame Street*, *Barney*, and so on? Where does gender feature in the research? How, for example, do the researcher parents of sons differ in their focus and interpretations from researcher parents of daughters?

In essence we have treated these documents as primary data, not unlike the way Dale Spender (1989) for her book *The Writing or the Sex?, or Why You Don't Have to Read Women's Writing to Know it's no Good* (1989) treats the acknowledgments written by male and female authors as evidence of how far particular authors are willing to go in terms of recognizing the intellectual contribution of spouses. In her work, she was interested in the ways that male authors, in particular, would acknowledge the emotional support their wives and partners gave them, but would seldom acknowledge their intellectual contributions, even though other biographical data would suggest a much more central support from many of these women. Spender's use of document analysis, then, provided a model for treating as primary data the "firsthand" narrative accounts written by researchers of their own children or of themselves.

As an example of "our children's childhoods," David Buckingham includes in his Introduction to *Moving Images: Understanding Children's Emotional Responses to Television* references to the responses of his son Nathan to the character of

Big Bird on *Sesame Street.* As he observes: "When Big Bird appeared, he would leave the room or turn off the set; and once he had mastered the remote control, he would rapidly skip past *Sesame Street*, adamant in his refusal to watch it – even if Big Bird was not actually on screen at the time" (1996: 1). And while Buckingham goes on to caution researchers about generalizing from our own experiences or those of our children, he notes the value, nonetheless, of these sources of insights: "I suspect that these kinds of responses will be familiar for many readers" (ibid.: 2). His commentary on his own family situation is representative of what many researchers working in the area of children's popular culture have to say about their inspirations. Stephen Kline, for example, in the acknowledgments in *Out of the Garden* makes the point that were it not for his own two children, the research could never have proceeded in quite the way that it did. As he states:

> Raising children can be a radicalizing experience . . . From the start my son Daniel made a major contribution by first inspiring and then informing the critical argument which is forwarded in this book. It was his fascination with Voltron and Transformers which first alerted our family to the real "power" of children's toy-marketing and helped us to recognize not only the importance of toys in children's lives, but the need to understand and criticize what was happening in children's cultural industries (1993: vii).

Kline goes on to write about the ways in which he and his wife began to insert themselves into the debates about popular culture:

> We were both enthusiastic about Daniel's imaginative play and wanted to encourage it, but as we watched and listened and played with him, we began to worry about the repetitive and aggressive ideas that underwrote that play. Like many other parents who thought in this way, we attempted to counteract this influence by limiting television, banning violent toys and talking to our children constantly. But being an academic interested in the criticism of culture, my instinctive response was also to try to understand why parents were being backed into a position where they were forced to resist the pressure of television (1993: viii).

Similarly, Henry Jenkins in his acknowledgments in *From Barbie to Mortal Kombat* writes:

> My son, Henry Jenkins IV, is really the one to blame for my involvement in this project, since he was the one who years ago begged and pleaded until we bought our first game system, who has been showing me level after level since he was five (and still at 16 is willing to take time out from life to walk me through "Nights into Dreams" at a

moment's notice) . . . who asks the questions about my work and about the media that get my creative wheels spinning, and who may someday surpass me as a writer. Henry, you are a tremendous pride (Cassell and Jenkins 1998: xi).

Ellen Seiter in the acknowledgments to *Sold Separately* notes the significance of her pregnancy in writing the book. As she observes:

The research for this book began during my first pregnancy, when I found, pushed through my mail slot every day, free magazines filled with cheerful advice and tempting offers for products that promise to cure illness, to provide good nutrition, to banish children's tears, and to turn my soon-to-be-born child into a person as clever as could be. Every time I watched television or picked up a magazine, I suddenly discovered that there were children everywhere: adorable babies in tender maternal embrace; laughing babies at play. Despite the fact that I am a professional media critic – a specialist in daytime television, in fact I had never really noticed how many children and babies were selling not only diapers and baby food but soaps and detergents and shampoos and tires and automobiles (1993: 1).

For Susan Willis the behavior and observations of her daughter Cassie at age three, and her son Cade at age four contribute to her insights about gender and play:

I want to cite two people whose experience of the child's relationship to gendering and commodities is closer than my own. The first is my daughter whose comment, made almost a decade ago when she was three, gives simple and direct testimony to the young child's recognition of polymorphous, or multidimensional sexuality. When asked whether her teddy bear was a boy or a girl, she responded "My teddy bear is both a boy and a girl." Later, when I came to write on Toni Morrison and wanted to characterize the author's portrayal of childhood sexuality, I remembered my daughter's remark and referenced her in my essay (Willis 1987). Many readers have told me that what they most remember about that essay is Cassie's comment. Such response registers acceptance of the way professional women and their children can work together in critical pursuits . . . I want to compare Cassie's comment to a response made just the other day by my 4-year-old son. Cade was playing with some foam-rubber dinosaurs, whose lack of sexual characteristics makes them comparable to the teddy bear. I asked him whether his dinosaurs were girls and boys. "No," he said "just boys and boys." In its syntax, his remark suggests the possibility of masculine and feminine even as his words affirm that boys can only be boys and play with boys (1991: 25–6).

For Henry Giroux, his extensive writing about the world of Disney comes out of his experience as a single father to three eight-year-old sons. He claims:

> Before becoming an observer of this form of children's culture, I accepted the largely unquestioned assumptions that animated films stimulate imagination and fantasy, reproduce an aura of innocence, and, in general, are good for kids. In other words, such films appeared to be vehicles of amusement, a highly regarded and sought-after source of fun and joy for children. However, within a very short period of time, it became clear to me that the relevance of such films exceeded the boundaries of entertainment (1997: 53).

While many of the extracts noted above, not unlike those offered within our section on "collectors," appear to be offered less as self-reflexive comments on the research act itself, and more as acknowledgements and "background to the study" statements as part of a convention of academic writing, we see that the political space of researching children's popular culture is one that might be enriched by a greater recognition of the dynamics of the insider position of the parent researcher.

We have also found many examples of researchers' own childhood experiences woven into various analyses of children's popular culture, a phenomenon we explore more fully in Chapter 2. Like the examples from "our children's childhoods," they provide, we believe, an additional reading on achieving insider status. They also, however, speak to the difficulties of accessing childhood directly. Valerie Walkerdine's work, for example, on the class-based features of the eroticizing of popular culture for little girls is something that is more directly accessed through her own childhood experiences. As she observes of her own working-class childhood in *Daddy's Girl*:

> This story has only been possible because I have interrogated my own and felt anger and a desire to tell another story, to set the record straight. No doubt someone else reading this will want to offer their own record in opposition to mine. But at least let's not operate under the illusion that the next protagonist has scientific right on their side, to demonstrate the truth about what happens to human beings without a flicker of intruding emotion, without a shadow of a doubt (1997: 189).

In a similar way, Suzanne de Castell looks back on her own girlhood experiences as a way to contest the conventional expectations that are often placed on girls. In referring specifically to the possibilities for girls to engage in video play, something that has been associated more with boys, she, in a sense, sets the record straight in other ways from Walkerdine: not all girls want to play with dolls. As she writes:

> I remember I cried the first Christmas I got a doll, a baby doll, from my parents. When they asked why I was crying I remember telling them I was "just so happy," when what I was was terrified and appalled at the realization that this was what I was supposed – biologically supposed – to like. To love, even. How on earth to *play* with this diapered apparition into which you squeezed water on one end and mopped it up at the other? Unlike my friends (who had Barbies) I never abused "Baby Wet-ums" who in time, after what I must have imagined would be a respectable period of intense maternal guardianship, lay dusty on her flannel-sheeted metal bed (in Bryson and de Castell 1998: 232).

For Henry Jenkins, the issue is one of comparison – looking at his own childhood in relation to that of his son's:

> Sometimes, I feel nostalgic for the spaces of my boyhood, growing up in suburban Atlanta in the 1960s. My big grassy front yard sloped sharply downward into a ditch where we could float boats on a rainy day. Beyond, there was a pine forest where my brother and I could toss pine cones like grenades or snap sticks together like swords. . . . Between my house and the school, there was another forest, which, for the full length of my youth, remained undeveloped. A friend and I would survey this land, claiming it for our imaginary kingdoms of Jungleoca and Freedonia. . . . Of course, we spent many afternoons at home, watching old horror movies or action-adventure reruns, and our mothers would fuss at us to go outside. . . . Often, something we had seen on television would inspire our play, stalking through the woods like Lon Chaney Jr.'s *Wolfman* or "socking" and "powing" each other under the influence of *Batman* (1998b: 262).

These memory-work pieces are interesting in that they point out the significance of invoking our own autobiographies in the study of youth cultures, something that Chris Richards (1998) also refers to in his discussion of teen music. Our point in drawing attention to this work is really to support our position that researching children's culture is not a neutral position. As adult researchers we not only set an agenda in our work, but we have an agenda that is informed by our experiences with children, including our own, and, as well, as we explore in the next chapter, our own childhood memories.

Chapter Two

Memory Spaces: Exploring the Afterlife of Children's Popular Culture

And Roy Rogers is riding tonight,
Returning to our silver screens.
Comic book characters never grow old,
Evergreen heroes whose stories were told,
The great sequin cowboy
Who sings of the plains,
Of roundups and rustlers,
And home on the range,
Turn on the T.V.
Shut out the lights –
Roy Rogers is riding tonight.
[Sound of hoof beats of Trigger galloping off into the night]
(*Roy Rogers*, Elton John).

Elton John's poignant 1970s ballad of cowboy heroes from the silver screen is a reminder of the enduring nature of the cowboy hero in adult memory. Indeed, if you ask many adults in North America and the U.K. born between the 1940s and early 1960s the question "Who did you want to be?", they will respond, even without the added prompt that this choice should be based on movies or television shows that they watched, with the name of a Western hero: Roy Rogers, Gene Autry, Zorro, Wyatt Earp, Bat Masterson, Hop-along Cassidy, the Lone Ranger, the Cisco Kid – and occasionally, from a female respondent, there will be a reference to Annie Oakley or Dale Evans. Many will go on to recall a particular photograph of themselves decked out in a cowboy/cowgirl outfit, a Davy Crockett jacket or coonskin hats and so on, or will relate a particular incident of playing cowboys. However, unlike many enduring characters of children's popular culture – Nancy Drew, the Hardy Boys, Barbie, Archie, Winnie-the-Pooh – which "live on" in the sense that their adventures continue to be produced over several generations, the cowboy/cowgirl hero is one whose time has mostly come and gone. We have discovered relatively few people who were born in the late 1960s and onwards who have any association with cowboy memories whatsoever. At least that was the case prior to the release of the highly successful Pixar–Disney *Toy Story* movies which feature the Cowboy Woody doll as the protagonist (along with Jessie the Yodellin' Cowgirl who appears in *Toy Story 2*).

Whether or not the success of the *Toy Story* movies, however, heralds the return of the cowboy is another matter. It is unlikely to be more than a co-incidence that shortly after the release of *Toy Story 2*, Madonna released her album *Music* featuring her all-new revamped cowgirl look. A more likely interpretation of the popularity of these films is that there is a nostalgia factor operating: they are produced principally by and for the baby-boomer generation, the parents and grandparents of today's children.[1] As the Flick Filosopher of the Internet observes: "The *Toy Story* movies aren't about our childhood toys as much as they are about the nostalgia for our childhood toys. And adult nostalgia is precisely what fuels *Toy Story 2*" (1999: 1). This is something that Henry Giroux describes more generally in writing about Disney in all its various manifestations:

> Disney's appeal to pleasure and the "child in all of us" is also rooted in a history that encompasses the lives of many baby boomers. These adults have grown up with Disney culture and often "discover some nostalgic connections to (their) childhood" when they enter into the Disney cultural apparatus. In this sense, Disney can be thought of as an "immense nostalgia machine whose staging and specific attractions are generationally coded to strike a cord with the various age categories of its guests." Disney's power lies, in part, in its ability to tap into lost hopes, abortive dreams, and utopian potential of popular culture (1999: 5).

In keeping with the overall focus of this book, we are interested in methodologies for exploring childhood culture within the space of memory. In this chapter, we address a number of questions related to memory work and children's culture: Why focus on cowboys since even by the early 1970s they were already memory material for an Elton John song? Why work with adults if we are really interested in children and childhood? How can we mine the contemporary cowboy/cowgirl movie *Toy Story 2* in its self-conscious "reading back" on popular memory, corporate culture, and contemporary childhood? How can children's popular culture as mediated by the nostalgia-marketing strategies of the toy industry contribute to memory-work studies? These are broad questions that have to do with exploring memory as phenomenon and method within the context of researching children's popular culture, and we believe that however briefly space allows us to deal with them, they speak to the complexity of the relationship between the rememberer and the experience or thing being remembered – and of course to the complexity of childhood in relation to adulthood. We cannot just talk, of course, about working with adult memories; we need to consider adult memories of specific things or events. Then "what" is remembered spills over into "how?" and "why?"

This spilling over from "what" to "how" is precisely what we see in the memory as phenomenon and method approaches of a variety of researchers working in the area of memory work: Frigga Haug and associates (1987), June Crawford et al. (1992), Erica Rand (1995), Annette Kuhn (1995), and others. The phenomenon under study, for example by Haug and her associates, is female sexualization as remembered through specific body parts: hair, breasts, hips, calves, mouths, and so on. Their method – collective memory work – incorporates the idea of body as both personal and social; June Crawford and her colleagues focus in their memory project, which also uses collective memory work, on the childhood holiday memories of males and females in order to examine the interplay of emotion and gender. Annette Kuhn and others who have explored memory work through photography have looked at the ways in which the image of the picture both captures and contests particular moments of childhood identity. Erica Rand's memory project on Barbie is one that looks at the "queerings" of Barbie – the transgressive uses of Barbie, and the ways in which Barbie becomes a pedagogical tool for her rememberers. In each of these projects there is a deliberate remembering about a deliberate phenomenon.

Why Focus on Cowboys?

Cowboy memories, we propose, have a *particular* significance in the study of childhood memory because, unlike memories of texts that have endured such as Barbie or the Hardy Boys, they have not been sustained over the years by direct contact with contemporary childhood. The cowboy hero offers a *particular* case for investigating nostalgia as a feature of memory work, not just because of the so-called Boomer movies *Toy Story 1* and *2*, but because of the vast range of images evoked by the cowboy hero. As Sean Griffin (1999) points out in his work on Davy Crockett, the popularity of the cowboy hero within postwar North America cannot be easily separated from the phenomenon of suburban spaces, the protection of children within the wide open spaces of the suburbs in the 1950s, Frontier Land within the Disneyfication of American culture. All of these are features that children's author/illustrator Dayal Kaur Khalsa manages to capture in a children's picture book, *Cowboy Dreams*. The book conveys a sense of nostalgia for the cowboy genre through its 1950s-looking illustrations as well as the text (Figure 2.1). As can be seen in the brief excerpt below, the story is told from the point of view of a little girl who desperately wants to be a cowboy and who desperately wants a horse. Page after page of illustration has her riding a wooden rocking-horse, riding on her father's back, riding on a merry-go-round, a coin-operated mechanical horse on the sidewalk, a horse on wheels, and always in her cowboy regalia of a Stetson, cowboy boots, and fringed jacket.

> When I was a girl I wanted to be a cowboy.
>
> My earliest memories are of lying on the living room rug, listening to "The Lone Ranger" on the radio. "Hi Ho, Silver! Away!" were practically the first words I ever said.

Figure 2.1 "I built myself a horse on the basement banister," illustration from *Cowboy Dreams* (Dayal Kaur Khalsa 1990) (Reprinted courtesy of Tundra Press).

> All day long I made believe I was a cowboy. I galloped everywhere, slapping my thigh and yelling, "Giddyap!" to make myself go faster. As I grew older I developed a bowlegged walk and tied my blankets into a bedroll at the foot of my bed. My whole life revolved around being a cowboy. I called my bike Old Paint, my brother Pardner, my supper chuck and my bedroom a bunkhouse. Whenever I went on a merry-go-round, I pretended I was out riding with a posse, chasing bandits (Khalsa 1990: n.p.).

A good example of the images of cowboy culture as nostalgia and childhood within the academic literature itself may be seen in the cover art of two key references on children's popular culture: *Out of the Garden: Toys and Children's Culture in the Age of TV Marketing* by Stephen Kline (1993), and *Moving Images: Understanding Children's Emotional Responses to Television* by David Buckingham (1996). Both covers include a television western scene. The Kline cover (Figure 2.2), which could even be an image of Roy Rogers and Trigger, contains a 1950s television set in the foreground surrounded by a fading western backdrop. Also in the foreground is a child's pinto-marked rocking-horse and a child's rim-stitched cowboy hat and bandanna. The faded western wash is reminiscent of the landscapes of Canadian prairie artists such as Terry McLean who are likely to include an image of a herd of deer or buffalo roaming across the land instead! The Buckingham cover (Figure 2.3) also includes a 1950s or early 1960s television set with a stylized cowboy on the screen and a 1950s "poodle-dog" rug in front of the television. The cover, though, also includes several children who resemble cherubic British tots: one in the

Figure 2.2 Cover: *Out of the Garden* (Stephen Kline 1993) (Reprinted courtesy of Garamond Press).

Figure 2.3 Cover: *Moving Images: Understanding Children's Emotional Responses to Television* (David Buckingham 1996).

foreground looks as though he or she just walked out of a book of knitting patterns, and the other child, whose back is to us, is dressed in tartan woollen shorts held up by suspenders. In the background a June Cleaver character who seems to be a stay-at-home mum, still in her dressing gown, is arranging flowers. On the floor are several toys that one would be likely to see in a store such as the "Inner Child" nostalgia toy store in the movie *Small Soldiers*: a teddy bear, a top, an antique van, and a generic Babar-type book. The background – a 1950s-looking shade of cake-frosting, Barbie-doll pink – is also suggestive of "back then," and we are reminded of the perfect match between the pink of the Buckingham cover and the pink that is used throughout *Cowboy Dreams* as described above.

It is worth noting that there are numerous personal references to cowboys in other academic writing on children's media and popular culture childhood. These personal accounts, offered somewhat unselfconsciously, might be regarded as examples of the "Kitchen research/family ties" that we spoke of in Chapter 1, and signal, we think, that the cowboy image is one that lingers in the background of contemporary popular culture. Murray Nelson, for example, in his analysis of trading cards in an essay in *Kinderculture* (1997), makes reference to collecting cowboy trading cards of Zorro and Davy Crockett. Dan Fleming writes about the significance of the Lone Ranger in his memories of childhood:

> I had a toy Lone Ranger figure on a rearing white horse – that horse galloped through my childhood dreams for years. It was the single most potent image that I returned to in fantasy throughout much of my childhood, and my stomach still turns over just a little when I see a white horse (1996: 1–2).

For Fleming, this cowboy memory feeds into an exploration of images of power more generally within children's popular culture.

More self-consciously rendered is bell hooks' very poignant description of a snapshot – now gone missing – of herself in full cowgirl regalia. This has particular significance, as she observes, because it captures a moment when she felt some personal worth.

> My favourite childhood snapshot then and now shows me in costume, masquerading. And long after it had disappeared I continued to long for it and to grieve. I loved this snapshot of myself because it was the only image available to me that gave me a sense of presence, of girlhood beauty and capacity for pleasure. It was an image of myself that I could genuinely like. At that stage of my life I was crazy about Westerns, about cowboys and Indians. The camera captures me in my cowgirl outfit, white ruffled blouse, vest, fringed skirt, my one gun and my boots. In this image, I became all that I wanted to be in my imagination (1994: 45).

She takes the snapshot with her to show her father's cousin, but unfortunately it gets lost:

> His was a home where art and the image mattered. No wonder, then, that I wanted to show my "best" image. Making my first big journey away from home, away from a small town to my first big city, I needed the security of this image. I packed it carefully. I wanted Lovie, cousin Schyler's wife, to see me in "all my glory." I remember giving her that photograph for safekeeping; only when it was time for me to return home it could not be found. This was for me a terrible loss, an irreconcilable grief. Gone was the image of myself I could love. Losing the snapshot, I lost the proof of my worthiness – that I had been a bright-eyed child capable of wonder, the proof that there was a "me of me" (ibid.).

Her description is an important one here for its relevance to looking ahead or engaging in what she calls working with the "usable past." For hooks, this missing photograph serves as a starting point for exploring the importance of remembering through visual images the lives of African Americans. As she observes: "Using these images, we connect ourselves to a recuperative, redemptive memory that enables us to construct radical identities, images of ourselves that transcend the limits of the colonizing eye" (1994: 53). Far from being some sort of "useless longing," hooks regards this memory work as being in the service of working towards an understanding of the present and the future. Nostalgia, itself, is so often described in disparaging terms as though it were a weakness, based on an untruth and best not indulged in. However, as discussed in *Reinventing Ourselves as Teachers: Beyond Nostalgia* (Mitchell and Weber 1999), writers such as Susannah Radstone (1995), Mary Jacobus (1987), Janet Flax (1987), and the poet Adrienne Rich (1978) are working to rehabilitate the idea of nostalgia, preferring to treat it as "future oriented remembering" based on what they describe as "the half remembered and half anticipated." These writers use the term "feminist nostalgia" to refer to a kind of yearning that is at one and the same time both nostalgic and utopic. Yearning for a past that never was, they argue, can be an impetus for future action.

Notwithstanding the issue of "days gone by" and the end of the cowboy hero in popular culture, the whole terrain of the cowboy hero is an obvious memory-work minefield in relation to colonization and dominance (cowboys and not Indians, white male Anglo-Saxon culture, individualism, macho-heroes). It is also a potential minefield for women who are looking back on their childhood play as cowboys and not necessarily cowgirls. Griffin's discussion of the image of the cowgirl offers a reading on the gendered notion of what was an approved area for girls who liked to play at being a cowgirl. He writes:

> This was ostensibly endorsed because it took the cowboy icon and accentuated its feminine aspects (particularly the emphasis on costume,

> with tassels and fringe). The "cowgirl" was supposed to accompany the cowboy, without ever supplanting him in dominance. Such folkloric figures as Annie Oakley and Calamity Jane were reworked in the postwar years to express femininity in Western garb, instead of a challenge to male dominance. . . . Yet, to say that this is precisely how girls used the "cowgirl" image, is to deny much of what Jenkins, Spigel, and others have noticed about the "negotiated" use of cultural objects by children. It is just as likely that girls used the "cowgirl" in order to complicate the gender boundaries that were already impinging on them (1999: 115).

Griffin uses this analysis of the cowgirl to explain some of the popularity of Davy Crockett among girls. While, as he points out, there were ads for girl-paraphernalia associated with Davy Crockett, these fads never really caught on. As he concludes: "*Life*'s essay on the Crockett phenomenon included a photo of a young girl in coonskin cap brandishing a rifle. Clearly, at least some girls were ignoring how the adult world would have preferred them to use Davy's image" (1999: 116). What is important, we believe, is the fact that notwithstanding the dominance of the white male hero in popular memory – after all, as Yvonne Tasker observes in her feminist analysis of the image of cowgirls, the cowboy in popular culture *is* a "spectacle of masculinity" (1998: 52) – there is something of a negotiated space for women looking back on girlhood. As Tasker discerns, the possibility for cross-dressing, for example, in the form of unrestricted dress is but one of the features of this negotiated space. While there is not sufficient space here to take up all of the concerns Griffin raises, the cowboy hero site is clearly one that brings with it a complexity in relation to questions about nostalgia, issues of gendered memory, and the possibility that the images themselves can have symbolic value in relation to childhood past.

Why Use Adult Memories to Study Children's Popular Culture?

In posing the question "Why study adults, anyway?" we are acknowledging, of course, that accessing childhood past by working with adult memory is as fraught, albeit in different ways, to working directly with children. Indeed, as we have also found, for every adult who will be able to offer some sort of response to the question "Who did you want to be?" with the name of a cowboy hero (or, as it sometimes turns out, a Halloween figure), there are just as many who may recall very little of childhood play. Colleagues have even said "I don't remember anything about that time in my life. What does that say about my childhood?" In some cases there is almost a resistance to being asked to remember, as Georgia Tsakalis (1998) discovered when she set up memory-work groups with a group of friends all in their mid- to late twenties who were viewing, as part of a focus group, the movie *Toy Story.* "Some respondents (both male and female)," she observes, "were determined that they had no memory of their childhood play and initially refused to acknowledge the use of memory work as research. Ironically, during the discussions it was these respondents who spoke at length about their most favourite toys (e.g. Easy Bake ovens, Curious George) and reminisced about the 'good old days'" (1998: 28). She goes on to note that "[O]ther group participants spent a great deal of the interview complaining about the 'unfairness' of life" (ibid.). Remembering, forgetting, and even resistance to remembering, however, are all central to the study of memory so that the responses of the participants in this memory-work group are particularly interesting in relation to their disparagement of nostalgia noted above. We regard it as ironic, however, that many of them ended up discussing how unfair life is now. The implication is that things must have been much better back then!

Far from regarding memory work as a corrective strategy ("after all what can children know?"), we see it as giving researchers access to components of the "afterlife" of childhood that are not otherwise available, either ethically or conceptually. Ethically, as we noted in the previous chapter, there are a number of issues about what it is that adult researchers can ask of children in research settings. This is more than just getting informed consent – or even about gaining entry and trust. Conceptually, however, as we explore in this section, the point is that there are dimensions of childhood that can be understood only in a *post hoc* way. While David Buckingham quite rightly points out that too often in research settings we trust adults' judgments over children, we are also moved to point out the converse: it is tempting to privilege the child's voice over all others, or to attribute to children an adult consciousness. Gender, for example, is something that children can demonstrate at a very early age; and as early childhood researchers, such as Karen Bailey (1993), Bronwyn Davies (1989), and Vivian Paley (1984) point out, children as young as two and three can both express preferences and opinions about gender relations. However, they have a limited ability to articulate what they mean about the significance of gender. Beyond being able to articulate what they mean, however, there cannot be an adult consciousness within which to give shape to a particular experience.

Neil Sutherland notes in his study of Canadian childhood between the 1930s and 1940s that "adults no longer subject to sanction by parents, teachers, or peers can now tell us what happened to them at home and elsewhere and what they felt about these events" (1992: 244). Sutherland's observation makes sense, in the context of our arguments above regarding the ethical and conceptual concerns about working directly with children. At the same time, however, it is important to acknowledge that childhood remembered in adulthood is anything but straightforward, something that we see represented in the vast range of writings on autobiography, life-history, memoir, and literature in which the space of childhood-in-memory is hotly contested. As novelist Marguerite Duras observes: "I realized that, while I was writing about my childhood, about a certain year of my childhood, I was writing from everywhere, writing about my whole life, all years confounded, of this life, as I had never done before" (cited in Cristofovici 1999: 285). While Duras was, of course, not writing about the specifics of remembered Flintstones paraphernalia or cowboy heroes in her discussion of childhood, she is nonetheless drawing attention to the fact that childhood and images of the past do not simply begin or end at some particular chronological moment. Claudia, for example, thinking back to when she taught fourteen- and fifteen-year-old students in a small fishing village in Nova Scotia in the early 1970s, recalls the ways that the *Sesame Street* television show, even then, only three or four years after it was first launched, and long after these students had passed the prime of preschool viewing, had already achieved the status of memory and nostalgia in their lives:

> Rubber Ducky had a particular nostalgia appeal for this age group, even though the show had never been part of their own preschool viewing. Theirs was a world of *Romper Room*, *Mr. Dress-up* and *Mr. Rogers*. The Grade Primary students in the school, however, regularly watched the show every day at 11:30. I remember that the ninth graders were always wheedling and cajoling in relation to watching the show. "Aw just once!" They all sang the Rubber Ducky song on the bus when they went on sports outings. As a special treat towards the end of the year, I remember allowing them to watch one episode (fieldnotes).

The students are in a sense remembering something that they never had!

But one's children's childhood experiences of popular culture also spill over into one's own consciousness and memory space. Consider, for example, the following analysis of a multigenerational family photograph commercially staged within a *Sesame Street* backdrop. We call the photograph "which ones aren't like the others?" (Figure 2.4), so named from the familiar *Sesame Street* saying. The photograph, taken from Claudia's family album, might be read on one level as a straightforward artifact/spin-off product from the well-known children's television series. It contains the array of familiar *Sesame Street* characters – Big Bird, Oscar the Grouch and so on, the same characters who regularly appear on lunch kits, children's clothing, educational materials, books, videos, and so on. Because there really is a *Sesame Street* magazine, the picture might be taken as a real cover. It isn't. The photograph is actually staged in a *Sesame Street* "set," assembled at the World's Fair in Vancouver in 1986. It is not unlike the kind of set that might be seen in a Disney theme park or in a dress-up studio where participants can be captured on film in some other time or place. The success of the *Sesame Street* initiative is based on the willingness of adults to spend a few dollars to have their children become cover people.

When one looks more closely, one can see four people "who aren't like the others:" an adult, two older children – one who is a teenager and the

Figure 2.4 Which ones aren't like the others?

other who is just turning eleven – and a toddler, along with characters who really do belong – Bert, Ernie, Big Bird, and Oscar the Grouch. What is interesting about the participants in the photograph is the fact that in some ways no one belongs. The two older children, Rebecca at age fourteen and Sarah at age eleven, are well past the *Sesame Street* age; Dorian the toddler is the closest in terms of age-appropriateness but even she is slightly on the outside since she has just turned one and has not quite grown into being a viewer of the television series yet; the adult, Claudia, is pre-*Sesame Street* having been born long before the show's launch in 1968. What is equally significant though is that, in fact, everyone belongs. For the two older children, the pose is a playful memory enactment in which they willingly participate, ostensibly to humor their baby sister, although she is too young to care. While they have never known a life without Oscar the Grouch, they are sufficiently past the *Sesame Street* age that there is no chance they will be taken as being socially regressive. They are old enough to "look back." The toddler, like her sisters, was born into *Sesame Street* – even if she is unsuspecting at the time of the photograph. She has already worn *Sesame Street* pyjamas, has Cookie Monster in her toy chest and has a whole set of *Sesame Street* artifacts to grow into in the form of hand-me-down toys, records, and books. Even though Claudia, the adult, can have no childhood memories of *Sesame Street* herself, the years of relying on *Sesame Street* to amuse young children, the memory of their hopes for a Big Bird birthday cake, the viewing of the Jim Henson's *Muppet Movie* with them, and so on, have ensured that there is space in memory that is activated when it comes to buying a place on the mock-up cover.

Beyond these blurrings of boundaries that can only really be studied *post hoc*, what people remember of their childhood, as we know from the vast body of work on memory, is mediated by a range of factors: class, gender, the age of the rememberer, the time of childhood, the emotional state of the rememberer or of the time being recalled, and so on. Memory is mediated both by the "critical space" within which one experiences a particular event as well as by the ensuing period of time. It is no small thing that the bulk of the work within the area of memory has been carried out by women, first of all, and women in particular of working-class background (Walkerdine, Spence, Kuhn, Zandy), and women of color (hooks). Crawford and her associates who studied the memories of men and women of childhood holidays through collective memory groups note that the kinds of memories the women reported were more likely to contain accounts that were *not* the fun-filled experiences normally associated with childhood play and pleasure. As she observes:

> In our memories, as girls and as adult women, we noticed and described the work done by women, by our mothers and aunts and later by ourselves as adults. Holidays were a lot of work. The everyday tasks of cooking and cleaning and making beds, of children, of organizing outings, were not always, but mostly, done by women. These tasks were constantly referred to – in our childhood memories we were already engaged in helping perform them. . . . None of the boys' memories mentions any work; certainly they do not appear to have done any, or to be expected to do any. Nor do they refer, or appear to be aware of the work performed by their mother. Each refers to the other people and the place as part of the given of the holiday – the backdrop against which their own private drama was played. In essence this drama revolved around their own private excitement and

> pleasure at play. The memories were predominantly carefree and pleasurable: "every day was fun and new", "a sack of toys was at the end of the bed" (1992: 143).

Here we are thinking of the differences that might exist for men remembering themselves as boys playing with G.I. Joe or more recent Action Figures, and women recalling themselves as girls playing with Barbie. Although there is a context for interrogating childhood play around war toys (Carlsson-Paige 1987) – generally boys' toys – the moral panics about boys playing with such toys tends to wax and wane. The criticism of Barbie (and of her fans) has never waned, although, as we explore elsewhere (Mitchell and Reid-Walsh 1993), it has changed over time. At various points Barbie has been associated with excessive consumerism, at other times with causing eating disorders. The controversies surrounding G.I. Joe and the controversies surrounding Barbie are not experienced in the same way by males and females. Not surprisingly, then, as John Michlig points out in his analysis of G.I. Joe in *G.I. Joe: The Complete Story of American's Favorite Man of Action*, males and females *apparently* recall G.I. Joe and Barbie differently. Michlig writes:

> Since his appeal is often compared to that of his close relative, Barbie, it should be noted that men's memories of GI Joe seem free of most of the angst attached to Mattel's fashion doll. "Body image" is a nonissue; as kids, we boys had no desire to grow up looking like GI Joe, and in fact we pitied him for his spindly legs and arms. Unhealthy materialism resulting from the pursuit of endless accessories? Sure, we yearned for the latest adventure equipment, but GI Joe did not need a gleaming townhouse as long as your parents allowed you to dig a dirt fort in the backyard.
>
> And the "war toy" argument? Virtually irrelevant in hindsight, since GI Joe existed as a military man for a mere six of its thirteen-year original product run. Still, if exposure to olive drab and miniature armaments before puberty indeed leads to a malformed adult psyche, the damage to millions of former GI Joe owners has managed to keep itself well hidden.
>
> Furthermore, philosophic debate among members of the GI Joe generation regarding the toy are most often limited to pro and con discussions of the "coolness" value of Kung-Fu Grip, or whether it was possible to successfully shave the flocked beard of an Adventure Team member.
>
> Purely and simply, GI Joe was fun. (1998: 198–9).

We highlight the word "apparently" in relation to this analysis, since to date boys' popular culture texts have been subjected to much less scrutiny in both the popular and the academic press. However, we would concur with Michlig that generally there is much less "hype" about boys' play and the extent to which the freedom to "just get on with play" ensures a relatively fraughtless environment, for play is likely to contribute to what is recalled years later.

Women, however, are much less likely to look back on childhood play in such a "free-wheeling" way, as we see in the memory account of Avra, a beginning teacher in her early twenties, who recalls the ways in which class was an intervening variable in her Cabbage Patch doll memory. As she writes:

> When I was young, I wanted a Cabbage Patch Kid so much because everyone had one. But my parents were very reluctant to spend $45.00 for a toy. I strongly remember finally convincing my mom to purchase me one, and out of desperation, I said she could even take the money out of my savings account. She said "all right!" So, we went to the pharmacy (because they were sold almost *everywhere* at that time) and purchased a brunette doll. When I finally brought her home, I admired her so much. I was thrilled – until my father found out that I had spent all that money on a doll. He said it was "unheard of" and ordered my mother to return it! I begged her not to, but I had no say in the matter. A couple of days later I got home from school and found a beautiful Cabbage Patch Kid on my bed! I was so excited until I checked her behind. There was no cabbage patch signature on the bum! From that point on, I knew that she was a fake, and I refused to fall in love with the doll. During recess and lunch time in school, the kids who did have dolls would get together and role play. But I was always left out because I didn't have one and I was too embarrassed to bring in an ugly fake one. Luckily, it was not too long until they stopped allowing the dolls to school (personal communication).

While we do not want to suggest that it is only women who have memories of childhood play that are marred, Avra's memory compared with the G.I. Joe memory raises important points about studying the critical space of children's play through memory. What Avra's account provides is some recognition of the narrow range of possibilities that children (here, girls) must be aware of in negotiating a social space for play. These power dynamics, regardless of whether they are in relation to siblings and peer pressure at school or gangs are not something that most children can so easily describe – at the time of the experience. Interestingly, Tsakalis (1998) found in her interviews with males and females in their mid-twenties to late twenties who had watched the first *Toy Story* film that their responses had a gendered dimension to them:

> The women's reactions were much more critical, realizing that every part of their play was centred around the home and their appearance. The men were definitely more nostalgic, less critical, and much happier about the memories of their childhood. By and large they remembered a childhood full of adventure and excitement, something they

> said is now lacking in their lives. They all expressed the feeling that although they "liked" their jobs and their personal lives, the vigour and excitement they now remembered feeling when they were children is no longer a part of their lives. When I questioned them, the participants likened that "excitement feeling" that is missing to the scene in the movie *Toy Story* where Andy anxiously waits for his birthday guests to arrive and then even more excitingly opens his gifts (1998: 53).

How memory is interpreted by the rememberer is of course the point of this work. In speaking of her work with Barbie players, Erica Rand considers the tendency of her respondents to see a direct progression from childhood to adulthood as itself an adult construction which often employs the plot of the destiny narrative. She compares the chronological structure of the Barbie narratives which read the present from the past to the structure of psychotherapy and the *bildungsroman* (1995: 112). Rand also notes that memory is selective: what is remembered is because of its significance, while what is forgotten may be because it is commonplace. She observes that the main interpretative point of "even back then" may also be the main catalyst for the retrieval of memory and/or fabrication (ibid.: 137). However, she also cautions that while many adults assume that one's present can be explained by identifying incidents in one's past from which the present appears to be a logical outgrowth, the frequency with which they unravel under scrutiny supports Freud's idea that these narratives are a mixture of *history and myth* (emphasis added ibid.: 114).

On Memory Work

We highlight the term "history and myth" above because we regard it as particularly relevant to understanding the role of the cowboy hero in memory work. As Tasker (1998) and others observe, cowboys are already imbued with history and myth. While many of the television heroes are based on real life (Annie Oakley, Davy Crockett), they have taken on larger-than-life mythical status. In popular culture they are meant to be spectacles of sharp-shooting, heroic courage, and omnipotence. In their larger-than-life status, then, they are ideal sites for memory work, since it is "history and myth" that is precisely at the center of conducting memory work.

What differentiates memory work from simply collecting accidental memory accounts, testimonials or confessionals centers on the word "work," and the fact that the person remembering is the one who "works back" or "works through" the memory, engaging in what the novelist Toni Morrison describes as "deliberate remembering." As Morrison writes, "Memory (the deliberate act of remembering) is a form of willed creation. It is not an effort to find out the way it was. The point is to dwell on the way it appeared and why it appeared that particular way" (1996: 213). In approaching memory as a deliberate or purposeful act, the various methodologies that we discuss here – ranging from what we call "first draft/second draft writing" to a strategy for working with photographs – fit with the distinction bell hooks makes between "nostalgia, that longing for something to be as it once was, a kind of useless act, and that remembering that serves to illuminate and transform the present" (cited in Maingard 1994: 240).

While there are a number of different approaches to working back through memory, ranging from the collective "writing in the third person" memory work of Haug and associates or June Crawford et al., to the individual remembering of Annette Kuhn (1995), Naomi Norquay (1993), Mitchell and Weber (1999), Weber and Mitchell (1995), Zandy (1995), all the approaches have one thing in common: a strategy for moving from a "first draft" or unself-consciously mediated remembering to working back in a systematic way. An example is Patricia Hampl's work (1996) on memoir writing. The rememberer writes out the memory first in an early draft, and then goes over it a second time, looking for inconsistencies, out-and-out lies, misrememberings and the ways in which it wasn't quite the way it was first remembered. Jacqui, for example, having once accidentally remembered a cowgirl suit that she had as a child, writes a first draft of "Playing Cowgirl:"

> As an only child of successful middle-class parents, I always had lots of toys – boys' toys as well as girls' toys. Indeed, my father took a delight in toys and he made some (boys') toys and bought me many others – I, of course, did not think of my hand-made castle complete with towers and drawbridge, or crafted doll-house imitating an English "cottage" or toy train which was a replica of a famous steam engine as boys' toys or girls' toys – I just know I delighted in playing with them. Since I was growing up in the 1950s and 1960s, my leisure activities also meant that in addition to engaging with quality toys, I was also exposed to popular culture through television and then radio and records. My memories of television are mainly of watching westerns with my father – and indeed his interest in the American West has never diminished, in his active retirement tracing in car trips General Custer's route, and, now not as vigorous, reading historical books about the period or watching history shows. When I was little we watched all the frontier shows and westerns series together, the names run together: Daniel Boone, Bat Masterson, Wyatt Earp, and later Bonanza and we took trips to children's theme parks such as Frontier Land. There my parents who are always well-decked out, bought me a complete cowgirl suit.
>
> Talking with my parents, during the summer of 1999, of this period of my childhood, I am reminded of my cowgirl suit. I vainly look for old photographs. In my mind I am able to imagine myself again complete with red braids. The photographs, it seems, have either become submerged because of my parents' many moves, or more likely,

> are somewhere in my small apartment's locker. I asked them about the cowgirl suit. All I remember is the fringe on the vest, the holsters, with guns, and the hat. But apparently, I had boots, and a skirt as well. My parents related how we went to Frontier Land, and my father told how one of the lead actors of the television series – he played Bat Masterson I think – came and enacted a shoot-out on the streets of Dodge. The ritual of the men in the white hats and black hats, good and evil, would be played out – the bad would be shot dead by the good. Then when it was over everyone would get up and walk away to re-stage the scene a while later. We explored every area of the "land" with my mother patiently coming along. Apparently I even had my picture with my arms fixed in the posture of a "varmint" in a stock.
>
> My father tells me I was most interested in the girl cowboys – Annie Oakley and Calamity Jane and others – were there others? Indeed, one of my nicknames was the latter: I am Jane by birth and tend to be somewhat dramatic in my reactions to catastrophes. He likes to think my feminist leanings were thereby presaged by this early taste in heroines.

Jacqui then proceeds – somewhat more deliberately – to review the first draft. While the first draft contains a combination of description and reflection, the second interrogates the details, images, as well as looking for gaps, inventions, and so on. As she writes:

> After having written the above account of my cowgirl memories, I once again talked to my parents on the telephone during our regular weekly or bi-weekly long-distance conversations. It soon became apparent that I had mis-remembered the events and elided different periods from my childhood together.
>
> I was surprised and intrigued by what I had constructed. My parents were able to correct me about numerous specifics, for instance, the actor who came to Frontier Land was Hugh O'Brien who played Wyatt Earp, the other television shows that were westerns were *Roy Rogers*, *Hopalong Cassidy*, *Have Gun will Travel*, and my cowgirl outfit was specifically a Dale Evans outfit which was pale blue. Most significantly, as the differences between shows such as *Roy Rogers* and *Wyatt Earp* indicate that a collapsing of time has occurred in my memory. I was a little girl in the early grades of primary school when I liked the singing cowboy and his partner Dale Evans, and older when I liked the drama series *Wyatt Earp*. The trip to Frontier Land was at this later age in middle school.
>
> I wonder, what is the significance of the mis-remembering and the elision of the two periods? What happened to the picture (and indeed the little girl) in her pale blue cowgirl suit? Apart from a frivolous

early establishment of fashion tastes (I know I have always liked pale blue denim, and jean skirts) what does my nostalgic image signify? It is again interesting that I identified with the female (equal) companion to *Roy Rogers*, but nothing else specific comes to mind reading this image as a symbol. Perhaps the act of connection is as important as the image, for it is a way of connecting with my now quite aged parents, and talking about our past. Perhaps, in a Gilligan-inspired move I am attempting to move back in my own life to a period before the shutter of adolescence was erected, to connect with the earlier "child" and discover who she was?

As an aside, while I was talking about looking for early photographs featuring my engagement with popular culture, my daughter started going through her photo album and showed me images of herself in costumes that I had bought her for Halloween. One was of her in kindergarten dressed as Ariel from *The Little Mermaid*. What she remembers was the embarrassment of having a long dress with a train – the tail – people looked at her and commented on the tail. Doing a liberal feminist reading – is there a difference between my early autonomy and freedom in my little cowgirl suit and her restricted mobility in her evening dress? What is the difference between growing up in the 1950s which I maintain, contrary to popular opinion, was not necessarily repressive for young girls and the post-modern, some would say post-feminist 1990s? Also she was younger than I was in her costume and expressed no interest in it – I bought her the Ariel costume for Halloween because she loved to dance to the calypso songs in the Disney film, and I quite enjoyed the matriarchal under-sea-world of the middle sections of the film, before the conventional Disney ending clicked in. On the other hand, a cowgirl costume now, with guns no less, would be considered to be encouraging violence, and as resurrecting a colonial history of oppression against the Native Americans. Yet the Disney film which inspired this costume (a rewriting of Hans Christian Anderson's brilliant and disturbing representation of nineteenth-century European femininity) can perhaps be considered as another manifestation of the same fantasy genre: stories where there is a battle between good and evil where reassuringly good people (guys or gals, cowgirls or mermaids) "win" over overpowering odds, no matter how this is defined.

The two drafts provide examples of some of the ways that misrememberings within the space of memory can be "worked through." They also illustrate well the ways in which working with the memory can contribute to theorizing childhood culture more specifically.

Memory Work and Photography

As we see in Jacqui's memory piece, photographs – both those currently in existence as well as those lost – can play an important role in memory work and indeed can also be regarded as another type of "first draft/second draft" approach to memory. While on the one hand they can serve as prompts to memory, they can also be regarded as providing corrections to memory. Family squabbles are occasionally settled by photographic proof: "See, I was the one who received the Barbie." Annette Kuhn (1995) includes an analysis of the inscriptions, on the backs of snapshots, as part of the corrective component when she explores a disagreement over what her mother wrote on the back of a photograph and what really happened.

Drawing from the extensive literature that already exists on the use of photographs, especially family snapshots (Annette Kuhn 1995; Jo Spence 1995; Marianne Hirsch 1997; Carol Mavor 1999; Judy Weiser 1999), along with the previous work on school photographs (Mitchell and Weber 1999), we are interested in how family snapshots can be used as the raw material of memory work in looking at children's popular culture. Photographs of popular culture artifacts, as we take up further in Chapter 3 on children as visual ethnographers, are likely to be abundant within the photo collections of families in Western countries simply because holiday occasions such as birthdays and Christmas are "high season" for gift-giving, dressing up (including taking on masquerades), and of course taking pictures.

Claudia, for example, in revisiting the family album, discovers a number of cowboy/cowgirl photographs, both from her own childhood in the 1950s, and from that of her children from the early 1980s. One is of herself in a family holiday snapshot from 1959 when the family is heading off to the Calgary Stampede (Figure 2.5). Claudia is the only one who is recognizably in costume; what she recalls was a brand-new white straw cowboy hat complete with striped cord and a whistle. In another snapshot, this time from a twenty-fifth anniversary family gathering in 1957, her brothers are in their Davy Crockett jackets (Figure 2.6). The third is of her middle daughter Sarah, who at age five decided that she wanted western paraphernalia for her birthday (Figure 2.7). She received a black felt cowboy hat with rim-stitching and cowboy boots, and a western-inspired pink and grey polyester shirt. While there are several snapshots from that time period with Sarah in her cowgirl regalia, the snapshot here captures Sarah in a cross-over outfit of sunsuit and western regalia. Any one of these photographs could provide the raw material for engaging in memory work. Sarah, for example, whenever she looks at the photograph of herself, mourns the loss of the cowboy boots. What image does she hold of those boots and that attire? Where does it fit with her sense of self now?

What follows is a protocol for working with photographs that has been adapted from Kuhn's *Family Secrets: Acts of Memory and Imagination* (1995).

Figure 2.5 En route to Calgary Stampede (photograph by Leslie Skinner).

Figure 2.6 Davy Crockett jackets: family gathering 1957 (photograph by William Skinner).

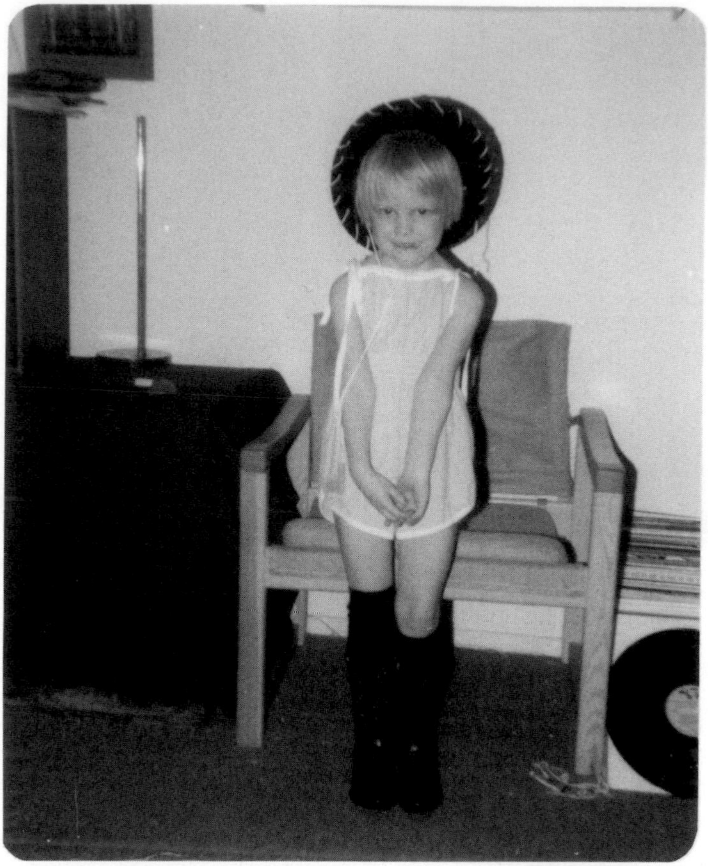

Figure 2.7 Sunsuit cowgirl (photograph by Claudia Mitchell).

1 Consider the human subject(s) of the photograph. Start with a simple description, and then move into an account in which you can take up the position of the subject. In this part of the exercise, it is helpful to use the third person ("she" rather than "I" for instance). To bring out the feelings associated with the photograph, you may visualize yourself as the subject as she was at that moment, in the picture; this can be done in turn with all of the photograph's human subjects, if there is more than one and even with inanimate objects in the picture.
2 Consider the picture's context of production. Where, when, how, by whom and why was the photograph taken?
3 Consider the context in which an image of this sort would have been made. What photographic technologies were used? What are the aesthetics of the image? Does it conform with certain photographic images?

4 Consider the photograph's currency in its context or contexts of reception. Who or what was the photograph made for? Who has it now, and where has it been kept? Who saw it then and who sees it now?

(Mitchell and Weber 1999: 99).

Claudia works with a photograph of herself reading an Annie Oakley book. The memory account, prompted by this photograph – a missing photograph – first appeared in *Reinventing Ourselves as Teachers: Beyond Nostalgia*. However, the act of "fixing it" in print in no way ensures that it is "fixed" for all time. Claudia, for example, adds in a title for the photograph so that it is no longer "just a memory"; it is now "Danger at Diablo," named after the Annie Oakley book that she is reading. In using this title, however, she is also drawing attention to the interpretations she is placing on the memory. The fact that it is not just a photograph but rather is a missing photograph takes on more importance, so she adds in "Lost photograph."

"Lost photograph: 'Danger at Diablo'
Taken Christmas Day, circa, 1959
(Photographer: Dad or Auntie Nell)"

It is a black-and-white photograph. She is around eight or nine years old, and she is sitting by herself on a couch at her aunt and uncle's place, reading an Annie Oakley novel, *Danger at Diablo*, a book that she received that day from her grandmother. In the picture, she seems engrossed in the book and it is unlikely that she knew the picture was being taken. She can only vaguely remember reading the book that day, although she remembers reading it over and over again later. She is interested now in its gender-appropriateness. Annie Oakley for a girl. She would never have been given something that wasn't exactly for a girl, and clearly distinguished from what "the boys," her two older brothers, would receive. What did they receive? Was that the year they received Jules Verne's *Twenty Thousand Leagues Under the Sea* and Mark Twain's *Huckleberry Finn*? The books were all part of the same series: shiny, plasticized contemporary-for-then covers, neatly laid-out table of contents, newsprint-like pages, but with red edging. The endplates always had some sort of content-related design. What interests her now is that she was allowed to engage in such a solitary activity as reading on a social occasion like Christmas. Where were the boys? Is she excluded from being with them (again) or does she want to be reading? But she is also now intrigued by the title: *Danger at Diablo*! What could be dangerous? Being eight or nine – the last good years as Carol Gilligan and her associates would have it – the years just before she loses voice. But is it already too late? Does she want to be reading Annie Oakley or is this another case of "second best" – taking what they (her brothers) don't want? Has she already lost her voice? Can the fiercely independent cowgirl Annie Oakley save her?

> Who had the foresight to capture this moment on film? Who would have thought that a solitary subject – Claudia reading – was worthy? Somehow to take a picture of just one person was wasteful, indulgent: Get everyone lined up and posed – one shot fits all. Why devote a whole photograph to just one person unless it was the person's birthday? Get everyone lined up and posed – one shot fits all. As for taking an unposed picture – no one ever took candid shots! Is this where the construction of herself as "always reading" was conceived and formulated? To her knowledge, this is the only known photograph of herself reading until adulthood. The snapshot always lived in the photobox, a large Eaton's coatbox. It was not the kind of photograph that was displayed; snapshots never were unless enlarged (and even then only if there was no possibility of a studio photograph – for instance, if someone had died and this was the last picture). The only photos put up on display were formal shots of weddings or a studio portrait of some child, customarily at age one. Surviving to the age of one is the last major occasion until high school graduation. But being stuck in the coatbox did not mean that these less formal photos were never looked at. Going through the pictures was a regular family pastime for the women, especially when her aunts would come over. Claudia probably saw this same photograph two or three times a year and probably also heard as frequently "Oh there's Claudia reading!" It is not just Claudia who carries around the solitary image of herself reading. It is also their image; it fits in with life's events (Mitchell and Weber 1999: 100–1).

On revisiting the memory account, Claudia becomes interested in other details. The photograph, for example, may be lost, but the book itself, *Danger at Diablo* by Doris Shroeder, has been on a shelf in her office for ten years. There is something significant about the fact that there has been this western image in the midst of her working life all these years. At the same time she begins to reflect more on the significance of reading about a cowgirl – and what was deemed as appropriate literature "for a girl." Why had she not remembered that, in fact, she had delivered a paper years earlier on the very issue of wanting to be a cowboy?

> It is not as though I ever wanted to be Roy Rogers or Dale Evans . . . I don't think I ever wanted to play anybody other than Hop-along Cassidy, and the reasons for that, while vague, seem in my mind to have something to do with the fact that nobody else that I played with, chiefly my two older brothers, ever wanted to be Hop-along. Choosing someone like Hop-along, so clearly a lesser hero was my entry ticket to being allowed to play at all. I stayed outside all the major power struggles like who would actually get to be The Cisco Kid or Zorro. It was the same thing when we spent long hours carving

> out new towns and cities, building roads and bridges, and especially setting up territories, properties and "acreages." My brothers had landrovers and other all-terrain vehicles and a few flashy cars. I had the 1953 mercury convertible, which in retrospect sounds rather glamorous, and could even have rivalled Nancy Drew's roadster. However, it wasn't considered so much glamorous as wholesome, and in settling for this car, I was no threat to any of the power struggles. As long as I was willing to know my place, and to be content to aspire to nothing beyond the 1953 merc I was allowed entry to dinky toy play.
>
> My own play texts carried with them little cultural capital – a doll carriage, a wooden cradle and high chair, a decent if not huge supply of dolls, and a bride doll, carried absolutely no weight. Occasionally I might find that my play site was in the middle of "war" or "guns," or I would set up beside their meccano or Lincoln Log colony, or near their electric train. Generally, though, I was left to my own devices, not I am convinced, out of any respect, but only out of disinterest on the part of my brothers. I suppose they did not feel they were missing much. For example, the bride doll, to this day has never had her dress off, let alone her underwear. One could tie and untie her little leatherette shoes, and remove her netted socks, but that's about it. The only thing she ever really lost was her head a few years ago, in one of my moves. Otherwise, she was taken out of her box occasionally, admired and then placed back in her brown box with the cellophane window, where she would stay for months before coming out again. I don't recall that I was particularly dissatisfied with the state of affairs, but that at least was in part connected to the fact that my aspirations seem not to have been particularly high. I did not really expect them to play school, or house or paper dolls or whatever it was that I played; I merely wanted to be accepted into their play culture (Mitchell 1991).

The value of the single photograph, then, missing or as part of a collection, lies in its potential to help uncover layers of meaning – indeed to engage in an archival dig. In fact, selecting the appropriate verb tense for describing this memory work is not easy – "has worked with" "is working with" "continues to work with." When does the memory work end? Childhood memories, even after, or especially after, they have been retrieved, continue to unravel.

Reading Back Cowboy Memories Through *Toy Story 2*

"Some bright sociologist I'm sure, will one day pin down the exact moment our toys began to toy with us" writes Gary Thompson in a review of *Toy Story 2* (*Philadelphia Daily News*, November 24, 1999). Thompson's point is one with which Ian Wojcik-Andrews is likely to agree, pointing out as he does in *Children's Films: History, Ideology, Pedagogy, Theory* that children's films might well be taught from the perspective of ethnography (2000). *Toy Story 2*, in particular, is full of provocative entry points with regard to a number of issues related to theorizing childhood and material culture, ranging from the commodification of children's culture through collecting and collectors ("You're not a collector's item, you are somebody's toy"), to serving as some unofficial version of the history of children's television culture over the past forty years since it operates in time zones ranging from the 1950s to the present.

As a background to examining the ways that *Toy Story 2* reads back cowboy memories, we draw on the idea of a particular genre of children's films that have meta-filmic qualities. As described by Wojcik-Andrews, these are films which, through style, content and a degree of self-reflexivity, work to provide a meta-commentary on particular phenomena. In speaking specifically of such films as *Stand By Me*, *Last Action Hero*, and the first *Toy Story*, he observes that:

> metafilmic qualities [are] those that suggest innovation, experimentation, and a high degree of playful self-consciousness. These and other films draw attention to themselves as artifice by playing with the various filmic conventions and extrafilmic practices that constitute cinema as a whole, including children's cinema. In the process, they contest the very definition of what constitutes a children's film. They situate themselves within a category they themselves resist and blur a debate of which they themselves are the focus. To borrow from Jameson, these and other children's films offer a "commentary [which is] at the same time a metacommentary as well" (2000: 11–12).

In drawing on this idea of meta-filmic qualities, we ask, in this final section of the chapter, the question: "As a pedagogical tool how can we use the film *Toy Story 2* to 'read back' childhood and memory?"

For our purposes, we regard *Toy Story 2* as perhaps the "ultimate memory-work" film in relation to children's popular culture. Produced as a sequel to *Toy Story* and directed and produced by John Lasseter, *Toy Story 2* takes many of the same toys that appeared in *Toy Story,* but gives them a whole new adventure, one which has a high degree of self-referentiality where the protagonists Cowboy Woody and Jessie the Yodellin' Cowgirl engage in "studying themselves" in relation to their aging child-owners, Andy and Emily. The movie is organized around the theft of little Andy's Cowboy Woody doll by an obsessive toy collector Chicken Al, who has been amassing the whole collection of IMC (in mint condition) toys associated with a fictional TV series from the 1950s, Woody's Roundup. When Woody discovers that his real identity is to be found in this 1950s TV show tie-in, along with

Prospector Pete, Bull's Eye and Jessie, and at the same time is the "subject" of a huge rescue operation by all the toys from Andy's bedroom (Buzz Lightyear, Mr. Potato Head, Slinky, the dinosaur and others), he faces a major dilemma. Should he stay with the Roundup gang, thereby completing the collection which Al is selling to a Japanese toy museum (and ensuring that they will all live on together), or should he go back to his owner Andy who for the moment is still interested in him, but who is inevitably going to outgrow him and forget all about him? The complicating factor is that without Woody, Pete, Bull's Eye and Jessie are worthless and will be confined to a packing-case. Is it better to opt for longevity or to go with the ephemerality of childhood?

While there are a number of different life-histories present in the movie – a memory-work device in itself – Jessie's story as recounted to Woody just after he has told her that he is going back to Andy provides one of the most obvious examples from the film of the relationship between childhood and the afterlife of popular culture. Told with the backdrop of Sarah McLaughlin's singing "When She Loved Me," her story might be read as the decline and fall of her positioning in the life of Emily, her owner who has left her, as the song goes: "Lonely and forgotten. . . ." In the scene, which takes place on the window-sill of Chicken Al's museum room, Jessie tells the story that any abandoned toy could tell:

Woody: Hey what you doin' up here?

Jessie: I thought I'd get one last look at the sun before I get packed away again.

Woody: Look Jessie, I know you hate me for leaving, but I have to go back. I'm still Andy's toy.

Jessie: [sigh]

Woody: Well if you knew him you'd understand. You see Andy's a really. . . .

Jessie: [cutting him off] Let me guess, Andy's a *real* special kid and to him you're his buddy, his best friend, and when Andy plays with you it's like even though you're not moving, you feel like you're alive, 'coz that's how he sees you.

Woody: How did you know that?

Jessie: Because Emily was just the same. She was my whole world. . . . [song begins]

Jessie: [as song ends] You never forget kids like Emily or Andy but they forget you. (From *Toy Story 2*).

We see scenes of her life with her owner Emily, the way they played on the swings together, the way she was a feature of Emily's bedroom and others – and then we see her tossed aside, under Emily's bed – to be replaced by nail polish, a pink princess telephone, teen pictures, and so on. Finally, one day Emily packs her up in the family station-wagon and she is dumped at a recycling depot. Of all the toys in the movie, Jessie is the least childlike, almost disturbingly so at times. Her life however is based on being a survivor since she has survived abandonment by Emily, as well as years of being banished to a box, knowing that she can never be anything unless a Woody doll is found to complete the Woody's Roundup set. And then, just when she is on the brink of being rescued, she discovers that Woody is going back to Andy. She becomes hysterical, and pulls at her hair as only someone who has experienced great pain and anguish can do, and cries "I won't go back."

The poignancy of Jessie's song picks up on the longing, and even more so the yearning, for a time gone by. When we conducted our own version of "kitchen research" at the office, we played the song – seemingly randomly outside of any pre-established context – for several of our female colleagues. The respondents had no familiarity with the movie and were unaware of the origins of the song, but they made comments such as: "It sounds like a mother–child relationship," "Could it be a dog and its owner?" "It sounds like a very tender love song – perhaps written as a male singing to a female but recorded by a female." The comment that was most telling, though, was one which – although accidentally offered – was accurately descriptive of Jessie's emotional state: "In some ways it is like a small child feeling abandoned by its parents." Unlike Woody, who in his toy life is still "innocent" or "unknowing" in that he is still a beloved toy, Jessie has passed through rejection or into what William Blake would label "experience" and is struggling to survive by staying outside of the box turned prison. In the final scenes of the movie which take place in Andy's room, she is adopted. Like Andy's other special toys such as Woody and Buzz, who have the imprint "ANDY" on the bottom of their shoe, Jessie too has the stamp of Andy on her foot. She again has an owner along with the possibility of another girl who will take care of her: Andy's baby sister Molly.

If we take into account the tales of "two owners," Andy and Emily and their dolls, Woody and Jessie, what do the narratives suggest to us about gender and age(ing), and memory and nostalgia? Woody has not yet experienced being rejected by his owner, and has difficulty even anticipating a past. Until he meets up with Jessie and Prospector Pete, he has no sense that he was ever part of a television series. More significantly, he seems to have never wondered where he came from. Jessie, on the contrary, lives only with the past as very much a part of her present. If Andy is a boy who has not yet grown up, Woody can remain relatively innocent of suffering, except in his nightmares. Perhaps Andy is another Peter Pan figure, one who never ages. By contrast, only girl owners in this movie seem to age, or at least they age more quickly, and their dolls are discarded so that they can turn themselves into dolls through their use of nail polish, lipstick, and fashionable hair, a point that we return to in Chapter 6, "Historical Spaces: Barbie Looks Back."

The film "reads back" memory in relation to ephemerality and abandonment in other ways. The toy shelves in Andy's room, for example, are something of an archive in this regard, as we realize when we see the toys and books that are on an upper shelf: games such as *Clue* and *Twister*, storybooks which must have belonged to a previous generation in Andy's family (*The Little Reader Collection of Children's Stories*, *The Really Big Book of Trucks*), a Fisher Price ring-stacking set (with authentic-looking dust), that even Baby Molly has outgrown, and so on are all there. When Woody dreams that Andy comes back and decides to throw him out because his arm is torn, he imagines himself in a huge garbage can full of used arms, legs, and other body parts left over from broken toys. This "relegated to the shelf" type of existence is of course even more marked in Jessie's life since she really was cast off at a recycling, junk-yard-type depot. In her case, she is first cast under the bed – where she waits for Emily to love her again . . . "for the day when she'd say I will always love you." Other cast-offs join her, but her position under the bed is mostly her "final resting place" until she is thrown out at the recycling depot. The reasons for her being cast off speak less to the idea of new crazes and inventions and more to the fact that Jessie's owner, Emily, grows out of dolls and into nail polish, talking on the telephone, and other adolescent activities.

Toy Story 2 reviews the fluctuating market-driven value contained within the supply-and-demand ratio of children's popular culture, and in so doing "reads back" anticipation followed by forgetting. While as former children we might all have personal stories to tell of "short supply" toys that we did or did not manage to receive for Christmas or a birthday – the run on Cabbage Patch dolls, the dearth one particular year of Elmo dolls, and so on – it is Barbie, the tour guide who in the film takes the toys on a guided tour of Al's Barn, and who notes that it was 1995 when merchandisers failed to take into consideration the popularity of the Buzz Lightyear doll. This intertextual reference relates back to the first *Toy Story* movie which was released in 1995. In that movie where Buzz arrives on the scene as a birthday gift to Andy there is some tension when Buzz is told that he is a toy (and not a real space ranger). Now, of course, in the Toys"R"Us-type store that Chicken Al runs, there is an entire "oversupply" wall, floor to ceiling filled with boxes of Buzz Lightyear toys.

Another feature of the film which contributes to its "reading back" on childhood memory is through its use of time dislocations. The film works to destabilize our memory and time-consciousness in a variety of ways. For one thing, we are never really sure of the era in which the film is set, or whether, for example, Jessie's owner, a little girl, Emily, was a relatively recent owner – like Woody in relation to his owner Andy – or whether the early 1960s Ford-Falcon type woodgrain ranch wagon can be taken as indicative of an earlier period. But the seat belt that holds Emily snugly in place is more likely to indicate the 1970s. This same confusion also exists in the *Toy Story* movie. Ostensibly the movie has a contemporary setting but the major conflict in the storyline centers on the fact that the special status of Cowboy Woody as the favored play toy of Andy is threatened when Buzz Lightyear, a space toy, arrives on the scene. While we are not at all sure where Woody comes from (a cowboy doll in 1995?), even Buzz Lightyear is far from contemporary. At the same time, as Brown points out, in the first *Toy Story* movie there is a "jockeying" between the real and the virtual that might be taken as a meta-reading of generational conflict. He observes:

> Though the film personifies the tension between the latest battery operated space ranger (Buzz Lightyear) and the pull-string cowboy (Woody), what makes the movie anachronistic is that for pre-adolescent boys in the 1990s, video games and computer games (for instance Disney Interactive's own *Toy Story* CD-Rom game) threaten to render the toys depicted (including piggy banks and toy soldiers, Mr. Potato Head and Etch a Sketch) all but obsolete (1998: 962).

These mixed eras serve to leave the viewer in a potential time warp. However, the sheer volume of television tie-ins that appear as Jessie takes Woody on a tour of his previous life also contributes to disturbing our sense of remembering. As we noted in the Introduction to this book, when Leigh takes his two sons to *Toy Story*, there is a constant "I want." As an audience for *Toy Story 2*, the adult viewers might be inclined to call out "I had" or "I remember" or "Where is that now?" or "I wish I'd hung on to that!" If there are any adults out there born after World War II who have criticized today's generation of children as having too many toys or have lamented the dominance of materialism, their cover has been blown by *Toy Story 2*. While the entire script is "made up" in the sense that a whole fictional television series has been created for the movie, it also includes the vast collection of television tie-ins that go with the series – doll versions of the main characters, Woody, Jessie, Prospector Pete, and Bull's Eye, along with such artifacts as Woody's roundup lamps, lunch kits, yo-yos, radios, cookie jars, record-players, records, collector plates, breakfast cereal – a whole cardboard village, a larger-than-life cardboard cut-out poster, and so on. What is interesting, though, is that the Roundup dolls, themselves the tie-in for the fictional Woody's Roundup series, have become the tie-in for *Toy Story 2*. The fact that many of these artifacts were on the market long before the movie was actually released creates, of course, not only a demand for the products in the usual way that Disney does with other movies, but also a double sense of déjà vu. For the child viewer there is a sense of anticipation, but also a sense perhaps, when Woody, Jessie and the other tie-ins appear on the big screen, that they really are part of someone's past. It is a clever feature cinematically. It is also clever as a marketing approach.

Like Hollywood blockbusters generally, *Toy Story 2* has a different type of time-consciousness to it because of the advanced publicity provided on such production shows as *Hollywood Access* and *Entertainment Tonight*, and of course the official website of the movie, where it is possible to know almost anything there is to know about the production of the film or television text, the movie tie-ins, fan responses, and so on. In the case of *Toy Story 2*, in much of the information that is available about John Lasseter the director, there is an added sense of the blurrings of time and memory. For example, as we learn in various magazines and popular sites, Lasseter, a baby-boomer father of five sons is himself a toy collector. He and his production crew played around with a whole range of movie *clins d'oeil* transplanted from their favorite movies and directors: Spielberg's *Jurassic Park*, Irvin Kershner's *The Empire Strikes Back*, George Roy Hill's *Butch Cassidy and the Sundance Kid*, Guy Hamilton's *Goldfinger*, Paul Verhoeven's *Robocop*, Stanley Kubrick's *2001 Space Odyssey*, Renny Harlin's *58 Minutes to Live*. While these variations of well-known scenes are, of course, "playful" for the production crew, they also contribute to a sense of déjà vu for the adult viewer. We are meant to be remembering!

At the same time, however, it is important to recognize the extent to which these production texts highlight the notion of "origin myths," since so many websites and other sources simply reproduce the information found elsewhere. Some of the websites are "official" in that they contain numbers related to promotion and distribution; others are fan sites which often simply import information from other websites. In our own readings and rereadings of *Toy Story 2* we found ourselves returning to the origin stories, eager to see that yes, indeed, just as Lasseter is quoted in *Premiere* (2000), there really is an announcement at the airport for Lasset Air (Lasseter) Flight A1 13 (named after the classroom at Cal Tech where Lasseter studied) to Fort Richmond (his home). While, as he notes, it is not necessary for the audience to know these details in order to enjoy the film, the fact is that they add a layer of textuality to the viewing, which in this case also contributes to a sense of memory. Indeed, it is as though Lasseter had written the script according to Fiske's discussion of the various layers of textuality that constitute a cultural reading. Fiske proposes that there are really three levels of text: the primary text (television episode, the actual movie, and all the tie-ins and spin-offs), the reader text (how viewers respond to the text), and the production text (the various ways in which the producers market the text) all of which "leak into each other" (1987: 256) and hence demand to be read together if we are to understand the meanings that people make of them. Here the three levels of textuality leak into each other to create a memory text.

Finally, we draw attention to the role of the out-takes in *Toy Story 2* towards contributing to a memory text. The movie seems to end, and then, as the final credits roll on, we are treated to several more scenes. The inclusion of out-takes as part of the primary text is something that we have seen in a number of recent films for children (e.g. *A Bug's Life*). In the case of *Toy Story 2*, these out-takes go beyond the idea of production moments (although there are playful moments in the out-takes that appear to be production moments), or even play-backs of scenes from the film, to include references to sequels that then create the sense that we are already operating in a future–past moment. For example, in one of these out-takes we meet two characters from the movie, *A Bug's Life*, also a Pixar film, who think they are part of a sequel, *A Bug's Life 2*, only to discover that they are only part of the backdrop for a production of *Toy Story 2*. In another out-take Prospector Pete as a dirty old man is propositioning a couple of Barbie dancers who are inside his collector box – promising them parts in a movie. Because of the origin stories where we have been told that Mattel was more than happy – this time – to have Barbie involved (for *Toy Story 1* they refused permission for Barbie to appear), there may be an element of having "sold out." Somehow Pete's line is suggestive of the kinds of deals that might have been struck between Mattel and Pixar – but it also suggests future deals; *Toy Story 2*, then, is already history. In still another out-take, three little Martian creatures who appear in the final airport scene of *Toy Story 2* wonder how they can get a part in *Toy Story 3*. These last two out-takes are reminiscent of the "breeder" strategy that publishers of series fiction use where they publish three books in the series at a time so that readers can be sure to encounter them and engage with them (and of course purchase them) as a series. One of the final scenes of a video version is a live performance by the Riders in the Sky, a western cowboy group singing a number of "cowboy favorites" including the "Woody's Roundup" theme song which by this time has become part of the recent memory, at least, of the viewers. We feel as though we are hearing a familiar song from the past, even if it is really only from the past ninety minutes of the film! This "instant memory" is accentuated because the other cowboy songs that they sing are not even part of the movie. Somehow, the "Woody's Roundup" theme song has simply become part of our memory.

Toy Story 2, then, is its own memory-work project, building in through Jessie the idea of a yearning for the past, creating for Woody a sense of a past, and constructing for the adult viewer a sense of time that undermines any conventional chronology. In the context of "reading back" feminist nostalgia it has a built-in feature of future-oriented memory. Though Jessie has little choice, Woody, as a witness to Jessie's story, is able to imagine what is going to happen to him once Andy starts to forget. More importantly though, he seems to have a choice, at least for the moment. He can choose ephemerality over longevity if he wants to. The movie is more than just a version of "nostalgia ain't what it used to be." Rather, the point of the movie, and, as well, the point of the cowboy hero read as a memory piece is to suggest a future for nostalgia, one that takes into account the rememberer, the experience being remembered, and also a remembering which contains longing, loss, and desire within the whole process of commodification.

Chapter Three

Visual Spaces: The Gaze of the Child

Insider Perspectives on Children's Popular Culture

> What would it really mean to study the world from the standpoint of children both as knowers and as actors? (Oakley 1994: 25).

This question about children as knowers and actors raised by feminist sociologist Ann Oakley frames our investigation into an insider perspective on children's popular culture. While there are, of course, many "insiders" in relation to children's popular culture – parents who live with popular culture, teachers who might monitor its presence in classrooms, adult collectors for whom it has both personal and financial value, toy companies who must keep a particular line of toy afloat, academic researchers who must negotiate their study of Barbies and G.I. Joes – in this chapter we use the term "insider" to refer to the children – the players – themselves! While it seems obvious enough to think about children as insiders, the whole process of involving children in the study of popular culture, as we noted in previous chapters, is fraught. Studying Barbie play or the viewers of *The Simpsons* is not necessarily done the same way as studying skipping songs or childhood nursery rhymes. While there is an "insider quality" to these aspects of children's culture too, there is quite a different political context for looking at the corporate culture of childhood – often invented and maintained by adults – even if it is children who might determine the currency. Thus, the concerns that adults have for protecting children, even the silence that children might maintain ("don't tell the grown-ups") all put boundaries on what it is that children are willing to reveal, but also boundaries on what adults might think they even want to know about childhood. There is a curious irony to all of this, since children's popular culture is one of the areas where children themselves are likely to know something different from most adults about the culture under study. Sometimes this knowledge is only expressed in a covert act such as a visual exchange between two four-year-olds clutching Elmo dolls in a supermarket line-up.

We have been interested in developing ways of working with children where they are operating in naturalistic settings and where they are not cast as "other." The idea of adults who are not parents, babysitters or relatives having access to children in naturalistic settings – playrooms, bedrooms, backyards, and so on – already places on the research agenda the notion of a "contested space" in relation to the private and the public. Who can occupy – or even "lurk in" – such spaces and under what circumstances brings into question issues on the protection of children from adult predators, the rights of children to not have their culture tampered with, and of course, the rights of children and their families to privacy. As we noted in Chapter 1, it is perhaps not surprising that many of our accounts of young children and their popular culture, of necessity taken out of the public sphere and placed into the private, involve the work of researchers writing about their own children. Valerie Walkerdine's careful ethnographic work with one family in "Video Replay" (1985) and her work with young girls in *Daddy's Girl* (1997) are two notable examples of overcoming some of the challenges of gaining entry to the domestic (or private space) worlds of young children. However, gaining access to the private spaces of childhood, even as parents (or perhaps especially as parents) by no means ensures that we avoid colonization. As Berry Mayall points out, children are frequently conceptualized by adults as "developing [developing people/developing countries] . . . as objects of socialization . . . as lesser than adults in that they are progressing towards the goal of mature adulthood" (1994: 2). It might not be entirely accurate to compare the status of adults who study childhood to those who might study exotic settings, since all adults have been children (we have been insiders), and many of the adults who write about childhood (as we noted in Chapter 1) are steeped in the childhoods of their own children. At the same time, though, when it comes to understanding the pleasures of Ninja Turtles, Barbie, or G.I. Joe – right now – adults can hardly lay claim to the same expert status as that of the fans themselves: children. At best, we can use our observer status to make some sort of inferences, or, as we noted earlier, we can subject our own childhoods to the scrutiny of memory. In either case, we are acting on behalf of children. As Ann Oakley notes, the prepositions attached to childhood studies have been "about," or "on," and rarely "for" (1994). Even rarer though in the case of childhood studies has been the use of the preposition "with." Although it may be challenging to invoke an "insider" decolonized view of childhood, it is worthwhile to pursue it for what it can tell us about the expertise of children generally (in other words, children's knowledge when they are not being constrained by an adultist perspective), and of course, because of what it can tell us about children's popular culture.

In the first section of this chapter we examine briefly children's popular culture as a visual space. In so doing, we consider the ways that much of children's popular culture is already highly visual. In the second section of the chapter we explore the question "What can a child do with a camera?" In this section we look at children both as spontaneous photographers as well as participants in adult-organized photography projects. In the final section of the chapter we look at the role of new digital technology in the participation of the child as visual ethnographer.

Children's Popular Culture as Visual Space

When the French visual artist Christian Boltanski, well known for his work as a recycler artist in which he uses items of clothing, other objects of material culture, and photographs, invited the 264 students in La Lycée, a school in Chicago, to choose "the single favorite object of his or her lifetime" to be photographed and incorporated into a large artistic piece, many of the objects brought in by the students to be photographed were items of popular culture – a Transformer, a Barbie, and so on. Over the course of several days, Boltanski set up each plaything to be shot at exactly the same scale and angle, under uniform lighting. While Boltanski worked with the positioning of some objects – for example, posing a stuffed animal, or situating a Barbie – the objects are photographed in such a way that they receive uniform treatment; there is a democratization of the relationship between the camera and the object with the result that no one object stands out. The full installation "Favorite Objects" is made up of 264 black-and-white 8½ × 11-inch photographs of individual objects. What is of particular interest is the way in which all these favorite objects have a similar intimate look. Even the commercial objects become personalized in their appearance, maintaining their brand new "in the package" look. In so doing, the artist has managed to capture something of the relationship between the child and the object.

We regard Boltanski's "Favorite Objects" – installed in New York's Museum of Modern Art in December 2000 as part of an exhibition on Childhood Innocence – as significant for several reasons.[1] First of all, the artist has managed to capture something of the personal and intimate all-forgiving relationship between the child and the favorite object. At the time, as we noted in our analysis of *Toy Story 2*, particular material objects such as a Cowboy Woody doll or a stuffed toy often have a limited shelf life. What adults might find offensive – "Why can't my granddaughter play with her Baby Doll who is so cuddly, and not that Barbie with the hard plastic body?", the child looks at "without prejudice." Indeed, there is often cause for conflict when a parent will try to replace a tattered blanket with a brand new one. A second reason for our attraction to Boltanski's work is that he has managed to locate everyday play objects as visual art. A final point is that Boltanski, using an artistic eye, has *captured* an artistic viewpoint as if experienced by the gaze of a child, an achievement that is well recognized as a challenge for most adult artists.

In drawing from work in visual anthropology and the visual arts, we use the term "gaze" in order to draw attention to the ways in which self-definition through representation can be incorporated into the research process. While it is a challenge to invoke the gaze of the child, as we note above, we are concerned with the idea of the unique standpoint or perspective of the child in researching children's popular culture. We offer that because so much of children's popular culture is highly visual, ranging from the artifacts of popular culture themselves in all their "larger-than-life" forms of plastic, frequently brightly colored and so on, to the packaging that is specially formulated to attract the child, to methods of play, it lends itself to being explored visually. We regard it as noteworthy that specific artifacts of children's popular culture have been interrogated and celebrated by a number of photographic exhibitions ranging from the various installations on Barbie – as we see, for example, in *The Art of Barbie* (Yoe 1994) – to a recent exhibition in a Vancouver art gallery: *Joes I know* on G.I. Joe (February 2001). In that exhibition, consisting of thirty portraits – all with black frames – artist Lorraine Weideman uses the genre of the commemorative portrait to study issues of race, ethnicity, nationality, and masculinity in popular culture, based on a collection of G.I. Joes from the past forty years. She says of her work:

> In my adult life I have lived with a hundred or more of these "action figures" – they belong to my partner who reminisces fondly about his childhood days spent playing with them. We have always thought of displaying them in our home, but for the time being they are stored in row after row of clear plastic containers in my bedroom closet. As I dress every morning, they peer out at me; their tiny painted eyes full of fond memories, and perhaps wicked expectations. . . .

Figure 3.1 U.S. Navy sailor battle stations, G.I. Joe 1960s. Lorraine Weideman from *Joes I Know*, 2001 (courtesy of the artist).

> This body of work started as a photographic series of full figures photographed in diorama settings. The faces caught my attention because although they have identical modeled heads, each figure seems to have its own distinct personality. Such was my fascination with their sombre expressions, I decided to concentrate on their portraits. I considered painting the portraits but felt the photographs captured a certain unique quality that only a plastic face can express (personal communication, February 14, 2001).

But the work of Weideman and other artists in a sense "mirrors" only a type of everyday art in the lives of children and their play (and display) of popular culture. As is evident in much of the play of children, they regularly create narratives through the construction of tableaux which resemble artistic installations (or which inspire installations). Barbies are positioned "on set"; Transformers interact with each other; a Lego creation can be an artistic form in itself. In the case of Barbie, the very idea of the "set" or "scene presentation" is a product. As Rebecca Rupp (1996) notes in her *Treasury of Barbie Doll Accessories, 1961–1995*, over the years these scene presentations have included Barbie Fashion Shop, Barbie and Ken Little Theater, Barbie Goes to

Figure 3.2 German Air Force Pilot custom 1990s, G.I. Joe 1960s. Lorraine Weideman from *Joes I Know*, 2001 (courtesy of the artist).

Figure 3.3 Japanese imperial soldier, G.I. Joe 1960s. Lorraine Weideman from *Joes I Know*, 2001 (courtesy of the artist).

College, Barbie Olympic Ski Village, Barbie Photo Studio, Barbie Six O'Clock News, Barbie Hot Dog Stand, Barbie Post Office, Barbie Reservation Center, Barbie Work Out, Barbie Dinner Date. One can also see these scene presentations on Play Mobile packages. What is interesting is that even the packaging of children's toys is suggestive of an installation. Like record album covers, the packaging of children's popular culture is highly visual – usually very colorful and often offering visual narratives depicting children at play with the object, or the artifact itself presented in a narrative style – Transformers "at war" with each other; Barbie relaxing with her friends in the backyard, and so on.

The visual narrative on children's packaging is so much a staple of advertising that it is necessary to have ethical guidelines to regulate this packaging. Is the object the actual size or at least proportional in relation to the child who may be depicted playing with the item? Is the object represented doing things that it is incapable of doing, and so on? Packaging is supposed to give a sense of the anticipated fun that is promised when the child plays with the toy contained within the package. Increasingly, packaging is considered to be part of the primary text. For example, in the collecting world an artifact has added value if it is MIB (mint in box) or MOC (mint on card). Indeed, sometimes the packaging is even more valuable than the artifact since it is much rarer. However, the other point, and the one that is central to this discussion, is the overall visual appeal, the artistry of the packaging. As Zac, a long-time fan of Transformers and G.I. Joes, and now in his twenties, writes:

> Toy packaging was always a major part of the whole experience for me. Most of the series I played with as a kid had extensive box art and other extras incorporated into the packaging. I think GI Joe and Transformers were the big ones for that. Transformer toys always had a painting on the back of the box with all the toys released in the line that year, pictured together in some large "battle" scene. Both GI Joe and Transformers had little clip-and-save proof-of-purchase tabs ("Flag" points and "Robot" points respectively) that could be used as part of mail-away special offers, as well as the all-important file cards that detailed the vital info on that particular action figure's "personality." I also remember cutting out the pictures (paintings) on the boxes of each figure, and saving them too, so really, only half of the packaging was ever thrown away. Any larger items were boxed with little booklets that listed all the other figures in the series from that year, with photographs of each one. They would always be pictured in these somewhat abstract dioramic landscapes, full of little rocks and gravel, and tiny bushes. Occasionally this would include images of a happy-looking pair of kids playing with (or gazing adoringly at) whichever playsets carried the biggest price tags. These booklets became a commodity of sorts. My friends and I would save ones from each year, committing the figures to memory, owning them all in our minds, even if we couldn't in actuality.
>
> I think the early eighties were an important time for these type of toys, because the Sears catalogs would frequently feature full-page dioramas with toys and kids, similar to those in the booklets, though it used to bug me when they would get something wrong, like having the wrong figure pictured with an accessory (a "bad-guy" riding a "good-guy" jeep, for example). In the little booklets, the larger playsets always had other figures and vehicles placed within them, a kind of "suggested serving." Sometimes a vehicle that was sold without a figure would always be pictured with a specific character/action figure, implying a certain sense of ownership between the two, so that if you had one, you always felt that you should have the other to go with it.
>
> Another function of the box art in some cases, was to provide me with a kind of internal image of what the action figure was supposed to really "look" like. This was especially significant with the Transformers, which were often rather awkwardly constructed, or un-poseable. Instead, in the illustration, they would be in dynamic poses, and at dramatic angles. The illustration on the box told me how to imagine the "character" beyond the limitations of the actual molded plastic.

> Television commercials were also a big influence on how I perceived kids were expected to play with these toys. Usually the children on the ads had elaborate backyard set-ups, where their GI Joes or He-man figures could climb rocks, swing on ropes, or knock over leaf-and-twig constructions. Often this would all factor into some brief, action-packed play-acted storyline, that would be resolved by the end of a 30-second commercial spot. Naturally, no product appeared alone . . . other figures and accessories always found their way into the background, beyond the new product being highlighted (personal communication, May 9 2001).

In addition to colorful packaging as visual representation, children's popular culture also includes highly visual artistic representations in the form of trading cards that accompany many popular culture texts: Barbie, Pokemon, Spice Girls. Websites, too, both those commercially produced and those produced by children themselves, as we explore in Chapter 5, become obvious sites of visual representation and exploration.

But beyond these more commercial or specialized "markets" for the visual, the world of children's popular culture takes on a highly visual form through family snapshots. Given, as we noted in Chapter 2, that so many family photographs document birthdays, Christmas, and other gift-giving events where children are likely to receive artifacts of popular culture as presents, it is not surprising that children's popular culture features prominently in family albums. A typical Christmas Day event in many households, for example, is to have children pose with their loot. Even in homes where the camcorder has replaced the Brownie instamatic, there is often still a convention of "holding up" for the photographer particular play objects. Indeed, even very young children aged two and three, aware of the eye of the camera, might be regarded as the authors of their own photographs. In our role as parents we have no difficulty in validating the "Take me!" reference and the fact that the home photographer is not necessarily in control of the picture-taking. Young children, sometimes even pets, "insist" on being photographed a certain way – so that a coy expression on the face of a child might be read as "Daddy take a picture of me like this!" The child, then, is fully aware of the eye of the camera.

The potential for exploring how children see through photographs in this very personal way occurred in a photo-interpretation project involving school pictures with a group of five ten-year-olds (Mitchell and Weber 1999). Looking back at their school photographs from kindergarten and Grade 1 school pictures, the children revealed their understandings of how they were complicit in posing a certain way for the school photographer. They also revealed an understanding of the commodification process in relation to photographs. For example, the children hypothesized that the reason the school photographer had posed them with a book – in some cases, one that they would not even be capable of reading – was so the photography company could sell more photographs to parents who would be willing to pay money if they saw their children looked intelligent in the photographs. This conversation was included in *Reinventing Ourselves as Teachers: Beyond Nostalgia* as a demonstration of the ways in which even very young children can be engaged in memory work. Here we include the conversation to demonstrate the ways in which they became, in a sense, subjects of their own research, contesting the idea of the "colonizing eye" of the camera:

Abby: Oh Grade 2 – they made us sit at the desks with the open book – a geography book! [shrieks and screams]

Norah: Oh no – mine was a dictionary.

Interviewer: A dictionary?

Gretchen: Mine was an encyclopedia!

Norah: Mine was a Larousse dictionary.

Gretchen: That year I had forgotten it was picture day and I remember I was wearing a mickey dress.

Interviewer: What's that?

Everyone: A mickey dress – it has Mickey at the front and Minnie at the back.

Gretchen: It was so awful, plus I had to sit at this desk . . . uh . . . in front of this book that I would never read. I looked a bit stupid reading this book.

Norah: I remember my hair was going all over and I had these little strings attached . . .

Dorian: I guess they wanted to make us feel like we looked so smart.

Interviewer: Do you think that's why they put you in front of a book which you probably couldn't even read. Hmm – was it a difficult book? Was it a French book?

Gretchen: Uh yes some of them.

Norah: Some of them were English.

Abby: I remember my book was English plus they made me do this. [demonstrates how she had to look down at the book and point]

Interviewer: Oh you're kidding. You mean they actually made you point your finger like they do in kindergarten?

Abby: [offers another demonstration]

Interviewer: And is that what you were doing in the photograph?

Abby: [nods head]

Norah: You wouldn't believe what I was reading – because to make me look like I was reading they made me read it. I was reading the definition in French and the word was "alphabet" [laughter all round] . . . and the next word was . . . uh aqua . . . and it was all these weird definitions.

Interviewer: Imagine reading the definition of the word "alphabet" while you get your picture taken in front of a book so you look like you can read.

Norah: I remember they used these books for the kindergarten kids too and they couldn't even read!

Interviewer: Oh you're kidding. Did they make them look at the page with their finger?

Norah: [nods]

Gretchen: Well, they did not do that for me; they just made me look at a weird book . . . Then they made me hold the book like this [holds out her hands in the book reading position] and then I had to go like this. [demonstrates the way in which her eyes had to land on the page]

Interviewer: Why do you think they made you do that?

Gretchen: I think they were trying something out that year.

Dorian: Maybe it's because it was supposed to look like a school . . . I feel like it was kind of like to make the parents think we are really smart or something (Mitchell and Weber 1999: 76–7).

This awareness is something that has been explored in work with school photographs where children – away from parents nagging them to look or stand a certain way – will sometimes use the occasion of the annual school photograph session to make their own statement through their facial expressions, positioning in the group, and so on (Mitchell and Weber 1999). While a number of participants in that study of school photographs complained about being controlled, there were also several accounts of resistance and "sabotage" – not everyone complied with the pose! One person, for example, now in his twenties, recalls adopting an oppositional stance towards school photographs, which he saw as an opportunity to rebel against being "schooled" to look a certain way. One year, his mother insisted that he wear a particular V-neck sweater. Convinced that, in combination with his long hair, the sweater made him look like a girl, he decided to use the one thing his parents could not control – the expression on his face – to ruin the picture altogether, and thus he succeeded in asserting his autonomy (Mitchell and Weber 1999: 90).

What Can a Child Do With a Camera?

While we are by no means of the opinion that the only way to ensure a child-centered "insider" approach to studying children's popular culture is through the visual, our heading "What Can a Child Do With a Camera?" offers a concrete approach to invoking the visual space of childhood. In adapting this subtitle from Jo Spence and Joan Solomon's book *What Can a Woman Do With a Camera?* (1995), a work which also inspired a project with teachers-as-photographers, "What Can a Teacher Do With a Camera?" (Mitchell and Weber 1999), we locate the work on the gaze of children within a body of research that seeks to explore the visual in relation to understanding culture. As Jay Ruby notes of visual anthropology in *Picturing Culture*,

> [it] logically proceeds from the belief that culture is manifested through visible symbols embedded in gestures, ceremonies, rituals, and artifacts situated in constructed and natural environments. . . . If one can see culture, then researchers should be able to employ audio-visual technologies to record it as data amenable to analysis and presentation (2000: ix).

Thus, we focus on the significance of the camera in projects which range from the idea of the child-as-photographer through to the idea of the child working with photographs and adult photographers. At either end of this spectrum our interest is in the ways in which the camera – conventionally regarded in anthropological and ethnographic work as a "colonizing" tool – might become, in the hands of children, a tool of decolonization. As visual anthropologist Richard Rohde writes:

> Given the explosion of revisionist texts dealing with visual representation and colonialism, surprisingly few are concerned with the theoretical issues surrounding the appropriation of cheap visual media technology by recently "decolonized" people. Such a reversal in the roles of who represents what, has profound implications for social historians and anthropologists (among others) (1998: 188).

In making this observation, Rohde is commenting on how one of the very tools of ethnography that has been used to colonize particular groups – the camera with its "exoticizing" eye – can provide an "insider" gaze, one which contrasts with the more usual "outsider" gaze of anthropology. Contesting the idea of a *National Geographic* "take" on culture, for example,

Rohde describes a project involving sixteen Namibians who, with access to disposable cameras, turn the camera on themselves. Their perspective manages to challenge a gaze that has been almost exclusively white and European. It was also a gaze that has typically been male, as has been challenged by the work of Laura Mulvey in relation to film, and by the work of Jo Spence and Joan Solomon and others in their book *What Can a Woman Do With a Camera*? To this list of adjectives – white, European and male – we would add the word "adultist," noting that children are seldom the ones telling the story even though they are used as "great subjects" in photographs to sell everything from life insurance and relief aid to providing us with blissful images of happy holidays. Thus, if children's popular culture offers itself as a rich ethnographic site for visual documentation, it is children themselves who might be regarded as obvious ethnographers in its documentation.

Children as Spontaneous Photographers

The photograph of Little Becca (Figure 3.4) aged three with her Fisher-Price camera reminds us of the reality of the gaze of even very young children who "play" at being photographers. However, while the Fisher-Price play camera has been a standard item of the North American toy-box since the late 1960s,

Figure 3.4 Little Becca with Fisher-Price camera (photograph by William Mitchell).

along with the Fisher-Price crib mobile and activity center, fully functioning "toy cameras" have been around since the late 1800s with the marketing of the Kodak Brownie camera directed at children and their parents. As Nancy Martha West (2000) observes in her study of Kodak, the early Brownie cameras were featured as children's toys – "even a child can use them" – and as we see in ads (Figure 3.5), children are depicted as prime producers in the photography world. Johnson notes the campaign by Kodak, on the company's fiftieth anniversary, to put a Brownie in the hands of 500,000 twelve-year-olds in the U.S.A. and 50,000 in Canada with the idea of getting them hooked as photographers (Johnson 1998: 131). West also points out that in some cases the ads actually depicted children who were far too young to be able to manipulate a camera and that these images were meant to capitalize as much on the idea of "capturing (and selling) memories," or selling the idea of parenthood, and not necessarily only on selling the idea of children-as-photographers (though the widespread use of cameras by children also offered an important market). However, it is her description of Kodak's recognition of the child's unique perspective that interests us here. As she writes:

> one of the striking aspects of Brownie advertising is how often children are depicted observing events or objects that might ordinarily escape the attention of adults. They take photographs of their dogs at play, or their younger siblings struggling with getting on their winter clothing, even of Dad reading his paper on the front porch (West 2000: 85).

Indeed, in looking through our own family albums, and speaking with the children of friends and family, we have been struck by the range and quantity of photography projects that children have spontaneously initiated, and which often include popular culture artifacts. The resulting images, as we see in the examples in this section, are not, of course, professional quality photographs and are sometimes taken with very inexpensive play cameras, or disposable cameras. Focus, positioning, and so on give them a certain "illicitness," and it is only when parents get the photographs back from being developed that they realize that the child taken a snapshot. At the same time, however, they provide what might be described as an "insider" point of view that may challenge certain adult notions of children's play. Zoe, for example, now aged fourteen recalls a photography project that she initiated when she was six, involving her Beanie Baby collection and her Playmobile figurines. One of the points that we find interesting in Zoe's project, as she describes it, is the "genre-blending." We also see this same kind of "genre-blending" in several examples of other portraits produced by child photographers. In Figure 3.6, "Wicker Barbie," for example, nine-year-old Rebecca has set up a potpourri of figurines: one Barbie, one cloth ballerina, and so on. In a second photograph (Figure 3.7), the arrangement consists of one pseudo-Barbie, one Blueberry Muffin doll, one Transformer figurine, and a cloth baby with velcro

Figure 3.5 Advertisement for the Brownie camera, *Youth's Companion*, 1909 (reprinted courtesy of Eastman Kodak Company).

Figure 3.6 Wicker Barbie (photograph by Rebecca Mitchell, nine years old).

fastener (so that it could be attached to its mother). While both of these arrangements would appear to be composed from a collection of toy-box artifacts, we see that "Christmas 1985: A Cabbage Patch doll and two Pound Puppies" (Figure 3.8) offers more of a portraiture of convenience. The young photographer who is visiting her grandmother over the Christmas holidays must work with what she has. It is a portrait that is reminiscent of the kinds of family groupings-of-convenience that emerge at large extended family gatherings. The photographer has worked with what she has, somewhat like the groupings that regularly emerge on the occasion of extended family gatherings where someone will insist on "a picture of all the cousins," or "a picture of three generations," or "a picture of the men," and so on.

What are we to make of these "genre-blending" portraits? In each of these examples it seems to us that the child photographer in her installation is questioning the "single-item-ness" of various popular culture items and the tendency of adults to go after a particular popular culture item in either a celebratory way or in a condemning way, as though children – the players – encounter these objects in the same singular way. Barbie, for example, is regularly attacked by adults – but the fact that Barbie can co-exist with

Figure 3.7 Family portrait (photograph by Sarah Mitchell, eight years old).

seemingly "wholesome dolls" such as a satin-covered cloth ballerina doll with painted-on hair and face (and no obvious sexual markers such as breasts or waist), and occupy folksy wicker furniture designed for some other doll altogether as opposed to her usual "upmarket" plastic backyard patio set or Malibu living room, suggests that children do not see these worlds in unitary and undifferentiated ways. We have found examples in our albums of snapshots of Holly Hobby dolls mixed in with Barbies, or a tableau involving Lincoln logs and the plastic Fisher-Price Play People. However, as we also know from countless stories from parents overhearing the play narratives of their children, Barbie can just as easily be transformed from a fashion doll into a pistol, and a construction of Lego can become a coffin or a machine gun. This insight of genre-blending and multiple meanings may hardly be radical to anyone who has observed children playing in a bedroom or multi-toy area in a daycare center. It is only that such scenes are often short-lived; they are created as tableaux and then once constructed they are often immediately dismantled. It is only when they are photographed that they are frozen in time.

Some of the resulting photographs may also carry with them a very "knowing" quality. Here we use the term "knowing" as Ann Higonnet does to describe the ways that children and their creations disrupt notions of

Figure 3.8 Christmas 1985: A Cabbage Patch doll and two Pound Puppies (photograph by Rebecca Mitchell).

childhood innocence (1998). Indeed, as she notes in speaking of various child-photographer projects that go beyond the family album, the children themselves offer a view on the world which is not that different from the very controversial photographs that adult photographers such as Sally Mann take of children. Speaking in particular of some of the creations made by children in projects organized by Wendy Ewald, she writes: "There is nothing more brutal, carnal, tragic, or strange about any of the most controversial new photographs of children taken by adults than there is about the photographs children take of themselves under Ewald's aegis" (Higonnet 1998: 217).

In adult circles it is probably works involving dolls such as Barbie that have evoked the most "dramatic" of the brutal and carnal, as we see, for example, in many Barbie-inspired installations featured in *The Art of Barbie* (1994). In many ways we feel that in a sense these works also mirror visual representations that exist in the everyday world of the child. There are the scenes, for example, in *Toy Story* where Sid, the evil boy next door, manages to construct his macabre-looking mutant toys, "Babyhead," a cross between the head of a baby doll and a construction set, "Jingle Joe," made up of the head of Combat Carl and a jingle push toy, or "Legs," made up of shapely Barbie-type legs and a fishing-rod. Another installation (although never photographed) which would fit into Higonnet's "brutal" and "carnal" category would be nine-year-old Rebecca's "pseudo-Barbie with breasts cut away – in order to create a Ken," a project we describe in Chapter 1. While from a "parent-as-researcher" perspective this work speaks less to a deliberate sense of the macabre and more to a pragmatic interest in having a male partner for Barbie, it nonetheless seems to interrogate the idea of the permanence of sexual markers. Another scene, though, from the "toy stories" of our own children is a representation that has now come to be called "Alexander's head posed in an empty wine bottle" (Figure 3.9), and which speaks to the more brutal. Alexander, an example of a very realistic-looking 1980s baby doll with "real-baby" features, something normally taken to be "OK" by most adults – "ah, a baby doll and not one of those Barbies" – regularly, during the years that his owner played with him, was dragged behind a stroller and later carried upside down. Alexander often drew looks of horror from strangers before they realized that he wasn't real. Eventually his head, separated from his body, was placed in a wine bottle where it has stayed for many years on a bedroom shelf. Here we think of the work of the Swiss photographer/artist

Figure 3.9 Alexander's head posed in an empty wine bottle (photograph by Sarah Michell).

Pascal Wuest (2001), who in *Beloved* presents a series of photographs of dolls which reveal the scars of childhood – dolls with missing limbs, gaping eye sockets, and so on.

At the same time, other photography installations, while not set up to disrupt the innocent play of childhood, may nonetheless have "disruptive" results. A photograph, "Horse on fire" (Figure 3.10), of Sarah's ninth birthday party, complete with candlelit cake and Barbie-type horse on top of the cake, is taken just seconds before the horse catches fire. The disaster is caused when a paper napkin serving as the saddle blanket ignites. "Horse on fire" is a good example of a photograph yielding more than a thousand words. Indeed, as Richard Chalfen (1987) and others have noted, it is the verbal interpretation which accompanies the photograph – what lies behind the camera – that is important. The birthday photograph merely captures the second or two before the fire broke out. It does not record the fire itself, the way the party was ruined, or the words uttered by the birthday child to her mother: "I hate your seven-minute icing."

Finally, we regard the visual space of childhood as not being just about "taking" the photograph, as in clicking the shutter, or even about "taking" a photograph, as in choosing the object to be photographed or arranging the composition; it is also about "taking" photographs in the sense of "taking

Figure 3.10 Horse on fire (photograph by Claudia Mitchell).

them up" to work with, or even more literally taking them out of the family album or off the wall and using them in some new way. An example of this may be seen in the way that even very young children insist on having their own photo album of special photos arranged the way they want them – and with complete freedom to purge the album at some point of pictures of siblings, friends, or parents if there is any sort of "falling out." Children's photo albums, picture displays in their bedrooms or on bulletin boards might all be "read" or interpreted for what they have to say about popular culture. Interestingly Christian Boltanski says of his own work: "I never take photographs myself. I don't feel like a photographer, more like a recycler" (quoted in Semin et al. 1997: 25).

Adult-Organized Photography Projects Involving Children

In the above section our reference to child photographers has pertained largely to the spontaneous "projects" initiated by children in home settings. While we would argue that these spontaneous projects highlight some of the ways in which children act as researchers and informants in relation to popular culture, we are also interested in how a more systematic or structured approach to children-as-photographers can provide a child gaze on popular culture. Thus we return to the question "What can a child do with a camera?" and draw on the extensive body of literature that is emerging on projects involving child photographers as visual anthropologists. What is particularly significant about the work of Wendy Ewald, Kamina Walton, James Hubbard, and others who have set up child-photographer projects is the acknowledgment of at least two features of ethnographic methods in relation to researching children's popular culture. One feature is the recognition of the significance of the visual in self-expression, and hence the academic and practical nod to visual ethnography – vis-à-vis photographs and documentary film or video. A second feature is the commitment to a democratization of perspective or voice. As Wendy Ewald observes:

> From St. Augustine to Wordsworth to contemporary psychologists, thinkers have pondered the complex and seemingly uninhibited world of children. To ask children themselves to participate in exploring their world is to acknowledge that it is their experience, and that rather than being made to "mind their place" children might be helped to find ways of illuminating and sharing their inner lives (2000: 17).

In making such an observation, Ewald is speaking of the contribution of the child's gaze to an understanding of the world as children experience it. Her recent book *Secret Games: Collaborative Works with Children, 1969–99* (2000) serves to synthesize her camera work with children over a thirty-year period. These projects, each lasting one or two years, and described in *Portraits and*

Dreams: Photographs and Stories by Children of the Appalachians (1985) and *I Dreamed I Had a Girl in My Pocket* (1996), are based on the idea that a simple camera offers a straightforward approach to self-expression. In these projects, Ewald works closely with children – in a range of settings where rural isolation, poverty, and so on are already barriers to children having any power or voice. Thus she has worked in Gujarat, India, in the Appalachians of the rural U.S.A., northern Canada, South Africa, and so on. Typically she works first to develop with the children skills in camera usage, as well as dark-room printing and developing techniques. Normally, projects culminate in a public exhibition in an art gallery or museum. As noted earlier, it is in this work that Anne Higonnet and others note the "knowing" telling.

In Trish Brennan's photography project with a group of children on the Holly Street Estate in Hackney, East London, children were invited to take photographs of their home, family, and street. When their neighborhood was about to be demolished, Brennan worked with the students through both video and their photographs in order to document their feelings. A number of their photographs are now part of a photo-book on childhood, *I Spy: Representations of Childhood* (Fehily et al. 2000), along with work from Wendy Ewald's "If I Were Orange" project.

Kamina Walton (1995) describes a photo project in her essay "Creating Positive Images: Working with Primary School Girls" in which eight- to eleven-year-old girls explored issues of physical and verbal harassment in their school. Working with cameras in a studio context, they created photographic images and print which gave expression to some of their anger and frustration. The outcome of the project was a series of posters produced for display in the school library which carried messages like: "We hate you punching us," and "We hate you lifting up our skirts." The photography project thus gave the students a means not only to tell their story visually to everyone, but also to engage in a type of activism.

Walton's work is characteristic of the types of photography projects done with students within a resistance framework in Britain in the 1970s and early 1980s. A prominent example is the work of Jo Spence and Terry Dennett compiled in Spence (1995), the "mainstay" of the Photography Workshop project carried out in London schools. Their mission was to use photography in a cultural studies framework as a way to work with student resistance. Dewdney and Lister note of this work: "Without conscious and active engagement with the content of young people's resistance, teaching is bound to reproduce more than it transforms" (1986: 31). Similarly, James Hubbard's "Shooting Back" project with homeless children in Washington, D.C. and later in a project engaging native children (Hubbard 1994) involved children "taking pictures of their own struggle" (Hubbard 1993, quoted in Paley 1995: 118). The following excerpt about "Shooting Back" further highlights the importance of the exhibitions:

> The diversity of photographs and level of artistry displayed at this exhibition immediately placed Shooting Back in the larger public eye.

> The photographs taken by the young boy and girl photographers showed children enjoying themselves at play, either alone or with their friends; they showed children affirming and creating their identities by posing for the camera with directness and grace; they showed images of families taking pleasure in the simple movements of daily life and in each other's company (Paley 1995: 119).
>
> While much of the jolting power of this exhibition came from the juxtaposition of images that subverted cultural and media depictions that all too frequently represent the urban homeless as lacking in hope and promise, it also came from the subtle and often unexpected ways that photographers forced viewers to confront parallel issues of stereotypic attitudes and behavior, the tremendous – almost surreal – disproportion of wealth in the nation's capital, the vacancy of governmental promises during the 1980s about human rights, and questions of what should be done now (Moore, in Paley 1995:119).

The book *Shootback: Photos by Kids from the Nairobi Slums* demonstrates the range of work done by a group of thirty-one children between the ages of twelve and seventeen. Working with inexpensive cameras, the group have produced photographs which document not only the extreme poverty within which they live, but also a range of themes – sports, families, sickness, drugs, death, and play. Inspired by the work of Wendy Ewald and James Hubbard (the Shootback Team leader), Lana Wong notes in her Introduction to the book: "Two years ago these kids had never held a camera. Today, their photographs are exhibited, published and collected around the world" (Wong 1999: n.p.).

A project with which Claudia has recently been involved in South Africa, Project Off-shoot, modeled after the work of Wendy Ewald and others, resembles *Shootback* in that there, too, young people in a development setting have been involved in documenting specific aspects of their lives. In the case of Project Off-shoot, learners in several districts in rural South Africa, all of whom have been involved in programs related to youth leadership, have been visually documenting the idea of transformation and social change. The name of the project – Project Off-shoot – is meant to pick up on the references to a film shoot, but also its location within a larger project on school leadership and organizational change which involves principals and other adult leaders. Perhaps there is even a hint in the name of a peaceful approach to change as opposed to "shooting." The participants in the photography project are not just "the leaders of tomorrow;" rather they are all members of the School Governing Bodies, the management teams of their schools which involve community members, as well as parents and the principal. Given relatively free rein to explore the notion of leadership, their photographs have managed to capture images of the township in which several of their schools are located, a dramatic presentation on HIV/AIDS, pictures of local adult leaders such as a highly respected principal, and the new fence around their school. It is not easy for an outsider to say what makes "transformation." It is not easy for an adult – even an insider in their schools who only "works in the school" but does not "go to the school" – to say that it is particular curriculum or structural changes that make a difference in terms of transformation. Through the gaze of the learners, however, we are invited to see how they view transformation.[2]

In another adult-initiated learner-photographer project in Montreal involving young photographers at a girls' school, the girls are using their own black-and-white photographs to explore issues of gender and identity. "Project Untitled", as it is called, is modeled after the work of Ewald and others in terms of students as photographers, but also the work of Jo Spence and Joan Solomon in relation to gender and identity. The project places democracy at the center so that the girls were fully involved in selecting the images, working with the visual texts, and even working with the venue where they set up the installation.[3]

While none of the projects noted above has had at its center investigations of children's popular culture, it is not surprising that at least some of the photographs which appear in the various collections and anthologies emerging from Ewald's and others' work – particularly those within a North American context – contain snapshots of popular culture artifacts. After all, the idea that children are photographing the culture around them, or the culture that is important to them means that at least some of that culture is likely to come under the umbrella of "popular culture." It is fascinating to explore how these images are "played out" in texts which are themselves interrogative of poverty, isolation, and gender-based violence. Several images stand out from Ewald's *Portraits and Dreams*, based on her work with children in the Appalachians. Lisa Gray's "My cousin at Christmas," for example, depicts a young girl of ten or eleven standing in front of a Christmas tree, cradling a doll, but also sporting what seems to be a brand new vinyl jacket (Ewald 1985: 98). What is interesting about this photo is in relation to what it captures in terms of age. There is something incongruous about the cradling of the doll and the new, more adult-like jacket. We are not sure which is the girl – or perhaps that is the point. She is both little girl possessing a doll and wearer of a new vinyl jacket.

Denise Collins' work "My little sister and my dolls" offers, through the positioning of the baby sister, an interesting line-up of three dolls, the baby sister and cheerleaders' streamers (ibid.: 101). While we do not know very much about Denise's life, somehow the parallel positioning seems important. This could be interpreted as the baby as "just a doll," but it could also be interpreted as the dolls as "just babies." We would guess that the little sister, worthy of being photographed, is as important to Denise as are the dolls. Ewald says more about the photographer Denise Dixon in *Portraits and Dreams*:

> Unlike some of the other children, she never ran out of ideas. I visited her home several times. She had set up her room as an oversized

> dollhouse, with stark white walls and a few posters of animals and family portraits. On the bureau, the night table and the bed, she had created tableaux with her dolls – just as in her photographs where she made up fantasies involving her twin brothers, Phillip and Jamie. The meticulous arrangement of her room and the deliberate way she dressed were reflected in the care she took in composing her photographs (1985:18–19).

Two of Denise's photographs, "A dream about my doll" (Figure 3.11) and "I am Dolly Parton" (Figure 3.12) are positioned side by side in *Portraits*. In each of these photographs there is the care of positioning – especially the hands on the doll and the Dolly Parton hands. In the photograph of the doll we have no sense of its relative size – it simply takes up the space, although standing slightly to the side rather than occupying the center.

The "portraits and dreams" created by twelve-year-old Denise Dixon resonate with the imaginative images produced in the cultural studies work of young people working with David Buckingham and Julian Sefton-Green, and in the film-making of Sadie Benning, as described by Nicolas Paley (1995). Buckingham and Sefton-Green document creative photography projects in

Figure 3.11 Denise Dixon: A dream about my doll, *Portraits and Dreams* (Wendy Ewald 1996) (reprinted courtesy of Appalshop Publishing).

Figure 3.12 Denise Dixon: I am Dolly Parton, *Portraits and Dreams* (Wendy Ewald 1996) (reprinted courtesy of Appalshop Publishing).

which students "inserted" themselves and their photographs into popular television and film narratives. They conclude that it is the "dialogic play between the subjective self, and the social self" (1994: 106) that is important.

The work of Sadie Benning is one of the projects referred to in the literature. Interestingly, we think, Benning's work on her bedroom is in fact based on an artifact of popular culture – the Fisher-Price Pixelvision video camera that she received for Christmas when she was fifteen. Receiving the camera from her father, also a film-maker, Benning expresses her initial disapproval of the camera. Commenting on her initial reaction to it, she observes:

> I thought, "This is a piece of . . . [expletive]. It's black and white. It's for kids. He'd told me I was getting this big surprise. I was expecting a camcorder . . ." It looks like a space gun or something. There's no zoom or focus. It's really incredible – the focus is like the eye – automatic, with a huge depth of field (cited in Paley 1995: 69).

In fact, this $89.95 piece of equipment launched her career as a video artist. Her work, much of it an exploration of her emerging lesbian identity, has been viewed as part of experimental film festivals around the world and has been featured in a retrospective at the Whitney Museum of American Art.

Play Display: Can You Show Us Your Room?

Clearly there are many different ways to involve children in visually documenting their own popular culture. These approaches might range from encouraging children to provide a visual tour through a Toys"R"Us outlet to actually setting up visual installations, for example, along the lines of Zoe's "Beanie Babies meet Playmobile" noted earlier. One approach that we have found useful builds on the idea of the insider by inviting children to document visually their bedrooms – literally, to display their play! Indeed, as we see in Andy's bedroom in the *Toy Story* movies – and as we explore in more detail in Chapter 4 – "the child's room" as a phenomenon of Western culture tends to be a rich cultural site in terms of toys and play. Even if children have to share a bedroom – as is often the case – there is nonetheless the demarcation of "personal space": "my side of the room." "Can you show us your room?" then is the kind of prompt that usually reveals more than a sleeping area.

"Crisdan's camera work"

Six-year-old Crisdan, using a twenty-four exposure disposable camera, provides an interesting visual "take" on a boy's life. As his mother promised, his room is a haven for the multi-genred collection of popular culture artifacts, ranging from his oversized Buzz Lightyear action figure from *Toy Story*, to his *Lion King* bed sheets, to his Pokemon poster, to his space creatures to his large and prized *Star Wars* poster. It is in a follow-up interview with Crisdan and his mother where we use the photographs as the "center piece," looking at the pictures together, discussing the process of picture-taking, something that Richard Chalfen (1991) claims – in his work on family photography – offers a level of social analysis in and of itself. How do people look at photographs together? Who holds them? Who determines the order? How long does one look at each one before moving on to the next? Who decides? What are the social expectations in terms of these "narrative captions" as Chalfen describes them? Physically, who is "in control?" While in this case the photos are presented in exactly the order in which they have come back from the developers encased in an envelope, there are nonetheless a number of social constraints at the beginning of the interview. As Claudia writes:

> Our process of going through the photographs is awkward at first. I am holding the photographs up one by one, implicitly seeking commentary from Crisdan. Part way through the interview, I realize that this is an unsatisfactory way of proceeding. They are Crisdan's snapshots after all or are they? He has no control over the order of presentation or the length of time to be spent on each photograph. The interview up to this point has been very adultist. We begin again,

this time with Crisdan holding up each of the 24 pictures and deciding what to show, when and for how long (fieldnotes).

In the course of the interview, Crisdan comments on his various strategies in conducting the study. For example, he observes that he has used up his twenty-four exposures over two sessions, and that, with one exception, he has kept the room as it is as opposed to staging it. The only photograph that was consciously staged was one of his collection of dolls and stuffed animals, a photograph (Figure 3.13) that he took in his parents' bedroom.

Each of the pictures has a context. For example, wanting to give a sense of the magnitude of his space action-figure collection, but not wanting to disturb the order of the room, Crisdan comments that it made sense to photograph the inside of his closet where his space figures are kept. He refers to the difficulty of getting an "inside the closet" shot (Figure 3.14).

Crisdan could easily be a dolcet in an art gallery, providing an item-by-item description of the artifacts in the photograph: "And here we have Buzz Lightyear." In making such a statement there is a type of implicit invitation that says "you do know who Buzz Lightyear is, don't you?" He is prepared to explain anything that is unclear. He goes on to say more about many of the artifacts: "I saved up to buy this." Like the genre-blending of the photographs produced by Becca in an earlier section, Crisdan operates in a world where Disney, Pixar, Pokemon all overlap and converge. Indeed, asked to choose his favorite picture for inclusion in this book, he chooses, without

Figure 3.13 Dolls in my parents' room (photograph by Crisdan).

hesitation, the photograph that has the bulk of his favorite artifacts all together: the Star Wars poster, his Buzz Lightyear books, his Buzz Lightyear action figure (Figure 3.15).

Figure 3.14 Inside my closet (photograph by Crisdan).

Figure 3.15 Buzz Lightyear and other favorite objects (photograph by Crisdan).

"Jana as video director"

Crisdan presents his bedroom and his photo collection confidently and matter-of-factly. Similarly, eight-year-old Jana – teaming up with a small film crew – takes on the role of director in showing us her bedroom. As part of a project on children's popular culture in a course at McGill, a beginning teacher, Bounmy (B.) works with Jana (J.) to produce a thirty-minute documentary of the bedroom in which Jana provides direction to the camera person, as well as a voice-over commentary on the various artifacts and layout of the bedroom. In so doing, Jana offers a perfect rendering of an autoethnography of a bedroom – not unlike Steven Riggins' (1994) autoethnography of a living room that we describe in more detail in Chapter 4. She starts, for example, on one side of the room, just to the right of the doorway, and proceeds to direct the camera's eye "place by place" around the room. As we listened to her voice-over commentary we were interested in how she, like Crisdan, sounds like a trained dolcet in an art gallery or museum. She speaks confidently of the various objects: "Here is . . ." or "This is . . ." followed by an articulation of what Stephen Riggins would regard as both the denotative ("this is what it is") and the connotative features ("this is what it means") of a particular object.

> *J.*: This is the Backstreet Boys. His name is Brian (points). That's him. . . . And here's AJ. He's my favorite . . . my sister's favorite. That's Howie. That's Kevin. And that's Nick. He used to be my favorite.

At various points during the tour she has the camera pause and "gaze" over the image at hand. For example, at the time she is sort of a Backstreet Boys fan, although she is not as much a fan of theirs as she is of the Spice Girls. Nonetheless she pauses at her BSB posters.

Mixed in with Jana's commentary on Backstreet Boys, Spice Girls, and "Sailor Moon" is her commentary on the sports and dance artifacts in her life.

> *J.*: [Pointing to awards and trophies] This one I got last year and this one was my first time playing soccer.
>
> This one was the second one, the second, the second [picking up another] and this was the third . . . because I wanted to play soccer but I had a crap team because the little ones were like this small . . . [motions]

Springing from this commentary, she is back to popular culture:

> *J.*: Someone made this box for me. All my Spice Girls stickers are in here.

Then, picking up a toy clown:

J.: It's a little thing, it turns its head. [music starts]
My mom [got it]. Oh my grandma, my grandma, my grandma.
I was six years old.

J.: These are my twin-triplets.

B.: Your twin-triplets?

J.: Triplets. They all cry. I can't make it stop. I could . . .

B.: What?

J.: I could hit them on the head. Do you want me to hit them on the head? One, two, three. First one [hits doll on head], now the other one, there. [laughs]
This one starts with an A so it's Anastasia.

B.: Anastasia? Is that from the movie?

J.: Yeah, this one is B for Brian [pointing to the BSB poster] which is his name. And this one is Chelsea.

B.: Chelsea? Why did you name her Chelsea?

Figure 3.16 Jana: "Twin Triplets" (still captured from video).

J.: 'Coz it starts with a "C".

B.: Ah, any particular reason. Like you know someone named Chelsea?

J.: Oh yeah all of them it's from something [pointing to her dolls one at a time], her, it's from a movie; her it's from the guy in the Backstreet Boys. And her it's from one of my friends, one of my cousin's friends.

These two examples of children as photographers, one of Crisdan with his disposable camera, and one of Jana working as director and narrator with an adult videographer, give a sense that children navigate the world of popular culture in very personal and confident ways. But there are other points uncovered in the "visual spaces" of childhood that bear underlining. For example, going beyond the point that popular culture is seldom encountered or experienced as a single item in the life of a child, it is important to recognize that in fact this is more than just genre-blending in relation to popular culture but is really a sense of the blending of "favorite objects" more broadly. Popular culture collections, figuratively at least, and sometimes literally, blend into other collections. Gifts such as jewelry boxes can occupy the same status as the mini-Barbie picked up as part of the kids pack at McDonald's. At the same time, there are some specifics of the two photography sessions which warrant more investigation. We are interested, for example, in the unsentimental treatment of the triplet dolls which cried. The only way to stop them – Anastasia (from the movie), Brian (taken from the BSB), and Chelsea, named for a friend – was to slap them. The child's gaze, as Anne Higonnet (1998) suggests, is one that is generally unsentimental, and by exploring it in ways indicated by projects such as these, we may have a much better sense of how to free children from innocence-labeling, but also how to better understand ways of working alongside of children.

Future Directions for "Play Display"

Beyond the specific documentary work of Crisdan and Jana as visual anthropologists, we are interested in how the imaginative possibilities of children's work with photographs and popular culture – play display – might feature more prominently in an exploration of the "insider" view of children's culture. The artistic works of Weideman, Boltanski, the contributors to works such as the *Art of Barbie*, and other adults who incorporate popular culture into visual installation, as we have suggested, are important for what they say about the ways in which children's popular culture artifacts evoke particular fanciful and playful interpretations – and, at the same time, critical awareness. However, they are also important for what they say about the ways in which the idea of spontaneous or daily installation itself might be regarded as important entry points for understanding children as meaning-makers. Increasingly in the social sciences we are seeing a move towards the use of artistic modes of data display, as the work of Robert Donmeyer and Kos Raylene (1993), Tom Barone (2000), and others suggests, to understanding issues and concerns that have typically been studied through the conventions of positivistic research of that work. These representations now find their way onto the programming of such mainstream organizations as the American Educational Research Association annual conferences, into the establishment of virtual centers such as the Image and Identity Research Collective (Mitchell and Weber 2000),[4] and into academic literature as we see in, say, Paley and Jipson's *Daredevil Research* (1997). Clearly, there is a space to incorporate the notion of gaze. Moreover, as Nicholas Paley observes in his close reading of three projects involving young artists (including the work of Sadie Benning and the Shooting Back projects organized by James Hubbard): "it's clear that young people, in general, are capable of artistic agency, of producing artistic works which (echoing Maxine Greene) 'make it possible to see from different standpoints'," and which "stimulate the 'wide-awakeness' so essential to critical awareness" (1995: 182).

In this chapter we have tried to demonstrate some ways in which this artistic agency of children in relation to their own popular culture can occur both spontaneously as well as in "adult-organized" projects, presenting various approaches by which we can read and interpret the results. To return to Oakley's question at the beginning of the chapter regarding children as actors and knowers, in these visual projects noted above, we would see children as being centrally involved as both. We are interested, though, in other uses of new technology that can involve children with even more agency as photographers. Susan Entz and Sheri Lyn Galarza, in their book *Picture This*, document the use of the digital camera with even very young children. As they observe:

> The digital camera, instant photography, a scanner, a printer, and the computer are new teaching tools that can be used to create a curriculum that capitaliz[es] on the way young children learn. . . . Toddlers, preschoolers, and early elementary students are remarkably egocentric. The young child is truly the center of his or her own universe. Curricula must capitalize on the fact that young children are self-centered and self-absorbed.
>
> Photography is a useful tool for teachers of young children. It puts children right where they want to be, at the centre of the action (2000: ix).

We are particularly intrigued by the ways in which popular culture, itself, has taken the lead in developing and marketing these self-referential tools. Here, for example, we are thinking of Sadie Benning's Fisher-Price Pixelvision video camera, and of course, Kodak's first Brownie camera initially marketed to parents as a toy for children. It is worth mentioning that Mattel now makes a Barbie Polaroid I-zone instant pocket camera which little girls can use to create postage-stamp-size images. Modeled after the Toy-Joy sticker polaroid, the Barbie camera, part of Mattel's techno-girl campaign which also includes several CD-ROMs with Barbie software and the *Secret Talking Electronic Scrapbook* that uses scanning technology, has the added appeal of product association. While this is not the first Barbie camera – there has been the Barbie Glitter Star 110 camera as well as the Barbie for Girls Fun Camera, Outdoor 35mm Camera and Film in One – there is something particularly appealing about the idea of the Barbie Polaroid in terms of self-definition. We are not aware of particular photography projects that involve this camera, although, in light of the possibilities for Barbie as pistol or sword, as well as fashion doll, we would propose that a camera like this can offer imaginative possibilities that go "beyond Barbie."

Chapter Four

Physical Spaces: Children's Bedrooms as Cultural Texts

Introduction

Bedrooms, as the 1960s Beach Boys ballad "In My Room" goes, are places for "dreamin' and schemin'," and, as the bedrooms of Cristian and Jana referred to in the previous chapter suggest, are also often perfect havens of "hyper-consumerism" and popular culture fantasy. From Mickey Mouse sleepwear to Lion King bed linen, to Pooh murals to toy-boxes full of Polly Pockets or Etch A Sketches and Lego, children's bedrooms tend to be repositories for contemporary kids' culture. In one sense, children's bedrooms are controlled by adults in terms of overall design and layout, and children may be subject to rules of behavior around neatness or whether the door has to be open, and so on. And of course, the idea of the room itself can have a type of regulatory function. The imperatives of "clean up your room" or "go to your room," for example, may serve to counter any sense of the child being in charge of his or her domain – even if the room is filled with highly desired play objects. Being sent to one's room, as we see represented in the children's book by Maurice Sendak's *Where the Wild Things Are* (1983) is regarded as punishment; it is not the same as going there freely – choosing to be in one's room instead of in a more public space. At the same time though, the child's bedroom is the one official place of some privacy – and a place where there can be at least some expression of individual taste. Max's fantasy about the wild things can only happen in a space where Max is king. And in contemporary urban spaces, where children are more likely to live in small apartments and not in large, rambling houses with attics and basements or backyards (all places where unofficial private spaces can be claimed in the form of forts and so on), the bedroom takes on even more importance. As Henry Jenkins writes:

> My son, Henry, now 16, has never had a backyard.
>
> He has grown up in various apartment complexes, surrounded by asphalt parking lots with, perhaps, a small grass buffer from the street. Children were prohibited by apartment policy from playing on the grass or from racing their tricycles in the basements or from doing much of anything else that might make noise, annoy the non-childbearing

> population, cause damage to the facilities, or put themselves at risk. There was, usually, a city park some blocks away that we could go to on outings a few times a week and where we could watch him play. Henry could claim no physical space as his own, except his toy-strewn room, and he rarely got outside earshot. Once or twice, when I became exasperated by my son's constant presence around the house, I would forget all this and tell him he should go outside and play. He would look at me with confusion and ask, "Where?" (1998b: 263).

Taking up Jenkins' point, we posit that while children may have less access to the usual "No entrance," "Enter at your own risk" discourse for regulating their own private space compared with adolescents, or compared with children several decades ago who might have had forts on a deserted lot, or at the far end of the backyard, the notion of the bedroom space is still the one which offers the greatest possibility for children-in-control. Children's bedrooms figure prominently in children's culture: from the literary bedrooms of *Raggedy Ann*, the works of C. S. Lewis, and the Harry Potter books, to bedrooms within television sitcoms and movies, and within a range of genres, from the idea of "the toys come alive" to the pre-teen sleep-over. Indeed there are a number of notable "famous bedrooms" as physical sites for exploring children's popular culture – Andy's room in the Toy Story movies, the bedroom of Syd the evil "boy next door" in the same movie, complete with the mutant toy collection, Emily's "growing up" and "growing out of Jessie" room in *Toy Story 2*, the bedrooms of Matt and Holly in *Small Soldiers.* Even the closet/bedroom of Harry Potter to be found underneath the stairs of the Dursleys' as a space for Harry's free play has taken on an image within popular culture, particularly since the release of the movie *Harry Potter and the Sorcerer's Stone* in November 2001. And Mattel in its market wisdom uses the space of a girl's bedroom as the foyer for its official Barbie website. Within virtual space, *Toy Story* is referred to as "Andy's Room." Thus, in the context of a range of issues – from the danger zone of urban spaces, to "good parenting" to the need to put some boundaries on consumer culture (after all, where does one locate all of this highly differentiated paraphernalia of play culture) the child's bedroom is not just a repository of popular culture, but like the suburban shopping mall, McDonald's play zone, or Disney theme park, can be regarded as a cultural text in itself. Indeed, if one were to follow the dictum of *House and Garden* and other interior design publications, the child's bedroom would be a theme park!

We are interested, then, in looking at the ways in which one might do fieldwork in children's bedrooms. As a cultural text, we propose, the child's bedroom logically can be located in the field of social or human geography, similar to the way cultural texts such as shopping malls and video arcades have been analyzed in relation to youth cultures, and can therefore be "read." Thus, our focus is on employing strategies for engaging in semiotic readings of children's bedrooms as popular culture. In so doing, we adapt the semiotic approach of Stephen Riggins as a way to engage in textual analysis (1994).

We examine two different sites, associated with two different age groups: the baby's room and the girl's room as depicted in teen magazines, taking into consideration how the first site is a space for the expression of creative decoration on the part of the parents and other involved adults, and the second site is a space where the girl can exert some limited power over the arrangement of her physical environment.

Bedroom Spaces Within "Capital G" and "Small g" Geographies

Tracey Skelton and Gill Valentine in their book *Cool Places: Geographies of Youth Cultures* (1998) describe as "capital G" Geography, a social cartography. They use the term "small g" geography to refer more to the actual physical spaces. In the case of adolescent culture, this "small g" often refers to the kinds of public autonomous spaces that have come to be associated with youth – shopping malls, street corners, video game arcades, and the like – along with the idea of contested and regulated spaces associated with youth culture in relation to adult culture. Interestingly, as McRobbie and Garber (1991) point out in their study of the bedrooms of adolescent girls, the "small g" geography of public youth spaces prior to their study often excluded young women. In coining the phrase the "culture of the bedroom," they draw attention to a rich ethnographic site for investigating the subculture of adolescent girls in youth culture studies. McRobbie and Garber were moved to use this term in order to comment on the "presence of absence" of girls in much of the work on youth subcultures in Britain in the 1960s and 1970s. In that research, largely given over to street-corner youth (such as Willis' lads), the studies are primarily about males. McRobbie and Garber hypothesize that perhaps girls were not so much absent as present somewhere else:

> It might be suggested that girls' culture of the time operated within the vicinity of the home, or the friend's home. There was room for a great deal of the new teenage consumer culture within the confines of the girls' bedrooms. Teenage girls did participate in the new public sphere afforded by the growth of the leisure industries, but they could also consume at home, upstairs in their bedrooms (1991: 6).

Subsequently, feminist researchers such as Griffiths (1995), and Dwyer (1998) have explored the culture of adolescent girls' rooms in terms of class, race/ethnicity, and age through using strategies of observation, participant-observation and in-depth interviewing. They determined that girls use different means to negotiate conventional, societal expectations of femininity while establishing their own sense of identity. Studying working-class British girls, Griffiths discovered, for example, what she considers to be a form of invisible resistance to the status quo in their use of CB radios to safely initiate mixed-sex

exist in at least two forms. Playgrounds, as the Opies found (1969), while being likely settings for encountering some aspects of children's culture, are at the same time settings where there is a particular type of public culture operating. There are some tastes that children cannot reveal in public. If a girl still plays with Barbie at age ten and none of her friends do, then there is no way that she can easily express this in a group. Moreover, as we have observed earlier, day-care centers and schools, which are likely to be informal public play settings, often openly ban artifacts of popular culture. Children, as they acquire school savvy, learn what they cannot safely talk about with adults, as well as what will incite adults to comment. As Allison James points out, children are fully aware of what they are doing by turning adult-accepted artifacts of play into "lower forms" – Lego to guns, and so on:

> From the child's perspective . . . the boundaries to the play world are neither fixed nor constant, for adults may arbitrarily intervene to put an end to play in both the class-room and the playground. The time for play may be cut short, styles of play disapproved of and particular games outlawed. In the nursery setting, for example, the building toys of Lego or Sticklebricks were seen by the staff as only suitable for creating technical or abstract constructions. They were deemed unfit for the more figurative representations used by children in their games. Firing guns made of Lego in a space-age fantasy and smoking "cigarettes" made from the plastic tubes of a construction set were both forbidden (1993: 172).

By contrast – behind closed (at least partly closed) doors – bedrooms-as-playrooms offer possibilities for exploring popular culture artifacts in ways that are less socially governed (it is acceptable to have a Smurf collection on an upper shelf of a closet even if one is not allowed to talk about it on the playground). For instance, in recalling their girlhood play with Barbie – privately in their bedrooms – several young women have told us of elaborate sex scenes they have carried out involving Ken and Barbie. As we noted in Chapter 1, in our own "public forum" of conducting an interview with four ten-year-old girls in a public library, the girls made reference to a "bedroom game" called Swan Prince. It was only later that we were told that the game included a part where "the prince had sex with the Barbie." In short, adult-organized "adultist" settings may not be the best sites for finding children's tastes and awareness of popular culture.

How to Read a Child's Bedroom

Our idea of reading or writing a child's space begins with the work on memories of dream-spaces in the *Poetics of Space* by the French philosopher Gaston Bachelard. He determines how:

> the reader who is "reading a room" leaves off reading and starts to think of some place in his own past. You would like to tell everything about your room. You would like to interest the reader in yourself, whereas you have unlocked a door to daydreaming. The values of intimacy are so absorbing that the reader has ceased to read your room: he sees his own again (1964: 14).

For Bachelard, it is these private recollections which are the most significant part of the reading, something that we also see in the work of social semiotician Stephen Riggins, who draws our attention to how to read a room – both denotatively and, in line with Bachelard, connotatively – by offering a field guide to reading his parents' living room in an essay called "Fieldwork in the living room: an autoethnographic essay" (1994). In explaining denotative information, Riggins uses the term "referencing" to describe "all of the content which is about the history, aesthetics or customary uses of the objects." He claims that this information is often "brief and superficial," with people knowing (or offering) very little of this information in the course of a regular interview (1994: 109). It is often either taken for granted, as, for example, by the fact that refrigerators or washing machines "are" coded as gendered objects, or their history is forgotten (or simply not known). Do we remember a time, for example, before television and hence the invention of the television? Or do we have sufficient perspective to be able to see sociological links between the invention of the television and its social uses? John Hartley, for example, in an analysis of the popularity of the television set, outlines some interesting links between the invention and mass distribution of the refrigerator and the television set. Not only did the invention and mass distribution of the refrigerator lessen the amount of time people had to spend purchasing and preserving food, but the television also became "sponsored" by food preparation, food clean-up, food elimination, and the like (1999: 100–2).

To illustrate his points about denotation with reference to his parents' living room, Riggins describes in some detail four mass-produced pictures done by the artist Paul Detlefsen which are hanging on the wall. He considers that the pictures

> present nostalgic versions of turn-of-the-century farming and small-town life. I would interpret these pictures as showing manual labour without drudgery, the reassurance of technological simplicity; the satisfaction of the harvest, and the excitement of firemen racing to put out an unseen fire in the distance (also reassuring because there is no hint of tragedy) (1994: 131).

In daily life, such pictures are seen, but not necessarily read as having a history. Indeed, it is often only when a visitor begins to query a particular object that this denotative referencing is invoked.

In contrast to denotative information, Riggins explains, connotative information is of a personal and connected nature and people tend to provide vast amounts of detail about this aspect of an object. He uses the term "mapping" to describe the ways in which objects serve as "entry points for the telling of stories about the self and its personal relationships" (1994: 109). Of this mapping feature, he writes:

> meaning by this that the self uses the displayed objects (gifts, heirlooms, photographs, etc.) as a way of plotting its social network, representing its cosmology and ideology, and projecting its history onto the world's map, its spatial spread so to speak. This is indeed what objects are – dots on a map and connecting links which can be retraced in any direction (ibid.: 109).

In exploring denotative and connotative meanings, Riggins points to the significance of taking photographs as central to the process of visual ethnography. He writes:

> Many of the subtleties of domestic artifacts will elude the researcher unless it is possible to closely examine photographs. Consequently, each room must be thoroughly photographed. Unlike the practice followed by the professional photographers employed by decorating and architectural magazines of removing all ephemeral traces left by users and inhabitants in order to avoid dating the photographs, ethnographers should make an effort to include the permanent as well as the ephemeral. Both are relevant to the research (1994: 110).

He then goes on to indicate the significance of utilizing a procedure for executing a written account. Again, the emphasis is on being systematic as opposed to being impressionistic. As he notes:

> One might want to begin the written account of a room with the first object visitors are likely to notice upon entering (something directly opposite the door or some other highlighted space) and from that point proceed systematically around the room. The same procedure should be applied to the contents of cabinets or shelves. Begin with the object farthest to the right or the left and proceed down the shelf (ibid.: 110).

Thus Riggins' work allows for both the denotative and connotative dimensions of interpretation. By drawing attention first of all to denotative information, we propose that there is a method for getting under what is normally taken for granted, and thereby not usually articulated in interviews. However, in our analysis, by providing a space for the connotative dimension, we leave ample room for the interpretive stories as well.

Children's Bedrooms: The Denotative

What kinds of denotative information do children's bedrooms contain? We start with the idea of children's sleep itself. As Stearns et al. point out, prior to the late nineteenth century, sleep was absent from discussions of childhood: "manuals for parents, produced in abundance, simply did not deal with children's sleep – in marked contrast to their counterparts by the 1920s" (1996: 345). The idea that children would have separate rooms accorded to them is of course another discussion, one which reflects a growing awareness by the middle classes in the early twentieth century of the importance of children's health, as well as the presence of a growing body of experts on childhood. As Stearns et al. state:

> Middle-class children [in the early twentieth century] were increasingly placed in individual bedrooms, in contrast to the 19th-century pattern in which the same-sex children had commonly slept together, usually sharing beds, even in the upper middle class. Throughout the 19th century, middle- and upper-middle-class children slept near a parent or nurse during infancy, and then were moved to share a bed with a sibling (sometimes in a room with other bedded pairs) thereafter (1996: 357).

As for play, seemingly a secondary use for a child's room, the idea of play in association with a separate domestic space seems to have come about as a function of the emerging idea of the "companionate family" in the first two decades of the twentieth century amidst the competing leisure-time pursuits of a more commercialized world of public movies, amusement parks, and so on. As Jacobson writes:

> anxieties about children's attraction to mass recreation and an autonomous youth culture provided an inescapable context for selling and interpreting the merits of children's play in a revitalized domestic sphere. Extolling the virtues of active play over passive spectatorship, child experts urged parents to provide children with adequate play space within the home and educational toys which stimulated the imagination. Together with interior designers, they advised parents how to transform frumpy homes into enticing play sites equipped with playrooms and backyard swing sets. Although psychological theories propounding the virtues of play informed these domestic reforms, the new understandings of play were also tied to the perils and possibilities of a consumer society. Revitalized play environments, experts believed, would help elevate children's taste and arm them against the sort of passive consumption that made them vulnerable to the attractions of mass culture (1997: 582).

While the advice of experts in the mid-1920s presented this need for space in the form of a specific playroom, as opposed to a bedroom, the practicalities of space within family dwellings along with the idea of the individualism of the child (the developing child needs his or her own "space") has meant that the contemporary Western bedroom has come to be associated with individual expression. What is interesting, of course, is the fact that what started out as protection from the demoralizing effects of the commercial world has in fact turned into the now-celebrated "children's bedroom" which, in its ideal is the playroom/sleep environment that is itself the ultimate in the commercial world of Disney sheets and coverlets, and popular culture toy artifacts. Indeed, as we observe at the beginning of this chapter, one of the most notable children's bedrooms/play sites in popular culture which is itself a bedroom full of popular culture artifacts must surely be Andy's in the movie *Toy Story*. Interestingly, some of the *Toy Story* spin-off texts that Disney has produced include artifacts such as sheets, pillowcases, posters, coverlets, and so on, all bearing images of Cowboy Woody and Buzz Lightyear, so that *Toy Story* fans can also occupy the *Toy Story* bedroom. Similarly, the baby's room in the movie *Father of the Bride Part 2* lays out the sleep/play space for baby as an over-the-top designer suite. Following from this, it is worth noting that children's bedrooms – like children themselves – might be read as status symbols. It is not just that this is still largely a world where heterosexual couples are expected to have children; it is also that children's eccentricities and fetishes (from being allergic to playing soccer to collecting Barbies) become part of the social world, located within the conversations of staffrooms and backyard barbeques. In the same way that there is a certain resignedness and pride to "Oh, no, we can't possibly come to the party; it is Chelsea's soccer game/figure-skating lesson/gymnastic class," so too there may be this same kind of resignedness and pride attached to "The room wasn't big enough to contain the whole of Damien's action figure collection so we decided to add on." Indeed, this is one material practice of the contemporary focus on the individual – one child equals one bedroom. If, in reality, each child in a family does not have his or her own room, then at least in the affluent, middle-class imagination of Hollywood, Disney and *Better Homes and Gardens*, he or she does. This is something that is often reinforced within the "checklists" of good parenting: "Does the child have his or her own room?" In reduced circumstances, parents, for example, will often sacrifice their own need for privacy to the needs of the child to have a room of his or her own. As archaeologists Buchli and Lucas found in their study of material culture in an abandoned British council flat, the traces of childhood – the Flintstones wallpaper, left-behind Crayola markers, and the like – are indicative of the dominance of children's physical spaces and material culture in the late twentieth century. As they observe: "The segregation of a children's sphere is confirmed, in practice, from the distribution of child-associated artefacts in the different rooms. One room was unquestionably dominated by children's artefacts, with almost no adult-associated artefacts present (the children's room)" (2000: 134).

Our discussion of Riggins' idea of referencing in relation to children's bedrooms has been, thus far, relatively general in that it has not addressed what we see as a key feature of children's rooms: that being their age-appropriateness and the fact that childhood (within the age range of birth to ten) is not some monolithic period. As David Buckingham writes:

> While I would agree that traditional developmental psychology of the Piagetian variety is both asocial and often mechanistic, there are certain generalizations about children's development which remain valid. Age, like other variables, cannot simply be reduced to a matter of "access to discourses". In their attempt to arrive at a "systematically non-cognitive psychology" (Potten and Wetherell, 1987: 157), discourse analysts risk throwing out the baby with the proverbial bathwater (1991: 244).

As a denotative feature of children's bedrooms, we see age most directly through the notion of agency. Clearly the infant or toddler has virtually no say over space, while the older child is gaining some autonomy over his or her space. Thus, the rooms of infants and young children, we posit, are in a sense much more like Riggins' living room in that they are not really private spaces the way the bedrooms of older children, adolescents, or adults might be; rather, they are more likely to be reflections of adult taste – or "repositories" for what parents want for their children. Given that the baby's room is often decorated even before the birth of the baby, it can even become part of the home tour: "Can we see the baby's room?" After the baby is born, visitors are often welcomed to peer in at the sleeping baby and, of course, the decor in which the baby sleeps. The choice of wallpaper, mobiles, crib bumper pads, the inclusion of nursery heirlooms, such as an antique rocking-chair or cradle, and so on, are all part of the vernacular decoration. Indeed, when we first announced to our colleagues and students that we were interested in babies' bedrooms, many people used the term "showroom" or "display room" to refer to the public function of these spaces. Historically, this has precedence in middle-class and upper-class American households. Indeed, referring specifically to the baby's bassinet in Victorian households, Karen Calvert compares its symbolic function to that of the wedding dress:

> In its appearance, costliness, and ceremonial nature, the bassinet closely resembled the elaborate white wedding gown that became popular at just about the same time. Both the white gown and white bed were sacramental artifacts, used for brief ceremonies consecrating the creation of family and celebrating the fact that the strength of the family lay in the innocence and purity of its components, particularly the virgin bride and innocent babe (1992: 143).

Children's Bedrooms: The Connotative

For slightly older children, the bedroom is likely to take on more of a connotative meaning as a play space where the presence of particular objects, toys, shelves, toy chest, and use of space reveals more of the individual interests of the child, even though it may still be the parent who is in control of the overall arrangement of the room. It is at this point that rooms tend to become very clearly gendered so that there are approved boys' room decor and girls' room decor. The bedroom of six-year-old Andy in *Toy Story* is a good example of this gender-differentiated space, with Bo Peep being the only female-coded text in the room, although there are what might be regarded as "cross-over" toys such as Etch A Sketch and Mr. Potato Head, and the Little Professor (even though these toys might be regarded as being coded male simply because they are open to either males or females), and then toys which are explicitly masculine – the toy soldiers, Cowboy Woody, Buzz Lightyear, and so on. For children beyond the age of six or seven, the bedroom becomes increasingly a private play zone, and, as we noted in the previous chapter, a display space for the child's individual tastes. In the context of this 'tween culture it is also, as we saw with Jana's bedroom, one that is closer to the adolescent bedroom as described by McRobbie and Garvey and others, complete with Backstreet Boys posters *and* dolls, and the "in between" bedrooms referred to by Karin Geiger (Scott 1997).

Bedroom Work

To illustrate our idea of doing bedroom fieldwork in which the room is read as a cultural text according to Riggins' broad categories of referencing and mapping, we employ two different approaches. The first is to turn to "Crissie's Pooh room" where we look at the denotative and connotative meaning of particular artifacts in the baby's room, showing the ways in which children are born into popular culture. Then, in extending our social semiotic reading to include the bedrooms of older children, we shift our focus to a reading of the bedroom-as-popular-culture in teen magazines.

"And here's the baby's room": reading Chrissie's Pooh room

The idea of the baby's room – and hence baby-appropriate vernacular interior decoration – is one that comes with its own relatively "invisible" set of referencing features. Indeed, so entrenched is the idea of the baby's room in the Western middle-class ideal, many people, outside of the LaLeche League and its advocacy of the "family bed," might not think of the sociohistorical significance of baby occupying his or her own relatively fixed sleep unit, a crib, as opposed to, say, a movable cradle, let alone the idea of a separate room.

Concomitantly, the origin of the extensive baby paraphernalia that is required, appropriately coded in terms of decoration – from the crib or junior bed with partial sides, to the jolly jumper, baby swing, bathing cot or mobile – is often invisible or taken for granted. Stearns et al., for example, draw our attention to the significance of the evolution of crib furniture. As they note, by the 1890s, infants were increasingly separated from adults for sleeping. This was possible and safe because of the invention of the crib:

> Cribs fenced a young child in for sleep. They were relatively immobile, which made placement in a separate room seem both logical and essential; unlike cradles, cribs could not be moved about depending on where a parent was. Only for a brief time, in the crib regime, was a basket used. . . . Finally, for an older infant, cribs provided safeguards from falling or wandering around; previously many toddlers graduated from cradle to sleeping with an older sibling whose presence had offered the necessary protection. A significant change in children's furniture, in sum, altered the age gradations of sleeping arrangements and above all prepared the experience of sleeping alone (1996: 358).

The development of the crib and the idea of baby in his or her own room, separate from all the bustle of everyday life, also speaks to the development of two new product lines based on the needs of babies: the need for stimulation, and hence the development of hanging mobiles and the like (ranging from musical nursery rhyme artifacts to those that are more obviously inspired by popular culture), and the need for safety. This latter point has led to the development of bumper pads which fully surround the interior of the crib, offering protection from both head banging as well as the bars of the crib, Fisher-Price monitors so that the parents can still be within hearing distance of the baby even if they are in another room, and so on. The need for both protection and stimulation speaks to the evaluation of appropriate decor for baby's room, something that is now taken for granted by most middle-class parents – especially those contemplating the birth of a first child – where decorating the baby's room is as de rigueur as pre-natal classes. Indeed, even in the case of furniture and accessories that are being "passed on" by friends and relatives, parents are often in the position to make selections according to what is appropriate, particularly in terms of sex, simply because there are often more people "passing on" baby paraphernalia than people having babies! A blue teddy bear motif will not do for a baby girl. Or worse, a Sweet Dreams pale pink motif will be unthinkable for a boy baby, and something deemed too "babyish" will simply not last.

For Chrissie, the motif is Winnie-the-Pooh. Barbara, Chrissie's mother, has first introduced us to Chrissie's bedroom through a series of photographs. Following Riggins' suggestion that we start with some feature of the room that is dominant, we might first look at the Pooh border glued on top of the regular wall covering (Figure 4.1). Produced under the Disney trademark and available through most major department stores in North America, it is derived from the original A. A. Milne characters which were "Disneyfied" in the early 1970s. The pattern that Chrissie's mother has chosen is one of several available – what we found ourselves referring to as the "real Disney" version, full of vibrant primary colors, as opposed to the more muted and subtle "classic Pooh" version based on the original Shepard illustrations.

While it is not obvious in the picture, Chrissie also has the crib bumper pads in a Pooh motif along with patterned curtains. Baby Chrissie may also be dressed in Pooh sleepers – domed terry cloth one-piece outfits, available in most major department stores which carry babywear and which usually go up to, say, size 2, so that it would be unlikely that a school-aged child or older would have such a garment with the Pooh motif – although adult-sized artifacts such as Pooh silk ties and vests as well as adult sleepwear have been available since the mid-1990s for the "nostalgia oriented." The only non-Pooh artifact in the room is a mobile, hanging over the crib. Mobiles, made popular in the 1960s in recognition of the findings of developmental psychologists that young babies' cognitive growth can be stimulated, are now a standard baby's room item. The Pooh mobile, a collection of small plush creatures, was not available at the time that the room was being decorated, and in its stead is a Sesame Street mobile made up of Big Bird, Ernie, and Cookie Monster. In a picture taken in Chrissie's bedroom two years later (Figure 4.2), after the family has moved, and after Chrissie has graduated to a regular single bed, we still see the Pooh border, but now Chrissie also has a full Pooh bed set of

Figure 4.1 Winnie-the-Pooh border on Chrissie's wall (photograph by Barbara Pyontka).

Figure 4.2 Chrissie's Pooh-paraphernalia-filled bedroom (photograph by Barbara Pyontka).

pillowcases, sheets, coverlet, again available from most major department stores. The Pooh pillowcase is in full view in the photograph. Out of sight, and at the other end of the bed, there are some Pooh stuffed animals.

In conversation, Chrissie's mother "maps" the evolution of the Pooh decor, in a sense offering a connotative reading on Chrissie's room. She reveals that Chrissie's "steeped-in-Pooh" ambience began with the Pooh border she chose before Chrissie's birth. It was chosen for its gender-neutral quality. While she observes that the Mickey Minnie border, would have also worked, the tone of the green would not have been quite right if the baby were a boy, whereas the bright red of the Pooh border was fine. A third possibility, a line called Precious Moments, seems not to have been in the running either because of its limited shelf life or its gendered coding. After the choice of the border was made, Barbara observes, the rest of the room unfolded according to the generosity of friends and relatives who loved the idea of purchasing according to a theme. When she itemizes the gifts from the baby shower held before Chrissie's birth she includes Pooh-based items such as a throw blanket, plush wall decorations of each of the inhabitants of Hundred Acre Wood, and a set for feeding the baby consisting of a baby bottle and matching bibs.

It is this Pooh theme that friends and relatives continue, collecting on Chrissie's behalf each one of the plush animals. As Barbara observes: "My girlfriend started it with Pooh which she bought for Christmas. And then my mother bought Piglet. And my sister-in-law bought Eeyore." Indeed, she notes that this "collecting" tendency of friends and relatives has now extended into other Disney artifacts so that family and friends inquire at Christmas and birthdays if Chrissie has the Disney video of *Beauty and the Beast* or *The Little Mermaid*, and so on, and if they should make the purchase.

The choice of Pooh as a relatively gender-neutral text is an interesting one, given that the protagonist is male and all the creatures of Hundred Acre Wood (with the exception of Kanga, Baby Roo's mother) are also male. Still, it is emblematic of the subtlety of choosing an appropriate decor so that no major gender boundaries are transgressed. As Buckley observes in her analysis of the clothing of babies and young children:

> for many parents looking for and buying baby clothes is more than a diversion. Aided and abetted by grandparents, aunts, uncles and friends it is part of the process of beginning to give an identity to the awaited baby, and trying to make sense of its likely needs in relation to one's own expectations, particularly in terms of the baby's sex. The most frequently asked question is still "what do you want, a boy or a girl?" And, after the birth, "is it a boy or a girl?" (1996: 104).

As Buckley goes on to note, while the big-price-tag items such as crib, pram, and so on tend not to be strongly sexed, or at least as in the case of Pooh not overly determined in terms of gender (and hence can be purchased before the birth of the baby, and passed on at a later point), it is the accessories – clothing, duvets, mobiles, etc. – that are more likely to be gender-coded. She points out, though, that the choice of these artifacts is more than just about the identity of the baby: "to some extent [it is] a reflection of that of the parents – indeed, the well-dressed [and groomed] baby or child is an attractive adult accessory, a cuddly status symbol" (ibid.).

In our own fieldwork in the baby section of several department stores, we have been interested in the relative absence of any obvious "girl-stuff" amidst the crib–bumper pad–coverlet paraphernalia, but the presence of what was either obviously neutral – for example, teddy-bear patterns in green and maroon and containing both male and female bears – or more boyish patterns which would still do for girls. Here we are thinking of the baby sets of blue teddy bears, *Sesame Street*, and so on, although at the higher end in terms of cost and specialty we found parents' popular culture invading the nursery through "Tommy Hilfiger for babies." These items (bumper pad, coverlet, etc.) with their bold, primary colored non-animal pattern seemed more directly marketed towards the parents of baby boys.

In this way the baby is steeped in popular culture even before its birth, as are the parents, grandparents, friends, and so on. What does it mean to participate in a child's "growing into" popular culture through vernacular decoration? In the case of Pooh bumper pads and mobiles, the popular culture of childhood, in all its supposed ephemerality and low status, is big business with adults. Babies, we must understand, however, could not care less whether they are sleeping, crying, being fed, changed, or being "goo-ed" at in a Pooh ambience, one of Precious Moments, or in the drawer of a bureau! Returning to Buckley's phrase "Aided and abetted by grandparents" (1996: 104), we see that there is a different kind of collecting going on than that which is normally associated with the collector (adult or child) collecting for herself. In the case of Chrissie, relatives and friends took delight in collecting on behalf of Chrissie or her parents.

What are people giving/choosing when they give/choose Pooh over Precious Moments or *Sesame Street* or Mickey and Minnie? Or rather, what are we being offered in relation to childhood? It is only when children are older and at the single-bed stage that they (and their parents) are offered a wider selection of Barbie, Ninja Turtles, Space Aliens, Mulan bed sheets and wallpaper. Indeed, short of embarking upon the cost of hiring an interior designer who will design "the" nursery, as Steve Martin does in *Father of the Bride, Part 2*, parents must either creatively "design their own" bedroom, "go alternative" based on baby-wear from specialty shops, or go with Pooh. In speaking of the baby-product market in Britain, Buckley observes:

> The conscious or unconscious representation of class or life-style is important in children's clothes [and decor], and the decision to buy from Laura Ashley or Next may indicate a greater design awareness than buying from Marks & Spencer or Littlewoods. Although some may reject the ostentatious display of money evident in Italian baby equipment or French baby clothes, they can nevertheless signify their alternative taste and style by buying from select shops which stock hand-made, "ethnic" or "heritaged" goods. In the provincial towns and cities in the North and the Midlands, taste and style are possibly more restricted because of fewer alternatives to the national chains, multiples and department stores. In these outlets design status is closely aligned with price: "how much" competes with fashionable design knowledge as an important selection criterion (1996: 104–5).

In our fieldwork in the baby sections of two department stores, one slightly more "lower end" and the other slightly more "upmarket," we noted that the Disneyish patterns tended to be less expensive than other patterns and often absent from the upmarket store.

Does the choice of motif offer some commentary on childhood itself? Buchli and Lucas in their study of a council flat abandoned by a single mother highlight the significance of the Flintstones wallpaper in the children's room, along with the blue stenciled figures of the little bears – a '"neverland." In particular they read the motif of the family portrait – Fred Flintstone, with his wife Wilma and daughter Pebbles in the context of the circumstances under which the single mother had access to the council flat, and the material circumstances of her children:

> The mother of the household clearly attempted to produce this segregated and highly differentiated "other" realm (neverland) in devotional anticipation of a familial ideal (ironically embodied by a prehistoric fantasy), whose reiteration was flawed in a crucial way – the lack of a viable opposite sex partner, the father (who would be the phantasmagorical Fred Flintstone). If this ideal were indeed successfully reiterable she would have obtained, according to British housing policy, preferential access to care, protection and support as a "wife" or cohabiting partner in addition to being a mother (Buchli and Lucas 2000: 135).

What meaning would we offer of Pooh? Does Pooh at least provide a connection to the past since he has been around since 1924, or some link to the personal pasts of today's parents of infants, most of whom would have themselves grown up with the Disney version of Pooh? As David Buckingham points out:

> it is hard to think of a fairy tale or a "classic" children's book which children will not now encounter first (and in most cases only) in its "Disneyfied" version. Symbolically – and in many cases legally – Disney now "owns" nearly all the fictional characters who have populated children's imaginations over the past century, from Sleeping Beauty and Cinderella right through to its most recent acquisitions such as the Muppets and the Ninja Turtles, A. A. Milne, Lewis Carroll, Rudyard Kipling, Hans Christian Andersen, J. M. Barrie and (most recently) Roald Dahl are only some of the children's authors whose work has been appropriated by the Disney empire (1997: 285).

And what does Pooh promise? A carefree childhood of lovable Disney/ A. A. Milne characters? Neither the brightly colored cheerful creatures from Hundred Acre Wood dancing on the border around Chrissie's room, nor the more muted "classic Pooh" designs reveal anything of the darkness that we now know of Christopher Robin, A. A. Milne's son. Like the photographs by popular child photographer Anne Geddes whose portrait of "Baby in a bunny crate," for example, consists of dressing up a baby as a bunny – so baby *is* a bunny, baby Chrissie is living "in" Hundred Acre Wood where she is surrounded by Pooh and Piglet and the House at Pooh Corner.

Teen Bedrooms in the Culture of Childhood: "What does your room tell about you?"

Our analysis of baby's bedrooms, however, says little about the agency of the older child, or the context within which children begin to exercise this agency, although clearly, as we saw in Chapter 4 in our discussion of the "bedroom work" of visual ethnographers Crisdan and Jana, children as young as five and six often have clear notions about the significance of the objects and arrangement of their bedrooms (or the private spaces they occupy within a bedroom shared with siblings). Given the significance of the bedroom as a play and creative space in contemporary culture, it should not be surprising that children's bedrooms might be read as texts of popular culture in and of themselves. Indeed, bedrooms are conspicuously a feature in popular North American teen magazines such as *YM* and *Seventeen* where there are regular articles and ads on room decor. *Seventeen* even goes so far as to publish a separate *Seventeen* supplement on bedrooms, somewhat akin to their Prom supplement. Articles on bedrooms figure prominently in ads and articles, ranging from "What does your room say about you?"(*YM*, spring 1997: 8–9) to "How to 'snoop-proof' your space" (*YM*, spring, 1997: 10) to "Does your room need a serious makeover?" (*YM*, spring 1997: 10) to "The hidden meaning of your stuff" (*YM*, spring 1997: 11) (all by Fitzmorris) to "Room to improve" (Lewin, *Girl*, Fall 1999: 128–9) – along with advice on how to organize and keep a bedroom tidy.

What can we learn by engaging in fieldwork with bedrooms in popular magazines (as opposed, say, to interviewing children themselves, as Brown, Steele, and others have done in relation to adolescent bedrooms)? Complementing our work in Chapter 4, where we interview Crisdan and Jana about their visual bedrooms, our research here draws on the vast body of work that has already been done on women's magazines (Winship 1987; Hermes 1995), but most particularly the work that has been done on girls' magazines. Dawn Currie (1999) and Angela McRobbie (1991) have carried out semiotic analyses of girls' fashion magazines as field sites for exploring codes of femininity, the codes of romance, and so on. Indeed, in looking back on the history of feminist scholarship and magazines for adolescent girls and women. McRobbie notes the ways in which magazines-as-field-sites have come to be taken as central to the study of feminist politics.

The position of teenage magazines in the study of children's culture, however, is less clear. The contents of these magazines rarely find their way into an analysis of children's culture since they are marketed towards the over-twelve or thirteen age range and hence are officially "out of bounds" to younger readers. However, we have been interested in what we see as being a downward trend in terms of age in the "unofficial" marketing of many "over-forty" girl-texts (including Barbie, who originated in 1959, and, Nancy Drew, who originated in 1929), particularly *Seventeen* which originated in 1944. *Seventeen* is a text whose very name suggests later adolescence and which, because of artificial boundaries that exist either in the research sites (early childhood, pre-adolescence), or in the research team (child studies/youth studies) tends to be studied only within adolescent culture. However, as one young informant – herself fourteen – observed: "Nobody who is seventeen would be caught dead reading *Seventeen*." What she doesn't say is that *Seventeen* magazine, currently designated by the magazine producers themselves as having a readership of

Referencing and Mapping Girls' Bedrooms in Teen Magazines

Since these magazines are read by young girls far below the textual age inscribed or suggested by the title of the magazines, one aspect we are interested in is how this readership or implied audience may be addressed in the language and presentation of the articles and advertisements. One thing that is immediately apparent, in girls' magazines, is the absence of extreme or exaggerated images of (hetero)sexuality – a prominent feature in magazines aimed at young women – in the presentation of the bedrooms (Farah Malik, personal communication May 12, 2001). Boys or men are absent as subjects from the photographs of the girls' rooms (unlike in women's magazines), but they may be safely present on the pages of the magazine as another image. For example, they may be present on the walls as pinups for the girl readers to admire, as in the poster of Antonio Sabato Jr. in the room featured in a *YM* special (spring 1997: 9). The function of the male star pinup in a girl's room may be similar to that in teen music and star magazines, where, as McRobbie notes, girls can safely stare at boys without being laughed at (1991: 171). Boys' images may be present as photographs of interpreters for the texts of girls' rooms, as in "Guys reveal what your bedroom says about you," where boys' interpretations of a girl's room are compared with the owner's comments (*Twist*, December 1998: 38–40). We speculate that the focus in girls' magazines, on girls' bedroom decor, and on girls' bedrooms as "spaces" for creative and individual expression, is something that is not evident in women's magazines. This could mean that girls' magazines present bedroom decor discussions as substitutes for the "sexual" content of bedroom discussions so prominent in women's magazines.

In the layouts for the photo displays of the rooms there are several recurring conventions. Often, the rooms are empty of their owners, with the emphasis being on the furnishings, in a way recalling the photographs of houses in decorating magazines. Or the owner may be present, standing in the middle of the room or posing on her bed among her possessions. As a correlate to the asexual nature of the rooms, the rooms are pristine, clean, and tidy, with the objects never crowded together but displayed in a tasteful fashion. The texts accompanying the pictures reinforce this presentation. For example, in a descriptive piece, such as the article on the Olympic gold medalist skater Tara Lipinski in *Seventeen*, the fact that she is sixteen years old appears to be irrelevant. She talks about her childhood decorating scheme being based on Walt Disney's *Snow White*, but how, when she turned sixteen, she switched to a sophisticated (very feminine) flower design. The article ends by making the comment about how "she hasn't completely boxed up her childhood. She kept one *Snow White* doll and a bunch of stuffed animals" (Glassman 1999: 70). In a similar way, we read of a bedroom make-over in *YM* (January 2002: 32) where eighteen-year-old Courtney Hamler unleashes "her imagination on her boring bedroom" to create an Aladdin creation, complete with a genie lamp and a papier-mâché dragon.

Many of the magazine articles contain commonsense advice about organizing and tidying bedrooms, not unlike advice found in home economics textbooks used in upper-middle school. In this way, the advice is continuing the parental voice of urging the young to acquire middle-class notions of cleanliness, tidiness, orderliness, and the attendant qualities of responsibility and pride of place necessary for the functioning of an orderly civil society. At the same time, however, these magazines extend this commonsense (and often much needed!) dimension in insidious ways. For example, in the special 1997 spring issue of *YM* there is a quiz entitled "What does your room say about you?" The article organizes the possible responses by categories: "clutter queen," "sentimental sister," "neat freak," "happenin' hostess" (spring 1997: 8–9). While, as might be expected, the first type is described in totally critical terms, the others contain negative as well as positive comments. What is disturbing to our eyes is that the writers state that the room is not only a reflection of the girl's personality but is somehow an equivalent of the inhabitant, existing in a direct one-to-one relationship with one's "inner self." Accordingly, in the same issue of *YM*, the pages which follow have sections of advice: the somewhat tongue-in-cheek "How to 'snoop-proof' your space," the serious "Does your room need a makeover?" (applying the minimalist Chinese interior-design philosophy of Feng Shui which hypothesizes that your surroundings radically influence your emotional state), and finally an illustrated section that "decodes" one's common keepsakes called "The hidden meaning of your stuff" (Spring 1997: 11).

If the articles are didactic pieces, they tend to be of one of two categories: they are straightforward articles giving advice about how to decorate a room or, as is more common, they give advice about how one's room is revealing of one's personality: "What does a room say about you?" In both, the mode of presentation tends to emphasize simplicity and purity. For instance, in "Room to improve" (Lewin 1999: 129), the article is actually a catalog section for pieces of inexpensive furniture. The examples, which are all small and/or portable, range from a clock to a phone to an inflatable chair to a stackable component for a dresser. The style of the pieces shown is modern or futuristic: an uncluttered, minimalist, spare style that is also very tidy and could be interpreted as virginal looking. In an article about decoding one's bedroom, if glimpses of drawers or clothes closets are shown as in "Your bedroom decor – decoded" (*YM*, spring 2000: 18–20) (Figure 4.3), the sweaters, tops, jackets, and shoes shown are all in modest styles and tidily arranged. There is no picture of any object that could not be owned by a pre-adolescent reader.

Behind this logic is the connection perhaps between tidiness and virtue and messiness and slattern (slut) that haunts girl culture and literature. The link is made apparent when we think of the genre of advice literature, that is, an old genre for young women in English. The didactic tone of the "how to" sections of magazine articles on bedrooms, the construction of the idea of the feminine in terms of domestic space, and the logic of a one-to-one correspondence existing between surface (objects, use of space) and depth (self)

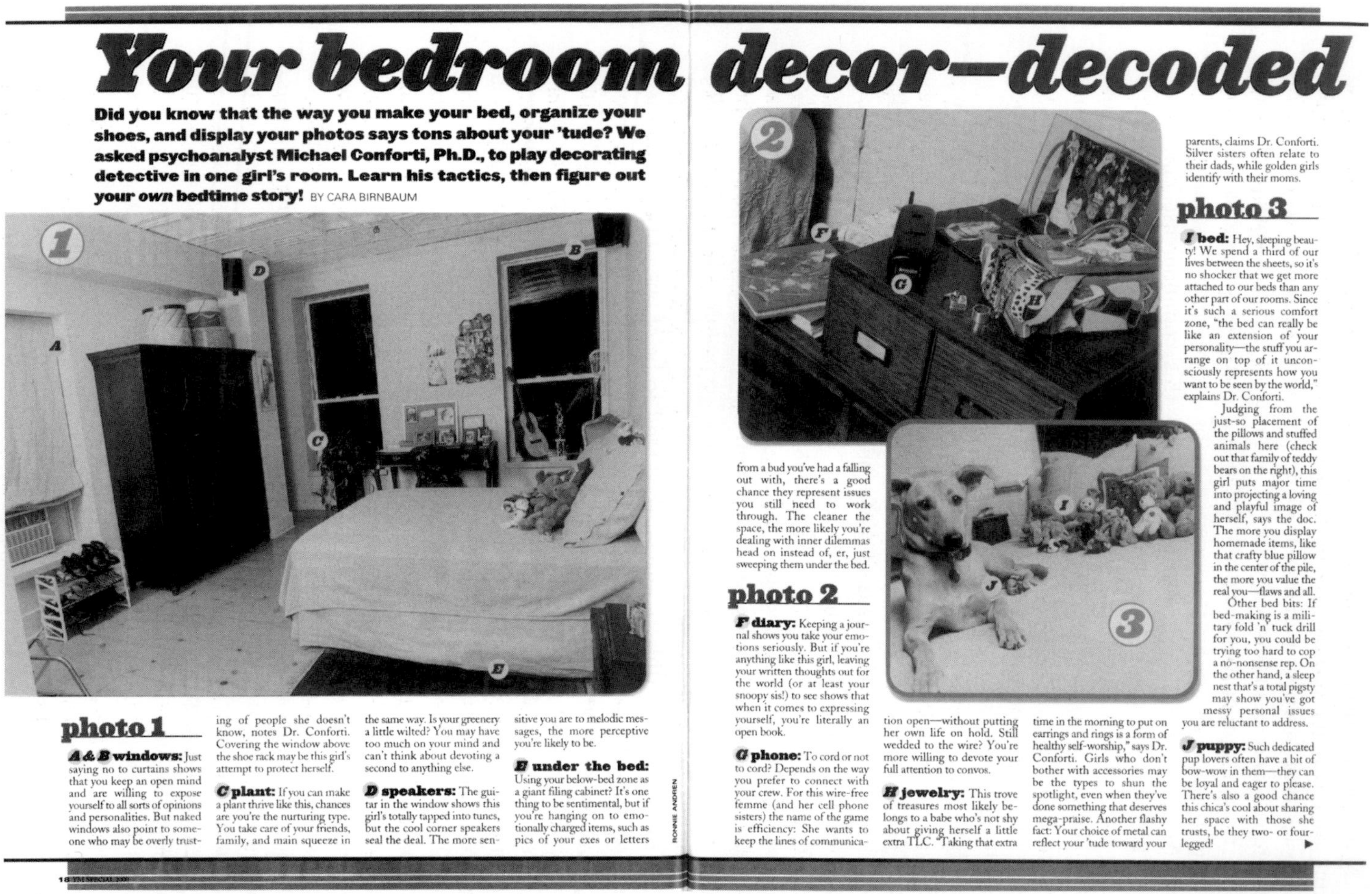

Your bedroom decor—decoded

Did you know that the way you make your bed, organize your shoes, and display your photos says tons about your 'tude? We asked psychoanalyst Michael Conforti, Ph.D., to play decorating detective in one girl's room. Learn his tactics, then figure out your *own* bedtime story! BY CARA BIRNBAUM

photo 1

A & B windows: Just saying no to curtains shows that you keep an open mind and are willing to expose yourself to all sorts of opinions and personalities. But naked windows also point to someone who may be overly trusting of people she doesn't know, notes Dr. Conforti. Covering the window above the shoe rack may be this girl's attempt to protect herself.

C plant: If you can make a plant thrive like this, chances are you're the nurturing type. You take care of your friends, family, and main squeeze in the same way. Is your greenery a little wilted? You may have too much on your mind and can't think about devoting a second to anything else.

D speakers: The guitar in the window shows this girl's totally tapped into tunes, but the cool corner speakers seal the deal. The more sensitive you are to melodic messages, the more perceptive you're likely to be.

E under the bed: Using your below-bed zone as a giant filing cabinet? It's one thing to be sentimental, but if you're hanging on to emotionally charged items, such as pics of your exes or letters from a bud you've had a falling out with, there's a good chance they represent issues you still need to work through. The cleaner the space, the more likely you're dealing with inner dilemmas head on instead of, er, just sweeping them under the bed.

RONNIE ANDREN

photo 2

F diary: Keeping a journal shows you take your emotions seriously. But if you're anything like this girl, leaving your written thoughts out for the world (or at least your snoopy sis!) to see shows that when it comes to expressing yourself, you're literally an open book.

G phone: To cord or not to cord? Depends on the way you prefer to connect with your crew. For this wire-free femme (and her cell phone sisters) the name of the game is efficiency: She wants to keep the lines of communication open—without putting her own life on hold. Still wedded to the wire? You're more willing to devote your full attention to convos.

H jewelry: This trove of treasures most likely belongs to a babe who's not shy about giving herself a little extra TLC. "Taking that extra time in the morning to put on earrings and rings is a form of healthy self-worship," says Dr. Conforti. Girls who don't bother with accessories may be the types to shun the spotlight, even when they've done something that deserves mega-praise. Another flashy fact: Your choice of metal can reflect your 'tude toward your parents, claims Dr. Conforti. Silver sisters often relate to their dads, while golden girls identify with their moms.

photo 3

I bed: Hey, sleeping beauty! We spend a third of our lives between the sheets, so it's no shocker that we get more attached to our beds than any other part of our rooms. Since it's such a serious comfort zone, "the bed can really be like an extension of your personality—the stuff you arrange on top of it unconsciously represents how you want to be seen by the world," explains Dr. Conforti.

Judging from the just-so placement of the pillows and stuffed animals here (check out that family of teddy bears on the right), this girl puts major time into projecting a loving and playful image of herself, says the doc. The more you display homemade items, like that crafty blue pillow in the center of the pile, the more you value the real you—flaws and all.

Other bed bits: If bed-making is a military fold 'n' tuck drill for you, you could be trying too hard to cop a no-nonsense rep. On the other hand, a sleep nest that's a total pigsty may show you've got messy personal issues you are reluctant to address.

J puppy: Such dedicated pup lovers often have a bit of bow-wow in them—they can be loyal and eager to please. There's also a good chance this chica's cool about sharing her space with those she trusts, be they two- or four-legged! ▶

Figure 4.3 "Your bedroom decor – decoded," *YM*, spring 2000: 18–19 (Reprinted with the permission of *YM*, Cara Birnbaum, and Ronnie Andren)

connects these present-day magazines with a much earlier Western type of advice literature also written by adult experts and targeted at young women. During the eighteenth century in England, Europe, and North America, "conduct books" extended an earlier tradition of advice literature into a practical, secular and domestic realm. Aimed at the emerging middle classes who were intent on self-improvement, these books attempted to define the position of women in society (Armstrong and Tennenhouse 1987: 4). Not being books of etiquette, they provided instruction for newcomers into society, and attempted to inculcate good morals as the foundation for correct behavior: manners were described as being the outward expression and indicator of morality (Hemlow 1950: 732–3). These books seek to define the feminine in terms of a domestic world or "province" which is set in opposition to the economic world of men (Armstrong 1987: 94). While claiming that this domestic realm is an equal but complementary space, the discourse suggests otherwise. The underlying assumptions were that appearances (conduct, dress, gestures, deportment) were all reliable indicators of moral merit, and that young women in particular had to be schooled into proper modest behavior in order to be successful members of their class. While, on the one hand, the aim was to create marriageable young ladies (the main "career" for respectable young women), the traits were extolled as possessing merit in their own right. The logic was that surface *is* depth, private *is* public, and that society works to create a "readable" world. With the space of some two hundred years between, these teen magazines similarly seek to create an easily "decodable" world, whereby objects and use of space can be openly "read" as were manners in the eighteenth century as reliable, indeed absolute indicators of personality. While elsewhere it has been posited that teen romance fiction, while masquerading as "love stories", are conduct books in modern dress (Reid-Walsh 1993), here we are struck by how these non-fiction texts, with a focus on apparently neutral "information," are continuing conduct book logic in a direct manner.

As this brief discussion of the conduct book suggests, the logic of anyone being able to interpret who the girl is from looking at her room may be seen as a regulatory device. In terms of Riggins' idea of mapping as being a narrative that accompanies personal objects, it would seem that these magazines are advocating one narrative. For example, in "Your bedroom decor – decoded" (*YM Special*, spring 2000: 18), the author, Cara Birnbaum, consulted a psychoanalyst, Michael Comforti Ph.D., in order to write the article. The approach in the piece is to give a positive statement followed by a negative or critical one. The author also appears to address the girl reader directly by using the second person. For example, the bedroom shown in the layout has no curtains. This is interpreted to signify that "you keep an open mind and are willing to expose yourself to all sorts of opinions and personalities. But naked windows also point to someone who may be overly trusting of people she doesn't know" (Birnbaum 2000: 18). Another picture of the room shows several significant objects in a window: a lacrosse stick, trophy, guitar, and skates. If one were to interview the girl owner and ask her stories about them, it would be fascinating to use Riggins' criteria as entry points for the telling of stories about the self and personal relationships (1994: 109). The author of this article, however, gives a limited, unitary reading: "The lacrosse stick hints at the aggressive streak, while the guitar hints at this girl's artistic awareness. But arranging them in the window may show she subconsciously cares more about the showcasing of these objects than playing with 'em" (Birnbaum 2000: 20). The rest of the article continues in the same vein.

This regulation and suggestion that all girls can be decoded by their rooms is the opposite of what photographer Adrienne Salinger observes about bedrooms being a space for individuality. As outlined above, she believes that rooms are places for self-expression and multiple storytelling based on narratives of the past and the present. Thus, we examine whether this sense of multiple storying may also be present in the articles and how this is presented textually in the words and images.

One article called "Messing up" in *Seventeen* magazine (January 2000: 60) concerns the multiplicity of meanings a room may convey through presenting contradictory messages between the photographic images and the written text. Indeed, if one looks only at the photos of the components of a "perfect" girl's room, with tidy bed, bookshelves, dresser, and so on, along with the photograph of the supposed owner of the room, one would suppose that this article is like all the others. However, the subtitle "Anne Hathaway knew that a room this neat wasn't the real deal" indicates that the article is about the actress in a teen show *Get Real*, and how she transformed the set into a high school student's room by "scattering clothes, pulling necklaces out of jewelry boxes, and unmaking the bed" (Charron 2000: 60). Hathaway goes on to describe her real-life room as being the opposite of the one in the show since it has "clusters of stuffed animals, dusty sports trophies and dirty dishes." In this way, a representation of a supposedly real teenager's room, although this in itself is a stereotype, is given a presence in the written text while the ideal or imaginary teen room is the only one visible in the pictures. This lack of variability of visual presentation images may not be surprising if the magazines are read as advice literature however, for conduct books were written expressly against what was actually occurring in society at the time. In the same way, on a much reduced scale, the articles in magazines may be written in opposition to the "fact" of clutter in many of the readers' rooms, teen or otherwise.

Two recent articles (March and May 2001), in *Seventeen* and *YM* respectively, take the point of view of real teenage girls, not the editors, in their presentation of actual bedrooms. The format of the layout is the same: the girl is shown in the middle of her room, a conventional form as we have discussed earlier. In these articles, the girls have literally transformed their spaces, not by focusing on the objects in the spaces, as the advice articles do, but by transforming the rooms into art spaces. For example, the recurring feature in *Seventeen* entitled "Your room" (March 2001) headlines a teenage artist Naomi Hancock, who has used her walls as a canvas and her room as a gallery space for her multidimensional art. Her room is described as an elaborate dream studio: "She painted the walls and ceilings blue and the skylights yellow. And with her favorite artist, Jackson Pollock, in mind, Naomi splatter-painted the floor" (Daly 2001: 154). Similarly, the section (called "Your room") in *YM* (May 2001) features another artist Samantha Lomuscio, who used her walls as canvas to re-create famous impressionist artworks such as Edvard Munch's *The Scream*, Van Gogh's *Cafe Terrace on the Place du Forum, Aries, at Night* and *Starry Night*. Samantha describes how she transformed her conventional girl's room into an art studio: "It was right before I turned 17, and I wanted to get rid of my pink room. I picked these paintings because of their vibrant colors" (Leonard 2001: 42). It is significant to examine how both of these young women artists modeled their work on male artists who were considered radical in their time period, but are now considered to be at the pinnacle of high art. Munch, Van Gogh, and Pollock all use vivid color and an almost anarchic or violent style. It is hard to conjure up images more opposed to the conventions of girls' room decoration! Indeed, even though their bedroom furniture is sparse and the style spare, the presence of artifacts of girlhood and adolescence such as a dressing table and stuffed animals creates a dissonant impression on a viewer. It is fascinating to speculate that the convention of girls' room decoration has become such a stereotype that, in order to subvert it, young women are going to male masters as their models for inspiration, and notably ones who were revolutionary thinkers.

At the same time, the implications of these creative room make-overs for younger girl readers, the positive examples of assertion, agency and creativity, become tempered by class considerations. On the one hand, room components, such as an inflatable chair, a neon plastic clock, or a generic lamp, are only a number of small discrete purchases that can be added to in a cumulative fashion. These objects can be arranged or perhaps modified by the owner in a way that reflects her individuality. Furthermore, these objects are small, portable, often lightweight, and can be moved easily to new apartments. Only elite girls can create their own art galleries. If the articles about real girls' rooms can be seen as an inspiration, it is perhaps as a way to suggest how other, less affluent girls can be aided by what we see as a unitary narrative of room decoration. Less affluent girls can break the rules according to their own tastes and use the space they have access to in an individualistic way that asserts their own (limited) autonomy. On the other hand, one common denominator that we have noticed in our analysis both of babies' bedrooms and representations of bedrooms in teen magazines is that the presence of popular culture items or images in decorating tends to be a populist phenomenon. Elite groups are disinclined to use popular culture motifs. No sign of the conventional popular culture of babyhood, for example, appears in the extensive magazine coverage of the nursery of Celine Dion's baby. The magazines include a vast array of photos of baby René-Charles' blue-and-white wardrobe of clothes, his huge bedroom, and the various items of furniture such as an antique cradle and, of course, an antique rocking-horse.[1] This absence of popular culture is apparent when visiting elite home-decorating stores and upmarket babywear boutiques, or viewing elite decorating magazines. How could girls or young women, or their parents, who are less affluent, either living in a rental apartment with mandatory rules about white walls, or sharing a room with siblings, implement any of these ideas? It is disturbing to see replicated here, in a girl's bedroom decoration, the cycle that has been criticized in liberal feminist actions. It is the middle- and upper-class women (or parents of young children) who are able to engage in such acts of rebellion and self-assertion because they are in a financial position to do so.

Equally problematic, of course, as we have noted throughout this chapter, is the idea of the bedroom itself in relationship to contemporary urban childhood and the spaces that children *are* or are *not* allowed to occupy. In some ways, the *Home Alone* movies work only because they are so beyond the imagination of most parents and children. Street children in the slums of Nairobi do occupy the streets; they do not, however, tend to occupy the kinds of bedrooms referred to by the Beach Boys – or any bedrooms at all for that matter. The rooms that the Beach Boys are singing about, on the other hand, are occupied by children who are not allowed to roam freely on any streets, often not even on a culdesac in a suburban neighborhood. This is not only because they have their lives organized for them – they are taken to specific spaces to play: to playgrounds where their actions can be regulated by care-givers who watch over them, and to homes of playmates where by prearrangement their leisure time has been planned for them – but also because of concerns about safety. "In their rooms," then, seems like a safe place for children to be. In this context, "room culture" and the geography of the bedroom take on new meaning in studies of childhood in the twenty-first century.

Chapter Five

Virtual Spaces: Children on the Cyber Frontier

In this chapter we examine websites for children and by children as a type of virtual popular culture able to exist because of the Internet. We consider the Internet to be an efficient vehicle for transmitting children's popular culture, a popular culture phenomenon in its own right due to children's imaginative uses of the Web, and a fascinating but problematic research tool for investigating children's popular culture. Our investigation of websites complements the burgeoning area of research on children and computer play that tends to focus on computer games, such as that undertaken by Kinder (1991), Friedman (1995), Buckingham (2000), and Macnamee (1998, 2000). Our approach is in some ways similar to that of Tobin (1998) and Walkerdine (1998a) in that we are interested in the Internet and the Web as a cultural space. We focus on websites because the Web is a relatively more accessible space for children to enter than the world of elaborate computer games. The Internet can be accessed in many places – at school and in public libraries – although most children tend to use it at home. For example, in Canada, the survey "Young Canadians in a wired world" (Environics Research Group 2001) calculated that ninety-nine percent of children aged between seven and sixteen have access to the Internet, and eight in ten have access at home. In the United States, according to the Pew Internet and American Life Project, one in five children and youth aged between twelve and seventeen has a personal website (Lenhart et al. 2001). Indeed, in acknowledging the household presence of the home computer in Britain, Buckingham and Sefton-Green have coined the term "digital bedroom."

Our focus in this chapter is on children's websites. We use this term in several ways. First, in the commonsense use of the term, as Zipes notes (2001), children's websites can indicate websites that are targeted at them. Second, in the less commonsense use of the term, children's websites can refer to children's own homepages. A third use of the term is to describe sites where children have substantial input into adult-organized sites. We thus organize sites into three categories based on self-evident description – according to whether they are widely accessible, public sites (usually commercially constructed by companies); whether they are the less accessible, private or semi-private sites created by children by themselves, without apparent adult involvement; or whether they are sites jointly created and owned by adults and children. In our investigation of commercial sites for children we are interested in the degree of interactivity which these sites offer and how limited the choices are. We consider whether there appears to be an opportunity for action, or resistance or subversion in the interactivity, or whether these sites limit the user to prepared and predetermined choices. In our investigation of child-produced websites we are interested in how these homepages often function as a kind of domestic space or "virtual bedroom" through combining ideas about "girls' bedroom culture" (McRobbie and Garber 1991), as we noted in Chapter 4, with ideas about boys' computer use in a domestic setting. Finally, in our discussion of adult- and child-produced sites, we explore how website space is negotiated in these joint ventures and consider the sites in terms of aspects derived from the two previous sections: the high degree of interactivity provided by these sites and the creation of a virtual domestic space.

When examining specific sites, our method is to consider a website as a special type of visual (and audio) text. In continuing with the child-centered approaches, we focus on what is immediately visible to the typical child leisure viewer, not the complex system of hyperlinks. Accordingly, in our textual analysis we provide a brief description of the site, and analyze it as a constellation of words, static images, moving graphics, and multimedia images. Where appropriate, we include a discussion of the multi-sensory appeal of some of the elaborate sites. We bear in mind, of course, that websites are not texts in the same way that other media texts are, due to their instability and the fact that they have no "real" existence beyond their representation on a computer screen. Because websites are continually in flux, they may be summarily altered or obliterated for various reasons to do with time-outs, production difficulties, server problems, or power cuts.

In order to provide a context for our analysis of websites, we consider briefly a number of general aspects and concerns about children's engagement with the Web. We hope that through our discussion and analysis of websites for and by children we can enter into the emotionally charged debate around children and the Internet in a balanced way. Moreover, we hope we retain an attitude that is optimistic without being naive, and a stance that respects the needs of actual children while being open to changing ideas about childhood. As David Buckingham remarks, much discussion in this area may be classified as creating one of two scenarios: a "nightmare" or a "utopia" (2000: 42).[1] Generally, a tone of pessimism dominates much critical discussion regarding children and computer technology. For example, one recent study about children and the Internet is Samuel Friedman's *Children and World Wide Web: Tool or Trap?* (2000). Despite the balanced title, the book emphasizes the "trap" aspect. By stressing the multiple dangers to children on the Web since it is virtual frontier world, with few or no "rules" protecting the naive wanderer, children are presented as vulnerable creatures in need of adult protection and regulation.[2] Other critics such as Tim Gill (1996), and Mary Bryson and

Suzanne de Castell (1995) stress how many child users of the Internet are from elite socioeconomic groups, are predominantly male, and are living in developed countries.[3] In contrast to critics of the Internet, defenders of the Internet, such as Howard Rheingold (1993), Mark Poster (1995), or Andrew Calcutt (1999), tend not to address the issues of children directly but stress instead the utopian possibilities offered by the Internet for rethinking democracy and power relations between the individual and society. One defender of the Internet who does discuss children and youth is Don Tapscott in *Growing Up Digital: The Rise of the Net Generation* (1998). As Buckingham observes of Tapscott, he is "relentlessly optimistic." Buckingham summarizes Tapscott's argument as follows:

> The argument is based on two sets of binary oppositions, between technologies (televison versus the Internet) and between generations (the "boomers" versus the "net generation"). Thus, television is seen as passive, while the net is active; television "dumbs down" its users, while the net raises their intelligence; television broadcasts a singular view of the world, while the net is democratic and interactive; television isolates, while the net builds communities; and so on (2000: 46).

Children's Websites: Commercial Websites for Children

> Faced with this world of faithful [imitative of adult realities] and complicated objects, the child can only identify himself as owner, as user, never as creator; he does not invent the world, he uses it: there are, prepared for him, actions, actions without adventure, without wonder, without joy (Barthes 1972: 54).

Barthes' criticism of elaborate toys can be applied to describe the limited choice available to players of contemporary, high-tech toys such as Ninja Turtles, Power Rangers, or Transformers, and to video games and computer play. Some children's culture critics, such as Susan Willis, have noted about Transformers that despite their apparent ability to change shape, "everything transforms but nothing changes," and that the toys actually "manage and control" the child's desire for change (1987: 415–16, cited in Nodelman 1996: 106). Other critics have applied a similar logic to criticize the limited successful or winning choices existing behind a range of apparent alternatives in video games (Skirrow 1986: 129, cited in Nodelman 1996: 106). This has prompted one critic, Perry Nodelman, to speculate whether "in Barthes' terms, the more players can be made to believe they invent the world of their play, the more it invents them" (1996: 106). Extrapolating from this, we are interested in whether the same criticism may be applied to the types of interactivity found in commercial websites targeting children.

If one is trying to locate children's websites by using a search engine, the sites that are readily listed are mainly commercial tie-in sites produced by companies, sites to which children can send away for free merchandise, or sites where children can obtain free images for their own websites. Each major popular culture text, artifact, or media form, be it Barbie, *Seventeen* magazine, Britney Spears, Pokemon, Buffy, the Vampire Slayer, or the Harry Potter books has commercial sites which are lavishly produced. While some of these sites are simply warehouses, others are not. Most of these sites provide interactive areas: they range from games based on the product, to fan clubs, to "rooms" where one can engage in online "chat," so even these sites encourage child participation in some way. Although these sites may be freely accessed, their obvious intention to the adult viewer is to promote products and encourage brand loyalty (Tapscott 1998). Since this is all they know, children see the dominance of the commercial Internet as the norm. Although Tapscott (1998) and Buckingham (2000) remark on the high level of disposable income of some young computer users, many children who use the Web possess little spending money. Therefore, our search was restricted to "free" sites pertaining to popular culture, sites which one young user labels "information" sites (Krista Walsh, personal communication). Because there is such a vast array of sites, we provide only a selection of the popular culture sites available to children. To encompass as wide a range of examples as possible, we organized the sites by considering them in terms of the "implied viewer" (adopted from Iser 1974) to include examples of sites apparently intended for children generally, for children of different ages, and for boys or girls separately. Our approach is first to describe the sites and then to analyze them. We look at these sites in terms of two main aspects: how they seek to appeal to a child user through the incorporation of different types and different degrees of interactivity, and whether, in this space of "play" provided by the sites, there is a space for individual creativity, resistance, or subversion by the child user that mitigates against, or overturns the aims of, product promotion. We examine a Warner Brothers site devoted to the film *Harry Potter and the Sorcerer's Stone* for girls and boys, a Pokemon site apparently addressing boys, a Barbie site presumably intended for young girls, an official Buffy site targeting pre-teen and adolescent girls and boys, and finally a catalog site for girls.

The Warner Brothers site devoted to promoting the film of the book *Harry Potter and the Philosopher's Stone* (1997) is located at <http://harrypotter. warnerbros.com>. It has sophisticated graphics, moving icons, Gothic lettering, and eerie lighting, all of which combine to create a "magical" effect. The site is very well designed to be not only interactive but also exclusive in terms of intended users, since only those who have read the books would understand the language. The viewer is engaged and challenged from the start to probe further into the site because of the elaborate multimedia activities that draw the user into engrossing play. It is a sophisticated and subtle marketing tool in that from the outset the Harry Potter fan is addressed directly, and drawn into engagement in different ways. For example, the child viewer is invited to join Hogwarts School online and can register as a pupil in one of the forms, and engage in online quizzes and games based on a general knowledge of the Harry Potter books. The child viewer is also invited to join an online community in which he or she can engage in threaded email discussions about each of the books, and about the interactive site itself as a "school." Only knowledgable insiders, readers and fans of Harry Potter, would know the information required to be accepted into the school, and would appreciate the titles of each link, such as Hogwarts, Diagon Alley, and Platform 9¾. In this way, while keeping nonreaders of Harry Potter out, it also creates a club for fans to join. It is being continually developed. When the film was released in November 2001 trailers were added from the film.

Through these strategies, the site created an audience for the film before the product yet existed. The film is a tie-in text with an already established audience (the readers of the Harry Potter books) and, by creating a website before the film had been released, the producers are using a web-based marketing strategy that has been used before with pre-teens regarding music promotion: a new "boy" or "girl" group may have a website before the group has given a concert or produced CDs. Yet the site construction is so highly interactive in multiple ways that the space of play may actually mitigate against the commercial aim. Visiting the site and joining the school culture of Hogwarts is such an enthralling multimedia event that it creates a self-contained experience, even if one hasn't seen the film.

In contrast to the Harry Potter site that appears to be directed at girls and boys equally, the site devoted to the Pokemon game at <http://www.pokemon.com> appears to be directed more at boys. We base our interpretation on the rhetoric of mastery and competition that dominates the site. The site is interactive in that not only is each section phrased as a direct address to the child viewer to do something, but the multimedia dimensions of Pokemon are emphasized. For example, there is link which can lead to a viewing of the trailer for the *Pokemon 3* film, as well as links to the cards, to how to become a trainer, to how to obtain a free strategy guide, to how to "rock" to music CDs. The site is limited in its own terms: often at the second level of access the viewer is shown something to purchase. For example, there are books to buy "if you want to become a trainer." At the same time the site has numerous contests, such as a school "read-a-rama" that would enable the child's school to qualify for a free screening of the new film.

This focus on mastery and contests in the Pokemon site contrasts with the type of interactivity on sites targeted at girls. If one looks at Mattel sites such as the Barbie site, <http://www.barbie.com>, or a sister site <http://www.generationgirl.com>, it is apparent that these sites are interactive in a different way. On the Barbie site, one can quickly see that almost all of the components of the front page of the site are interactive. The site gives an image of Barbie in her bedroom and she invites the user to play various games: one can click on different activities such as sending letters, creating a cartoon story, creating a photo album, or joining a club. In this way, the site reproduces virtually some of the "girl's bedroom culture" (McRobbie and Garber 1991) activities that girls engage in. In contrast to the Pokemon site, the activities or games are not competitive, but more creative and evocative of the sense of belonging to a group. The clothes-dressing activity is not highlighted immediately, for spatially it is located to the side of the screen through the clothes closet door. Again this activity is one of several options, the others being to create a friend for Barbie, or to engage with an interactive girls' magazine. There are four dolls: three multicultural and one white. The clothes tend to be modest and functional. In contrast to the actual doll, the proportions of the pants and sweater-clad Barbie on the front page seem less exaggerated, although the undressed image of the doll ready to be dressed possesses the attenuated waist of the physical artifact. It appears that the web manufacturers have addressed – to some degree – a few of the criticisms concerning Barbie being equated with ideal body shape, sexualized fashion, and whiteness. The space of play created by the site is extensive and limited at the same time. It is apparent that while there are quite a few alternatives available to the viewer, and they are interactive in terms of encouraging different types of domestic play, the choices are limited to a set number of options.

Other complexly structured and sophisticated websites directly address an older, pre-teen, and adolescent audience of girls and boys, and usually have numerous interactive elements. For example, another Warner Brothers site at <http://www.buffy.com> the site for the television series *Buffy, the Vampire Slayer*, had various interactive aspects that combine information with communication in different ways, and always within the tone of a mock-serious Gothic.[4] For example, the viewer could obtain information about four years' worth of plot lines in the appropriately named "Mortuary." There were high school and university yearbooks describing current characters, as well as a list of deceased characters and a "bestiary" of evil characters. At the same time, this site offered information and a source of secondary research, for in the "library" there are leather-bound (virtual) volumes with succinct entries on mythology, and vampires. The site had numerous interactive aspects ranging from the viewer being able to send postcards, engage in a game, and join a fan club, to being able to email the show's producers (who answered questions), to being able to join "The Bronze." This virtual community had various types of communication, including a linear email discussion and a threaded discussion on certain topics. As with the conventional email queries, the creators of the show became involved with the "fans" by posting comments on the website. Their interaction was not democratic or equal in that the show's producers' input was privileged in different ways: for example, they could post more often than other members and their comments would appear in a different color – and thus be emphasized – on the screen. This high degree of interactivity between the fans and producers was also apparent in the "Stage" where viewers were invited to send tapes or CDs of music to be used on the show. It appeared then that the original producers of *Buffy* were very knowledgeable about fandom and the types of connections and interactivity desired by fans, so they incorporated fan input in multiple ways. Indeed, they even provided space for an official Buffy community which was managed by a volunteer: here you could link to any tie-in media (videos, music, dolls, and comic books) related to the show, as well as to numerous fan parties and fan sites, official and unofficial. As we discuss below, at the end of this section on commercial sites, the high degree of interactivity in this site lends itself to various interpretations about the role of viewers in the production of the show.

Since pre-teen and young adolescent girls or "tweens" are now a central focus of marketing, both online and offline, one way that companies appeal to girls is through online catalogs. These catalogs appeal to the girl viewer and potential customer in several ways: all are attractive in layout, easy to use, and "girl-friendly" in terms of their appeal to different age groups. One look at the site <http://www.lisafrank.com> reveals that it appears to be targeting a younger girl through the format and cross-over activities associated with "girl-room-culture" activities. For example, there is a story to read and react to, tips on writing a journal, a chat room, and memory games to play, as well as links to commercial story-reading and -writing sites. Other sites directed at older girls' interests seem to be a cross between adult-oriented catalog sites and online girls' magazines. Here we are thinking of popular catalogs such as L. L. Bean <http://www.llbean.com> and *Seventeen* magazine <http://www.seventeen.com>. For example, in the Delia catalog site at <http://www.delias.com> there are lots of contests (as at the Pokemon site), a lifestyle page has magazine-like features: an article about singer Ashley Ballard, quizzes, anagrams, and advice about bedroom decor. The decorating feature is not necessarily related to buying anything from the catalog. Although the entire site is a commercial catalog, in order to retain the visual similarity to a magazine, the advertisements are set apart from the articles as in magazines. At another virtual store site, <http://www.btween-us.com>, there is even a virtual changing room where one can virtually take outfits off hangers and assemble them to see how they look.

The commercial catalog sites are obviously trying to encourage girls to think of themselves as consumers when "play shopping" and thus later become "real" consumers when they are wage-earning adults. We are interested in how there is a possibility that the cornucopia of images provided by the producers of the sites may unintentionally offer avenues for subversion: by encouraging the girl readers of the magazines to "play" with home decorating and catalog shopping on the Internet, these media texts are also creating possibilities for short-circuiting their own aims.

There may be some parallels between the play possible with virtual ads, and play in the nineteenth century when new modes and media for advertising were similarly being developed. In both periods the publishers are encouraging children, especially girls, to play with their texts and images. In *The Adman in the Parlor: Magazines and the Gendering of Consumer Culture, 1880s to 1910s* (1996) Ellen Gruber Garvey examines how the Victorian era invention of chromolithography with multiple color printing made advertising in

the site, or interacting with other fans, or even corresponding with the site producers through email or online chat. In some sites there appear to be possibilities for creativity, resistance, and limited subversion. In other sites aimed at fans, a dynamic exists that places the user in the role of co-producer, however subservient to the official producers of the popular culture product. In these ways, we consider that the "lines" or "boundaries" between consumer and producer start to become somewhat blurred, thereby increasing the possibility for active engagement by the children.

Children's Websites: Websites by Children

In this section we examine several child-produced websites, both personal homepages and impersonal sites, by exploring these sites as being a kind of domestic space or "virtual bedroom" through combining ideas about "girls' bedroom culture" with ideas about boys' computer use in a domestic setting. By applying aspects of Foucault's discussion of heterotopias (1986) to children's homepages, we explore whether the Web may be a postmodern space where oppositions of public and private, adult and child, once considered inviolable may be overturned. This overturning of opposites in cyberspace, while not without problems, may enable children to enter the public domain as knowledgeable computer users, asserting their role as active agents, not passive dupes of technology. Since we think homepage construction is a new visual art form engaged in readily by children of varying ages, we suggest that the process itself may possess attributes that make it especially appealing to children. We also see that it has important links to the notion of visual spaces and the child's gaze examined in Chapter 3.

The idea of there being a girls' bedroom culture was first coined by McRobbie and Garber to address the invisibility of girls as subjects in youth-based subculture studies. They considered girls to be "negotiating a different space" and to be "offering a different type of resistance" from the boys (1991: 221). Girls' subcultures, especially those of younger girls, tended to be based inside the home and comprised activities such as reading magazines, listening to music (Frith 1983), talking on the telephone, playing with two-way radios (Griffiths 1995), and so on. The location of these activities was largely the result of parental control, whereby girls' actions and activities were restricted more to the private sphere of the home, while boys were allowed more freely to roam in the public space of the street (McRobbie 1991: 12; Nava 1992: 79–80). During the mid-1990s, however, especially after the Jamie Bulger murder in 1993, as Valentine (1997) and Macnamee (2000) observe, parental concerns about public safety apply to both girls and boys on the street.

The idea of a "digital bedroom" was coined by Julian Sefton-Green and David Buckingham (1998) to account for the physical location of many children's cyber play. They observed that whether it be computer game play, surfing the Web, or homepage construction, this is usually done on a home computer, the site of which, as Sefton-Green and Buckingham observe (1998) is often a computer in someone's bedroom. What interests us more than the physical location of the machine in the home, be it bedroom, living room or hall, is the girls' mindset of playing on the computer as a popular culture activity in a private space.

It is interesting to think of how the two ideas, "girls' bedroom culture" and "digital bedroom" can be combined. We are intrigued, by the idea that by staying home, and not going out, but by surfing the (world) of the Web, both boys and girls of different ages are engaging in a kind of domestic or bedroom culture that takes place in virtual space. While Tobin (1998) tends to see boys' engagement with the Internet, whether it be software "hacking" or communicating via the Internet as two different types of masculinity, thereby revising Sherry Turkle's (1995) opposition between male hackers and female users. We consider both boys and girls, in a way, to be gendered as "female" because of their physical location in a private or domestic space. While hacking and sensational subversion undertaken by teenage boys has been much reported in the media, we are interested in the opposite: children's legal use of computer technologies in their construction of web pages.

We consider that girls' personal homepages may be seen as a form of popular culture. In our discussion, we briefly consider the following: how these sites are constructed, how they appear to be a type of multimedia text that represents or is a virtual manifestation of girls' bedroom culture, and how the personal homepage functions as an ideal and idealized space.

Although children (wisely) do not often give much personal information about themselves, we tried to find pages by girls of different ages from "middle" girlhood to adolescence and who live in different countries. Sometimes the homepage creator will give enough specific information that one can deduce his or her age. For example, this Canadian girl's page (although it has probably been abandoned because it has not been updated in a couple of years and some of the links are not working) by "Heather" tells us her grade and general location (Figs 5.1, 5.2): <http://www.geocities.com/EnchantedForest/Glade/9492/heather.html>. The guestbook is a prominent feature that will be returned to later in our discussion. Sometimes the age of the homepage creator can be deduced partly by the subject and approach to the subject. For example, when the Spice Girls were popular with young, pre-adolescent girls many sites featured links to them, e.g. <http://www.gurlpages.com/music/kristaw/index.html>. In 2001 "Neopets" are currently a rage among girls whereby you adopt and look after a virtual pet (Krista Walsh, personal communication). There are numerous homepages devoted to these pets and they tend to be those of girls. Some girls have started "Guilds" which are a type of virtual community based loosely upon the care and play with these pets. For example, <http://www.neopets.com/guilds/guild.phtml?oid=berri_yum> is a site organized by a twelve-year-old Australian girl, and features images and graphics that recall stickers, and miniature dolls along with a delicate blue background. Older girls' websites tend to have a more sophisticated appearance. For example,

"Tilla's page," a sparely constructed page by a fourteen-year-old girl who lives in London (at the time of her update) is quite autobiographical. At the same time she is employing the Web as a way of promoting her creative writing and her art. She employs visual metaphors literally in her structure, for she uses the professional and less intimate analogy of an art gallery to organize her art pages, and the equally sophisticated analogy of a poetry reading to promote her poetry: <http://www.reading.ac.uk/~veskeinr/watercol.html>.

When girls/children engage in constructing their own websites or personal homepages this activity often appears to be a virtual derivative of the logic and process of step-by-step building block construction popular with small children, and continued in more elaborate construction by older children. Buckingham and Sefton-Green, although with particular reference to computer art, consider this type of creativity to be a derivative form of art, what they call a type of "lego-creativity" (1998), and we are interested in extending the Lego analogy to encompass website construction. Because no knowledge of HTML is required, even small girls/children can build websites. It might be argued that the popularity of building websites by small children may be seen as applying skills learned from play with material objects to the virtual realm: not only the logic of building blocks, but drawing, making sticker albums, collecting trade cards, writing diaries, and so on, all activities associated with girls. Indeed, the basic building block comparison has been noted by web experts:

> If you asked most pre-teen or young adolescents what the significance is of "Geocities", "Yahoo" or "Tripod" the response will likely be that they provide space for free homepages as well as e-mail accounts. ("Free" in the sense that you allow them to put their advertisements on all your web pages). In addition, they provide tools that take the web pages beyond static pictures of "this is my family and this a picture of my dog." More importantly, these tools are simple to use and don't require knowledge of HTML; it's a simple "drag and drop" procedure. These sites provide templates, graphics, JAVA-enabled animation, counters, audio, search boxes, forms and back-grounds in a manner that requires nearly minimal knowledge of web-page development. Assuming you have a fast processor on your PC, a reasonable amount of RAM and a scanner web-page development is a simple procedure.
>
> In looking at children's web pages one can see how they have a firm grasp on this enabling technology; however, unless instructed, they often have a minimal understanding of what occurs beyond what appears on the screen. For instance, the concept of a web "page" when displayed on a screen is perceived as a material entity having both shape and form; much like a page on a sticker album or a blank piece of drawing paper. This concept is further reinforced when the "page"

> can be sent to a printer. When printed, the web "page" has the familiar physical form of any other printed material. Basically, it's a "surface view" of their perception of what appears on the screen. In fact, what appears on the screen, is not a "page" at all; nor is it stored in the same format in which it is displayed. Of little consequence to many young web-page designers are the processes that occur through their web browser to display a page. These would include, for instance, the HTML programming codes, cgi scripts, links to icons and other pages as well as JAVA scripts that provide the animation (Michael Walsh, personal communication).

The graphics and images on girls' homepages often resemble or represent the kinds of material culture stored in their bedrooms. If their physical bedrooms contain informal collections of treasured objects, their websites are often (immaterial) or virtual collections of images, representing the kinds of objects stored in their rooms, or images of wish-lists, or stylized or even idealized images of objects. For example, neopets seem to be a cross between imaginary and exotic animals and recall stuffed animals often arranged on a bed or a shelf. Significantly, though, in contrast to the acquisition of material culture items, which requires money, the images gathered by children and displayed on their homepages are free, as are the commercial homepage hosts they tend to use. This is a good part of the appeal, for the commercial outlay refers to the cost of computer equipment and the cost of a modem and Internet line. While most children playing in this way appear to be middle-class and working-class children in the developed world, children of lower income parents are also acquiring equipment either secondhand or by the ever-decreasing costs of equipment.

Girls' Homepages and Foucault's "Of Other Spaces" (1986)

The notion of the personal homepage with a guestbook not only reproduces the idea of a private, domestic space in cyberspace but also creates an idealized space of a leisured existence when guests signed volumes in the vestibule at the door. We consider the homepage not to be a utopia (which is literally a "nowhere") but more of a heterotopia that according to Foucault has a "real place" (1986: 24). Our approach is inspired by Macnamee's idea of considering the space of children's video game play in their bedrooms as a strategy for negotiating and resisting spatial boundaries (2000: 484). She considers video-game play to be a kind of heterotopia. Although children are located in a real place (their bedrooms) and engaging with a real machine (the computer), the space where they experience the adventure is not there but in one of Foucault's "other spaces" (2000: 484–5). In our discussion, we apply Foucault's ideas to the child's homepage both as a concept and as a structural principle.[5]

Written before the World Wide Web was accessible to the general public, and not specifically addressing the spaces created by computer technology, Foucault's article "Of other spaces" provides a brief historical overview of the Western sense of space, and presents some provocative ideas that can be applied to our understanding of the Web, and to the phenomenon of the homepage. Foucault begins his discussion by stating how in the medieval period, space was conceived of as a hierarchical set of places which were set in opposition to one another. He called this sense of space the space of "emplacement" (1986: 22). In the Renaissance, Galileo challenged this fixed set of space by presenting space as being "infinite" and "infinitely open." The place of a thing was only a point in a movement, called "extension" (ibid.: 23). In the modern era this sense of space was in turn replaced by an understanding of place as a site which he defines of "relations of proximity, between points or elements." In form they are described as "series, trees, or grids" and are connected in technical work with the storage of data (ibid.). At the same time, he observes that some spaces still seem sanctified to humans in terms of oppositions based on private and public space and between family space, and social space. Extending from this he cites the work of Bachelard who talks of inner space and the space of the fantasmatic – dreams, and passions (ibid.) – before turning to discuss external space.

Foucault then briefly considers but does not elaborate on the space in which we live by examining sites in terms of the sets of relations that may define them. For example, he observes that there are sites of transportation (streets, trains, etc.), sites of temporary relaxation (cafes, beaches, etc.), and closed or semi-closed sites of rest (house, bedroom). However, his main intention is to analyze sites that exist in relation to other sites, but in ways that "suspect, neutralize, or invert the set of relations they designate, mirror or reflect" (1986: 24). He distinguishes two main types: utopias and heterotopias. Utopias are by definition sites with no place, unreal spaces that present society in its perfected form. This may be in a direct or inverted relation to the way society is. Heterotopias are, by contrast, places that do exist, real places, but they are also counter-sites, a "kind of effectively enacted utopia." These sites exist outside of all places, although they exist in reality (ibid.).

In his elaboration of the idea of heterotopias, Foucault enumerates five principles. First, he considers heterotopias to be present in all cultures in all periods, although they take different forms. In early or "primitive" societies he considers there to be a type he calls "crisis heterotopias" which are "privileged or sacred or forbidden places" reserved for people in crisis, such as adolescents, menstruating women, pregnant women, the elderly. He sees these as being replaced in more complex societies by "heterotopias of deviation" such as prisons, rest homes, psychiatric hospitals, retirement homes (1986: 24–5). The second principle is that a society as it changes can make an extant heterotopia function differently. The example he cites is of the cemetery which until the end of the eighteenth century was located in the center of a town, next to the church, but then, to mirror changing views of death was moved to the outskirts of town (ibid.: 25). The third principle Foucault considers to reside in heterotopias is how they can juxtapose in a single "real space" several sites that are themselves incompatible, such as in a cinema, which in a rectangular space has a two-dimensional screen on which three-dimensional space is projected, and a garden, the microcosm of the Earth, and its representation, the carpet (ibid.: 25–6). The fourth principle he lists is that heterotopias are often linked to slices of time: either indefinitely accumulating time such as in museums and libraries, or the obverse, transitory time such as fairgrounds and vacation villages. The fifth principle he describes about heterotopias is that they "presuppose a system of opening and closing that both isolates them and makes them penetrable." He states how heterotopias are not usually "freely accessible, like a public place" (ibid.: 26). He gives examples such as barracks, prisons, and saunas. In the final section, he provides a paradoxical example that only *appears* to be freely accessible. Here, Foucault develops an analysis of a type of bedroom on great farms in South America that provides entry to travelers yet denies them access to the family. He describes these rooms in the following way:

> The entry door did not lead into the central room where the family lived, and every individual or traveler who came by had the right to open this door, to enter into the bedroom and to sleep there for a night. Now these bedrooms were such that the individual who went in to them never had access to the family's quarters; the visitor was absolutely the guest in transit, was not really the invited guest (ibid.).

Foucault concludes his discussion by stating that heterotopias exist in relationship to all other spaces, either as an illusionary space that reveals others to be more so, such as brothels, or to create an ideal but real space that is the opposite of life "as perfect, as meticulous, as well arranged as ours is messy." He calls these spaces "compensatory" and gives as examples the Puritan colonies of North America, and the Jesuit settlements of South America. The final example Foucault provides is that of the ship, "a floating piece of space, a place without a place, that exists by itself, that is closed in on itself and at the same time is given over to the infinity of the sea" (1986: 27).

Girls' Homepages as Heterotopias

Foucault's discussion provides a rich dimension of analysis for a discussion of cyberspace, the act of exploring the web, the construction of homepages and girls' websites in particular. In our discussion, we apply these ideas in two ways: as a general concept for web play, and as a structural principle, in which we consider the fifth and third principles to be particularly pertinent. Generally, it is fascinating to think how Foucault's discussion of "other spaces" could be related to cyberspace in so many ways. For example, it is intriguing to consider how we can collapse together Foucault's ideas about early and contemporary Western notions about space and apply them to virtual space. Notions of virtual space being an ever-expanding world resemble the ideas of external space in the Renaissance and early modern period when it appeared that the space of the world was indeed "infinite" and "infinitely open" to Western explorers, especially for seafarers. This ever-expanding sense of space seems to be transposed to cyberspace in the way we commonly think of the Internet and Web as an imaginary sea to be "surfed." The heterotopic image of the boat Foucault poetically returns to at the end, which is closed in on itself, yet open to the sea and visiting ports of call, evokes the image of a computer user with a mouse traversing the Web. In this apparently limitless space, the act of constructing homepages may perhaps be seen as an attempt to create an ideal space that is "compensatory" in a way similar to how Foucault described the early religious colonizers' efforts. Specific websites also seem to possess both the aspects of "slices in time" that Foucault mentions, for they often appear to be virtual repositories, somewhat like museums, yet at the same time they are transitory, fleeting, unstable, and fluctuating mediums.

Foucault remarks that despite our changing concepts of space, certain oppositions appear inviolable, namely the division between public and private spaces. If this observation is extended to include age and gender, this "inviolable" opposition would include how girls are usually associated with space inside the home and boys with space outside. We consider, though, that the space of the Web and the homepage may "unsettle" and indeed begin to overturn this opposition. Moreover, the opposition between outer and inner psychic space may be unsettled as well by the Web, for it is on the publicly accessible, personal homepage that one may find the expression of an author's innermost secrets, dreams, and passions.

Foucault's discussion of the fifth principle with his extended description of the example of the visitors' bedrooms on South American farms is particularly useful when applied to girls' personal homepages. He describes a structural situation where one seems to gain easy access to the private space of a bedroom. To enter a girls' homepage, as with any website, all one needs is the URL address. Moreover, to continue the analogy, many of the younger girls' pages appear to be virtual representations of their bedrooms, for they are decorated with floral and/or pastel patterns called "wallpaper," they contain representations of objects that resemble miniature stuffed animals or stickers from sticker albums, and images of pop stars one might find on their walls, and so on. If there is a music file playing, it may be that of a favorite pop star, such as a girl might listen to in the privacy of her room. At the same time, though, as Foucault notes, the visitor never has access to the private, family quarters. This situation of separation appears to be increasingly the case with girls' websites. While apparently private expressions or personal spaces, they are not often openly confessional. Their collection of artifacts which are obtained from public, free sites only have a personal application if one knows the owner of the site. Otherwise they appear opaque.

For example, at <http://www.gurlpages.com/music/kristaw/index.html>, a girl, Krista, has constructed a site that appears to be only indirectly autobiographical. The page is composed largely of images, both graphics and photographs, and of links to other pages. The illustrations have been "adopted" from other sites, and the text both provides correct site attribution and urges readers/viewers to adopt correct Internet protocol when using others' images. In some ways, the effect of these images against a pastel-blue, patterned background recalls other girl culture collections such as cut-out pictures from magazines in a scrapbook, or photographs in an attractive photo album. At the same time, the website is not a virtual version of a sticker album because of the multimedia graphics. For example, the first image is that of a gilt-colored (girl) angel with moving wings, which is Victorian in appearance, accompanied by period piano music. Some other images are also in motion, for example, a calico cat's tail twitches, a kitten snatches at a goldfish in a bowl, a teen mouse girl talks on a telephone while gesticulating. Other images are static, such as images of (girl) fairies called guardians. The images are modified seasonally.

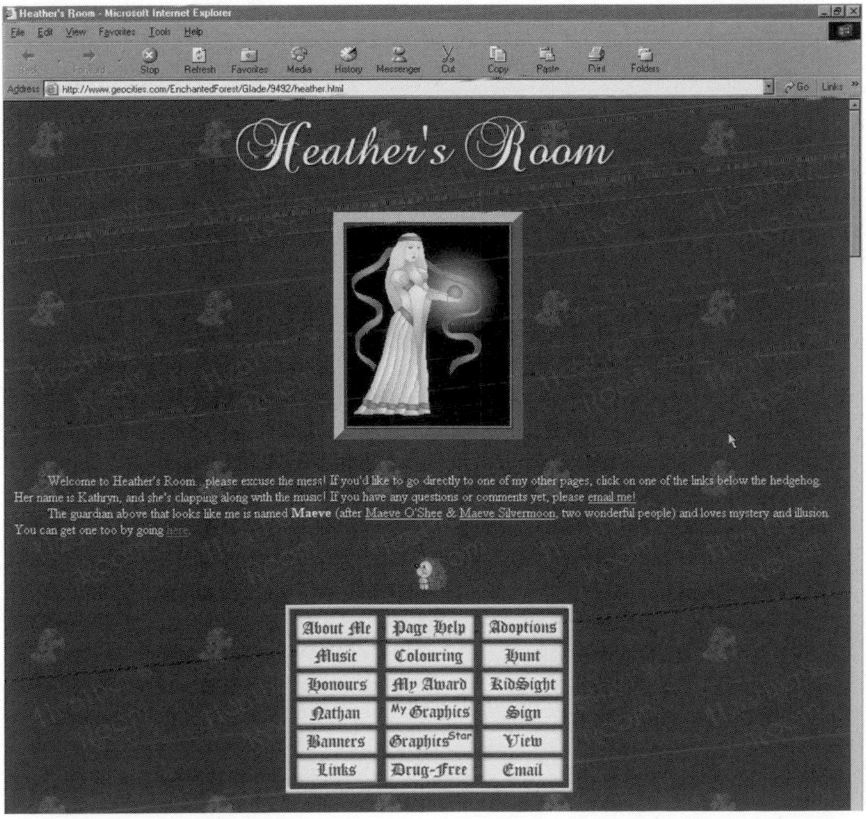

Figure 5.1 Heather's homepage.

For example, for Halloween, there are images of teen witches and ghosts. The photographs are in the linked websites devoted to girl rock groups such as the Spice Girls and Geri Halliwell, or popular music generally, with links to Much Music. There are also links to sites which have a combination of illustrations, photographs, and texts such as online catalogs and magazines devoted to girls, and to a "Games and Stuff" youth page. There is a Chat link as well as a counter for visitors and guestbook.

The site is mainly a repository or a collection of virtual artifacts. The theme could be said to be girl autonomy, which ranges from the choice of a parent site company called "gURL.com" to the almost exclusively female images (human, animal, and supernatural), to the links to women artists. The tone is light and playful.

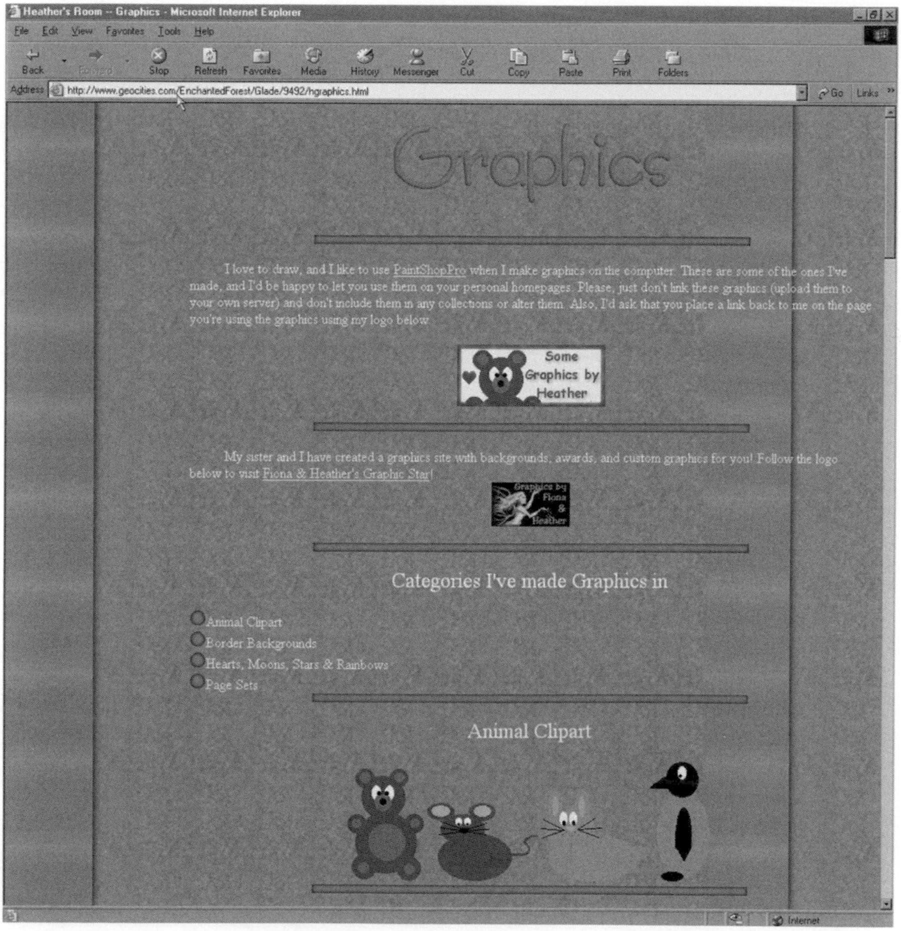

Figure 5.2 Website graphics page.

As in this site, many "computer-savvy" girls who build websites have learned not to give out too much personal information on their homepages, such as where they live or their phone number, although they will give an email address connected with the website. They may also not give their age, grade, or school. On the one hand, then, the impression on viewing their websites may be of being invited to see private aspects of these girls reproduced in a public domain. One may know her stated likes, dislikes, maybe even see a photo of her, and read her poetry, and look at her art. Yet, on the other hand, this domain of the Web is impersonal, separate from the "real" girl. She appears near yet remote at the same time. Gaining access to girls' homepages may create the impression of undergoing a contradictory experience: a viewer seems to be intruding into a private domain yet this access is an illusion. One may be allowed into a contained, "virtual bedroom" space, but a space that leaves the host – in this case the girl – inviolate. A viewer may sign the guestbook as invited to do so, but one is only a transient visitor, not an invited guest. In some ways the guestbook encapsulates the contradictions or incompatible aspects of a heterotopic space. It is a standard component of most website construction programs, yet by being personalized with icons that resemble stickers or decals, it evokes girls' culture. The invitation to sign the guestbook similarly recalls the popular practice of signing an autograph album. The presence of a guestbook evokes an imaginary leisured lifestyle far removed from any child's "real-time" existence, yet by being combined with a counter it is a way of recording statistics about visitors, and is one way to enable the homepage to be "recognized" by search engines. Through these means, the girls' homepage appears to be a kind of private space in a public domain.

Child-Produced Meta-Sites

The above discussion is not to suggest that all girls' or children's websites are composed of personal expressions or are virtual versions of bedroom culture. We have noticed how a number of children are interested in using the Web as a place to construct impersonal sites, especially sites that are of use to other children, such as providing links to other children's sites or constructing a place for children to post comments about something of interest to many of them, say, about Harry Potter. What makes these sites especially relevant in terms of our interest in children's agency being manifested on the Web is how children are using the Web as a way to practice ethical citizenship. Through the urging of proper attribution of text and images in their web traveling and web construction, and practicing this in their own websites, these children are "nomadic legal users." In addition, by appealing to one another as peers, children are participating in building a loose web community.

While "surfing" various children's homepages, we noted different types of information sites that are about the Web in some way, and because of this characteristic of "aboutness" we have labeled these types of pages "meta-sites."

Although much less common than adult-written web advice, there is some child-written and web-published advice from "kid" to "kid" as well. One excellent site is called "Lissa Explains it all" at <http://www.lissaexplains2.com/intro.shtml>.

She states she started the site in 1997 when she was eleven years old because there were no other websites available for kids to learn how to make their own site. Her instructions are well organized, clear, and direct. They are also quite comprehensive, covering the basics of web-page construction: HTML, frames, and tables. She combines a grasp of technical knowledge with user knowledge. As well as providing a section on web safety she gives comments from a child-user point of view about the pros and cons of adult-run "kidsafe" domains in terms of places to go for free web-page providers. Ultimately she does not recommend these "safe spaces" because the child user has to wait for adult approval to change his or her site. Rather, she advocates unrestricted page providers such as Yahoo at <http://www.yahoo.com> and "Geocities" at <http://www.geocities.com>. Not only is the site remarkable in relation to the extent of knowledge she possesses, but her idea of relaying this knowledge peer to peer is an effective teaching strategy, a fine example, we think, of Vygotsky's zone of proximal development. Since the site provides information about how to navigate the Web in an intelligent way, the audience could include anyone "new" to using the Web, no matter their age. Lissa discusses aspects of site construction, such as the difficulty for children to have their sites gain a visibility on the Web, in terms of having their homepages listed by search engines so they can be easily accessed. Accordingly, she gives instructions about how to insert "meta-tags" (keywords describing the site) on the page in order for it to be recognized by the search engines.

If this website is analyzed in terms of Foucault's ideas about heterotopias, it appears that the logic of established binary oppositions between private and public is somewhat overturned. Lissa's site is a public one, for it is a commercial site, a "dot com" with advertisements. It is also specifically a site of instruction. Yet she began this project as a hobby when only eleven, and has established herself as a young female expert in a male-dominated domain: indeed, CNN Science and Technology has awarded this site with a mark of approval. Both the appearance of the site and the rhetoric that Lissa uses are a blithe combination of incompatible modes. Not only will she write in an informal way as if talking to another friend, but she will combine autobiogaphical comments about her own experiences on the Web with factual, technical instruction of a fairly high order.

The following is an example of this mixture of personal and impersonal discourse from her first page. It is significant to note that the instruction is not only short, clear and succinct, which could imply a child reader, but the color of the words is in light purple print:

> Ideas: you need to come up with something original to make a really great page, something that no one else has done before. Here is a perfect example of an original page:

> *Fluffs Online:* When I started my page, there were absolutely NO other HTML help sites for kids. Now there are bunches hehe =) It's really cool to have something original. Coming up with something on your own will help you get lots of visitors. Maybe you can write about what you like to do, music, sports, whatever. Being original is definitely the key!! <http://www.lissaexplains2.com/basics.shtml>

The juxtaposition of these different modes of discourse does not seem out of place on Lissa's site, but rather provides a sense of the private and public existing simultaneously. The playful, informal, "childish" side is reinforced (one might almost say performed) by the careful use of color and decoration on the pages. On the front page, for instance, there are virtual decals of cats, flowers, butterflies, and so on, and there is a virtual arcade game of hitting moving ducks that waddle across the page. Two of the "how to" items listed under the "new" additions to the site include the apparently incompatible aspects of a technical aspect, how to build a "meta-tag builder" with a playful, girlish one, how to include "mouse fireworks." This combination occurs throughout the site. For example, Lissa has two different types of interaction with visitors. Not only does she have a public forum for teacher–learner types of engagement through enabling a visitor to register on the site and to engage in an exchange of ideas, but she has a personal, more childlike guestbook. Moreover, as an instructor and service to her viewers, she includes a page with links to different types of guestbooks so that child users can use her site to build their own. Ever cognizant of potential dangers to child users, she encourages them to use the type of guestbook where one can first pre-approve the entries.

Child and Adult-Produced Sites

In this section we look at websites produced by children and adults together, specifically when adults provide the frame and children the content. At the level of website construction, most sites with adult structure do not police the age of the visitor, but they are all openly labeled as "child-friendly" sites and so do impose restrictions in terms of the language and images used in the submitted material. The site managers act as moderators of listservs who scrutinize the content of the emails before sending them to the server. There are sites focusing on many icons of children's popular culture, such as Harry Potter, Sailor Moon, Aladdin or Pokemon. In terms of site construction, they range in sophistication of appearance and in degree of adult involvement.

We focus on two sites, one constructed by a parent and another constructed by an unrelated adult based on a shared interest. We do so in order to examine how the presence or absence of a familial relationship may be played out in the texture of the websites themselves. We consider several aspects when discussing a site: first, we approach an adult-structured website as a system of control by adults over children, in that the construction of the website may be considered as an attempt to try to reproduce virtually the power dynamics of life. If, as James et al. observe, "the central issues to be explored in relations to childhood space is . . . that of control" (1998: 38) then as play spaces websites can be seen as sites of virtual supervision and protection. Second, since these sites are constructed by both adults and children we consider these sites in terms of some of the points raised in the two previous sections. Although these sites tend to be modest, amateur constructions, unlike the company sites discussed in the first section, we are interested in how much engagement the children have in these sites. Are these sites truly interactive, or to rephrase in Barthes' terms, are children able to be creators, or inventors? In comparison with the child-created sites discussed in the second section, we also think briefly about these sites as heterotopic texts: do the child-produced elements (the images and words) attempt to accommodate, or negotiate the power relationships that are inscribed in the structure of the websites? As with children's own homepages, we are interested in exploring whether in joint, child–adult sites the oppositions of public and private may be overturned, or whether they are reproduced.

One joint site between parents and children is a British site co-owned by a father and his two daughters, Kate a young adolescent, and Peggy a pre-adolescent, at <http://cres1.lancs.ac.uk/~esarie/kate.htm>. The father's presence is invisible in terms of directing the content. He appears directly only as (literal) image, yet has a larger, less easily identifiable role in the background. The girls' pages are, as is typical, essentially attractively presented lists of links. The older girl's links are notably multimedia ones, especially for speech and music sites. Her sites include glimpses of the village they live in, the children's culture that they partake in: games, riddles, information about a famous great-grandfather, link to friends, a pony page, and a motorcycle page (her father's). Her pony page presents her to be "horse mad," and there are pictures of her riding her pony. The site is interactive not only in that it provides games, but also in that it includes a poll booth on a number of general and specific topics such as school, homework, smoking, favorite movie or TV show, boys, but also fox-hunting, keeping battery hens, and whether the Harry Potter books should be banned. It also invites users to suggest topics to be included. The guestbook section shows a wide range of guests, mainly children from across the developed world ranging from the U.S.A. to Hong Kong. The younger sister's page is an adjunct to Kate's. It is less sophisticated, but it includes multimedia games, such as a "fridge" on which you can move letters, a play dough recipe, as well as links to her pages on her sister's site devoted to horses, and to her family. In addition, there is a virtual photo album of the entire family that she has scanned in, both humans and pets.

Both of these homepages appear to serve as means of autobiographical expression, for the girls are sharing aspects of what interests them, or what they consider would be important for a potential viewer. The combination of images, text, and discussion creates quite a rounded sense of the girls as individuals.

At the same time, the open sharing of family photos with anyone who goes to the site appears problematic. As an adult viewer looking at the family album, one is placed almost into the position of voyeur. It seems to be an intrusion in the family's privacy to be able to see so much of the girls' lives.

If these pages are considered as types of "girls' virtual bedroom culture," it can be seen that the images are similar to those of the other girls' sites described above, except that they are more explicitly self-revealing. For instance, instead of a graphic image of a pet, they give a reproduction of a photo of the actual pet; instead of including mainly links to other websites of interest, the links are personal ones about their family and friends; instead of one photo, they give the contents of their album collection, and so on. In some ways, when one views the site, the impression is created of entering visually into an actual private space of the girls, not a virtual representation of one. In terms of Foucault's discussion of heterotopias, it seems as if the inviolability of public and private has been turned inside out. The girls are treating the public space of the Web as if it were a private space, or "internal space" by openly expressing their innermost "dreams" and "passions" (Foucault 1986: 23). If the site is thought of in terms of Foucault's fifth principle of heterotopias about access and separation from the family, it is as if the access has been granted not denied. Because viewers are transient visitors, not "invited guests" (ibid.: 26), they are placed in the role of interloper.

The question of why this impression occurs might revolve around the role of the father in the construction of the site. If the entire site is examined, one link appears disturbing: if a viewer clicks onto the phrase "touch not the cat but the glove" one goes to a site featuring the crest of the Scottish clan McIntosh, links to their site, and a phrase warning viewers not to "mess" with his children. This bellicose statement seems somewhat contradictory in intent, considering that he allowed the scanning of entire family photo albums on the younger girl's site which is most revealing in terms of identifying the girls. It makes a viewer wonder about his attitude – is he worried about their sites being too self-revealing? How does he see himself – as a warrior or protector of honor perhaps? Based on this question, we add an additional one: "Because the father thinks he is protecting the girls, does this enable them to treat the public domain of the Web as a private space?" Could this account for the impression that this website appears to be not a "virtual bedroom" but a domestic space or bedroom exposed virtually to the world?

A contrasting parental attitude to children's web life may be seen on a link on the older girl, Kate's page. Here, a highlighted section for parents that includes an article written by a mother of a pre-teen daughter, who presents balanced views about children and the Internet, including suggestions about how to explore the Web as a family and about how not to be overly worried about media sensationalism concerning the Web. The contradiction in roles highlights two different positions that parents of "web children" obviously hold and raises the issue of what responsible adults' roles should be, a topic we return to in the conclusion to this chapter.

In contrast to parent–child co-owned sites there are numerous sites devoted to child and youth fan creativity in which the adult is an (apparently) neutral host not only in terms of family relationship, but also in terms of commercial motive. For example, one section of a vast site called <http://www.fandom.com> is devoted to Harry Potter fans, and there are pages for fans to submit their fiction and art, which, they ask, should not be copied. While the age and often the sex of the authors cannot be detected from the headings of the stories, to introduce their artworks the child and teen artists usually talk briefly about themselves in relation to their interests, and especially their reading interests. They may give their age and grade as well. It is interesting to speculate why there is more transparency in the introductions associated with the art than with the fan fiction. Fan fiction has been established on the Web for some time as a genre, so the presentation has become quite sophisticated and anonymous. The texts "stand alone" as it were. In comparison, fan art is a relatively new genre online, so there are no established formats of presentation. Perhaps children are modeling their introductions on the captions often included with artwork in galleries.

Fan-produced creativity was initially associated with the fan fiction written by Star Trek fans (Jenkins 1992), but now the genre has spread to many popular culture texts and to many modes of expression. In addition to producing art and photography, fans compose music, lyrics, and poetry, as well as engage in constructive criticism of one another's work. For example, in the various sites directed to the television show *Buffy, the Vampire Slayer*, a series that has a wide cross-over audience in terms of age, the fiction is categorized in the way movies are with adult markers being attached to stories which contain sexual and violent content. There are also fans who write mock "children's literature" versions of *Buffy, the Vampire Slayer*.

One very interesting site to consider as a platform for children's own creativity is a site devoted to the Disney film *Aladdin*. This site may be interpreted as "growing" along with the creator as he ages from youth to young man. Perhaps because of this continuity he treats prospective child collaborators respectfully, as equals. This site is based in Holland, although written in English, and is dedicated to being a comprehensive site devoted to the children's film. Called "Agrabah's Market" at <http://www.agrabah.org> it was started by Marco Merkelijn when he was a student, as a place to share his fascination with the Dutch version of the Disney film and to "publish" his fan fiction. Only rarely are there links to products which can be bought, such as to computer games, or to "the Souvenir stand" which contains information about products including books. The bulk of the site is devoted to information about the *Aladdin* film, providing different forms of activity associated with the film (playing games, reading comics, listening to music).

There is a substantial portion of the site devoted to fan fiction (his and others) and art. By including coloring pages, and a virtual art gallery both for freehand art (including cross-over art with other popular culture media such as Pokemon and Titanic) and for collage art composed of the coloring pages, children who cannot draw well are included as "artists." Marco also gives links to graphics, clip art, wallpapers, and icons that he has gathered from all around the Web (world), for the viewers to use in making their own Aladdin sites. All sites are attributed properly; for example, one site for games and icons is a Korean site that is found easily by a viewer. The guestbook archives may be viewed, and the worldwide nature of the people who contribute to the site seems echoed by the global nature of the users, for there have been visitors from across Europe, Northern Africa, as well as America. All entries in the guestbook comment appreciatively on the interactive nature of the site, especially the coloring pages, the fan fiction, and the sing-along music.

Agrabah's Market is a modest site in terms of graphic design, but it is frequently updated and obviously the result of being a labor of love. By including scanned comics and scanned coloring pages, Marco Merkelijn appears to be consciously appealing to young writers and artists. He not only invites their submissions of art and fiction, but by including all the links necessary for the child viewer to construct his or her own Aladdin page, he is encouraging children to build their own websites. All he asks is that his site is linked to theirs. He also acts as overseer of the site for he states on the front page that it is a child-friendly site, and that he approves the material submitted. What is interesting in terms of our focus on children's participation is his inclusiveness: he is appealing to a young age group and encouraging them to "show" their work, and think of themselves as creators, not only with fiction, and art (freehand, collage) but also in terms of web construction. His function towards the young users of his site is one of a mentor. He does not intrude on their creativity but supports their efforts. In addition, by continuing to maintain his site through young adulthood, he serves as a role model for other web creators.

In some ways Agrabah's Market can be considered as a multimedia gallery recalling on a large scale the website of the teenage British girl Tilla mentioned earlier, where she has used the public structure of a gallery to present her private creations. The products of a bedroom culture – cartoons, coloring pages, stories, and so on – are turned into art by their being shown in a public forum, and the privacy of the individual child artists has been retained. The way this effect is achieved on websites could be explained by their ability as heterotopic spaces to juxtapose oppositional or contradictory aspects against each other, so the cartoons, say, are both children's private drawings and public art. Marco's respectful attitude to his child colleagues could stem from the fact that, like Lissa of "Lissa explains," he has grown with his website and retained his child-centered focus. He is not trying to exert any power relations over his collaborators. Rather, his site perhaps serves as heterotopic compensatory space, a "real space" that is "meticulous and well arranged" (Foucault 1986: 27), and transposes some ideas concerning the value of collaboration and respect into cyberspace.

Researching the Internet: Virtual Spaces and Children's Popular Culture

Associated with considering the Internet as a virtual space are a number of related issues about using the Internet as a research space. These issues could be categorized as child-centered, or adult-centered, but our interest here is more on the interrelationship between child and adult. We have no solutions for these problems, but simply wish to highlight some aspects of concern and some ideas they evoke in response.

One major child-centered issue revolves around the invisibility of children's sites on the Web and the attendant issue of protection. Many children's websites are invisible on search engines. This may be because of the fact that children tend not to put meta-tags on their sites; therefore, they are not recognized by the search engines (source: "Lissa explains it all"). The invisibility is also related to the circumstances of many children's web pages being hosted by protected page providers, which are invisible to search engines. Accordingly, to access any of these sites you have to know the URL (or the child). Invisibility can be seen as either positive or negative. For example, if a site is considered to be a safe space for self-expression, the relative privacy of a site may be a positive feature. By contrast, inaccessibility may be considered to be a weakness, if the value of a site is based on its popularity according to the number of visitors counted.

The flip side of invisibility is protection. As the instance of the father desiring to protect the security of his daughters highlights, what is the parents' role in relation to a child's website? What is the status of a homepage? Is it a private or a public domain? Once one has gained access, what is an adult doing when visiting a child's homepage? Is it an invasion of privacy? The action of "visiting" a private domain, indeed often a child's (virtual) "room of [his or her] own" is reinforced, of course, by the conventional terms used to describe a homepage. Indeed, as we discussed earlier, the inclusion of a "guestbook" where one can sign one's name and provide comments about the "host" site evokes a gracious, leisured world far removed from the constant bustle and pressure of being a (young) person today. As Foucault noted about visitors' bedrooms, the visitor to a homepage is just "passing through" another's domain, as would a tourist. Or, to use another analogy, perhaps a web traveler is an anthropologist, taking some time to survey each virtual artifact in a cultural space. As with visiting children's physical bedrooms or play spaces, the polite (adult) visitor looks but does not alter the arrangement of the child's environment; indeed, unlike a bedroom where one may be allowed to touch an object, here one relies on aural and visual cues. Significantly, a visitor cannot alter a website in any way; this is the right of the owner, although one could steal copies of the images. Nor is the host virtually present, unless of course one has purchased a Microsoft tour game that includes visitor and host on an interactive magical carpet ride! Yet, the personality of the host is suggested by the choice of image, sound, or multimedia clip. At the same time, by constructing a homepage and "publishing" it on the Web, a child is entering a public domain. Anyone with the right technology and knowledge of the URL can enter. To consider this issue on a general level, are there, irrespective of any theoretical examination of child-produced websites, any ethical implications of visiting a child-produced site when one is an adult visitor/researcher since the site was intended for a peer audience, not an adult one? Is it any different from reading other juvenile-produced texts?

Furthermore, there is the issue of the ethics of even visiting a protected "kids domain." Depending on the degree of security of the web-page provider, an adult may need a child in order to access the sites. This is the case, for example, when an adult wishes to look at the sites on <http://www.kidsdomain.com>. Here, because the adult (literally) is looking over a child's shoulder, the viewer is placed in the position of voyeur or lurker. On other child-designated domains, such as at <http://www.gURL.com> where there is no security, an adult can view web pages as easily as anyone else.

A related issue is the freedom allowed by the Internet to escape constraints or markers such as age (along with gender, race, sexuality, and, to an extent, ability). The possibility of assuming different identities is part of the adult appeal of the Internet, and must appeal to children as well. However, lack of age markers seems to be linked not with freedom from constraint, but with adult concerns about protection from stalkers. It is noticeable that children now tend not to share their age on the Internet – indeed, Internet advice literature tells them not to give out any personal information for their own protection. As a result, if one is studying homepages or fiction or poetry by children it is becoming exceedingly difficult to tell the age of the constructor/writer. The topic of a site does not necessarily indicate age, for a child and adult may both engage in the same fan relationship to youth popular culture. For instance, there are Sailor Moon sites and Sabrina, the Teenage Witch fan sites developed by girls and by women. To a degree, as we have seen, one can partly deduce the age of a site owner based upon the sophistication of the site construction in terms of graphics, by the topics posted on the site, and by the diction and rhetoric used.

Another contributing factor to the invisibility of children-produced sites is the drive to commercialization of the Web that can be seen not only in the proliferation of company sites but also in how children are turning over their amateur sites in whole or in part to companies. This aspect is particularly evident in the child-produced meta-site discussed above, for "Lissa Explains" is a commercial site with ads. As a consequence, in order to discover children's input on the Web one has to go more and more to commercial sites. When searching on a search engine then, the web addresses of many children's sites are not distinguishable from those of companies.

In some ways, children's websites seem to be an exemplary instance of present-day "youth culture" centered around social relations organized not by geographical scale as much as it is structured by a "constellation of temporary coherence" around a passing activity or product (Massey 1998: 125). We consider that the homepage's or website's virtual life as a construction (and under construction!) in various ways unsettles the commonly understood binary opposition between public, visible spaces and domestic, private spaces, especially as it pertains to children, and particularly girls, being relegated to the "domestic sphere." Indeed, perhaps their "symbolic creativity" (Willis 1990) and literal activity may suggest ways of how the binaries of public/private spheres with the attendant characteristics of production and consumption may themselves be (partly) dismantled. As we discussed, Internet use as a popular culture activity is in some ways similar to other engagements with popular culture modes such as listening to music, or attending to the latest style of dress. Each activity seems to cross age boundaries, since young or middle-aged or older are all participating in "youth" culture. Accordingly, in practice, as a leisure activity age-based distinctions seem almost irrelevant. Regulation of and participation in the Internet, as it is battled over by business and education, is the same for all users, no matter their demographics.

If we interpret the individual homepage and meta-site in terms of their existence in virtual space as a "work in progress" or a space which is continually "under construction," some of the ideas employed in the field of social geography prove insightful. Especially provocative are the ideas employed by those geographers such as Stuart Aitken (1998) who are turning their attention to the public and familial spaces of childhood. They discuss how many middle-class and working-class children lead restricted lives. As we discuss in Chapter 4, all aspects of children's physical existence, including leisure and play, comprises fairly circumscribed boundaries of home, school, and community centers. However, when we take these ideas which Aitken uses to describe a physical realm and apply them to a virtual realm, a different, more complex landscape of constraint versus freedom emerges. For instance, according to Henry Lefebvre's notion of "trial by space," "value" is accorded to individuals or groups who generate or produce a space "that is marked by them as theirs. Moreover, this space is on a world-wide scale" (cited in Aitken 1998: 99–100). Applying this idea to a child's homepage or website, these sites seem to be marking virtual territory within the wild frontier of the Internet realm, homesteading as it were, in a virtual world. These homepages and metapages have virtual spatial existence on the Web as valid or legitimate according to Lefebvre's idea of staking a claim as that of a university or corporate website. Although size as measured in computer storage terms makes this type of site much smaller than a company site, neither have any dimension in "reality" anyway. It is interesting to note that while children may be using strategies associated with colonization, based on the invisibility and immateriality of the realm in material terms, and based on their ethical approach to use from sites in terms of attribution of graphics and links, children's homesteading does not appear to be occurring in a bellicose way. Moreover, the child meta-sites are teaching other children how to homestead in a legal, collaborative, and fair way. These strategies or tactics appear to be the opposite of what Lefebvre describes as the staking of space being based on "confrontation with other values and ideas it encounters there" (cited in Aitken 1998: 100). Instead, homepage construction appears to be a non-confrontational assertion of territory.

As has been seen, we interpret these child-created sites as virtual spaces, which in various ways unsettle the binary opposition between public and private spaces, along with the attendant attribution of the former as the domain of the adult, and male, and the latter the "province" of the immature and female. The activity of site construction may by itself also help unsettle the binary opposition between consumption and production. Furthermore, in the practice of "creating" a website or homepage, the child is engaging in activities that undo the representation of children as culture dupes. By reconstructing and transmitting visual and auditory images the child is producing information, which is the prime cultural capital and monetary currency of the present-day information age. In addition, by engaging in being her or his own transmitting network through the mounting of a homepage, the child may be participating in helping to undo the power imbalance which exists between senders and receivers in the old broadcast model of telecommunication (Poster 1995: 38). By inviting visitors to sign a guestbook and encouraging chat, the child also promotes the building of a possible virtual community which again is considered by some Internet theorists to be one of the democratic powers of the Internet (Poster 1995: 33; Abbott 1998: 86). Although the duration of existence may be ephemeral, the child is becoming a producer of digital information, not just a consumer, however well informed.

Based upon our interpretation, it may be seen that through the Internet children and youth may become involved in different types of community building. Like fans grouped around a popular text, they seem to exist in what Paul Willis (1990) considers to be "proto-community," a group which emerges as a result of contingency because of a number of individuals who are spontaneously sharing interests with one another. For example, these communities may be seen as operating in the many chat rooms, fan clubs, and even the Harry Potter "school" where children communicate with one another about their consuming interest. Yet the children may never meet fact to face, and the population of this community is not a stable group, always shifting and recombining in makeup (Willis 1990: 141–2). At the same time, the Internet may also enable different types of communities to form. For example, it may encourage the formation of an "imaginary community" which may exist as a unifying idea, although, just as with the members of a nation, the members never all meet, they may be united by the idea of a place (Anderson 1983, cited in Jones et al. 1997: 384). As we have seen, to a degree, child-produced content and structure often emphasizes this community function. This is seen in relation to some children who insist on proper attribution of sites and in their nomadic but non-poaching approach to others' images. Perhaps adults should work to support this ideal of non-bellicose homesteading as opposed to competitive, combative, frontier "marking." We need to encourage this so that the Web does not become solely another domain of (macho) virtual (cowboy) "muscle-flexing" or size comparison. As mentioned above, in the apparently limitless space of the Internet, the act of children constructing homepages may perhaps be seen as an attempt to create an ideal, oppositional space similar to how Foucault described some of the colonizing efforts of the early religious groups, whereby they sought to create a space that is "as perfect, as meticulous, as well arranged as ours is messy, ill constructed and jumbled"(1986: 27).

This type of technical "user" knowledge or literacy can be complemented by critical knowledge, not only in a consumer society sense, but also in an ethical and moral sense. It is our duty as adults to support children's knowledge in this area as well. At the same time, adults need to accept that the Web can never be a "protected garden." This is soon discovered when roaming the net. As one young user tells it, when she was a little girl (six or seven) playing on her dad's computer at work, she typed in her name as a commercial address. To her shock she was linked to a Nordic porn site. (Protectively, she waited until she was a teenager before telling her mother!) She said, "not to worry, Mom, I quickly left the site. . . . Sometimes these websites have links that say 'if you don't belong here, here is a list of interesting children's sites you might want to go to'" (Krista Walsh, personal communication). If this anecdote is read as a moral fable, perhaps the Internet may be seen as a virtual return to a ("wide" "wild") common society. The Internet does not or cannot safely partition or protect children from experience, like the ideal of protected innocence or ignorance which was a dominant feature of the middle-class Victorian world and is still evident today as commonsense assumptions. The Internet is simply a realistic reflection and product of today's society and society's mores with all of their contradictions.

Chapter Six

Historical Spaces: Barbie Looks Back

"in due time she will be her own doll"
Jean-Jacques Rousseau, *Emile* (1762).

"As to the women, why they are mere dolls"
Frances Burney, *Evelina* (1778).

"We Girls Can Do Anything"
Barbie game (1991).

In this final chapter, we focus on the ways in which Barbie may be seen as a current instance of a long line of fashion dolls that have been available for well over the more-than-forty years of Barbie's official existence. Through obvious links to the collecting world, Mattel presents ways in which the history of Barbie is being recorded and valued. A brand new Barbie sells for around nineteen Canadian dollars (although there are some that are priced in the $9.99 to $14 range). A vintage Barbie *circa* 1959, still in her original box, sells for $2500. However, we have also seen signs of how Barbie history is inserted into the very play-artifacts of Barbie, as in the case of an episode in *Barbie* magazine, a magazine marketed at six- to nine-year-old girls. In this episode the young reader is treated to a retrospective on Barbie at the Museum of Modern Art. "Retro-spect-tive – what's that?" ask Nikki and her school friends who are on a field trip to the museum. "A retrospective is looking back," replies the museum curator. The young reader, through the eyes of Nikki, embarks upon a tour of Barbie fashions from 1959 to the present. The reader is also taken on a tour of some aspects of the dominant discourses embodied in Barbie over the years – from Barbie as pure fashion, to Barbie as career woman, to Barbie as a signifier of "we girls can do anything." An instance of Barbie possessing a self-consciousness towards her history may be seen in the comic book episode when young Nikki strays away from the school tour group and encounters the "real Barbie," so that Barbie-as-Barbie is used to explore the phenomenon of Barbie. It is an interesting meta-device not unlike the role of Arnold Schwarzenegger-as-himself in the movie *Last Action Hero*. In this movie the young boy accompanied by Arnold Schwarzenegger visits a video shop where there is a whole section devoted to Schwarzenegger-the-legend. In the comic Nikki meets the real Barbie:

> *Nikki*: Wow! I can't believe I'm meeting the real Barbie! But why were you sitting so still at your computer?
>
> *Barbie*: The museum is throwing a grand ball for me, and I was asked to give a speech about my show . . . I'm a little nervous – Lots of people will be listening because I'm going to be on TV. So I was sitting at the computer trying to figure out what to say.

This exchange draws attention to the perceived transhistorical reality of Barbie for so many girls.

Thus, in this chapter, we propose a history of the Barbie doll in the context of the emergence of Western, middle-class women's and children's fashion consumption in the eighteenth century. This history sets out to counter the notion that the doll emerged fully formed in the late 1950s as part of the baby boom, by presenting a "history of beginnings" as Foucault puts it, of Barbie that is not tidy or linear. In so doing we aim to complement the extensive body of literature on "Barbie culture" (Rogers 1999) that already exists in relation to Barbie the doll, and Barbie and her players.[1] By situating Barbie doll history as part of a longer time-frame, we aim to demonstrate that children's popular culture can, and should, be viewed from a longer range perspective that will encourage a more measured and nuanced critique of such culture than is usually the case. Our stance aims to question the belief in the present as the sole source of authority on children's culture that is common in much criticism of popular culture. We also hope that we will contribute to the redirecting of focus away from the "moral panic" that has accompanied, in every generation, so many events in the history of children's popular culture. This is apparent not only in each new generation, but in each new season of commodity as the latest artifacts are condemned: Nancy Drew, *Archie* comics, hoola hoops, Cabbage Patch dolls, and so on have all come under this moral opprobrium.

Specifically, we keep in mind Ruth Perry's warning to let the materials historicize our conceptions of childhood, "rather than fitting descriptions" from the eighteenth century to "twentieth century conceptions of childhood" (1997: 108). A useful example of this may be found at <http://www.uampfa.berkeley.edu/exhibits/newchild/toys.html> of the art exhibit "The New Child: British Art and the Origins of Modern Childhood, 1730–1830" which was on display at the University of California at Berkeley in 1995 and which contains a segment devoted to children's play, toys, and recreation. One picture, *The Children's Party* by William Hogarth (1730) depicts four well-dressed, obviously affluent children in activities that are either typically associated with childhood or conventionally symbolic. At the left side, a little soldier boy plays with his drum, a young girl opposite rushes towards him with outstretched arms, another girl sits at a tea-table with a standing doll (as a small dog overturns the ignored tea-table), and in the center of the picture, a young girl points at a mirror. Commentators have usually stressed the irony and symbolism of the picture, seeing in it a reference to children pretending to be grown-ups, noting, for example, the traditional use of the mirror to represent vanity, and how the iconography of the overturned tea-table with a young beautiful woman will be used later in the satiric sequence *The Harlot's Progress* (Paulson 1971). However, the curator of the exhibit, James Steward, prefers to focus on the significance of the picture in depicting a separate world of childhood, for there are no adults in the picture, and the children are engaged in play activities, not work. He argues that this painting helped depict the notion of childhood as a separate state that was evolving during the eighteenth century.[2]

In following Steward's lead, we find it fascinating to see that the well-dressed, miniature woman doll next to which the child sits at a table occupies a separate space just as the children do. Moreover, the doll stands at a tea-table that is constructed to her scale, not to the children's. To view the respective costumes of the doll and girls is somewhat disturbing to a modern sensibility, for, following the fashions of the day, the children are dressed as miniature adults: the girls are dressed in beautiful, tightly laced long, full dresses with caps, since they are in a domestic (if outside) setting. The doll is similarly dressed but in a more formal style. Significantly, while the children's figures are undeveloped, the doll is a representation of a slim adult woman, with a small waist, developed bust and with dressed blonde hair. Except for her scale – which is hard to determine – the doll is the miniature adult, and this stands in sharp contrast to the children's nondeveloped bodies.

This depiction of a fashionable lady doll as a plaything is interesting in terms of our historical project to revise Barbie history. Since the painting is dated 1730 it suggests that (affluent) girls have played with fashionably dressed, shapely dolls for a very long time. In the spirit of Erica Rand, then, who suggests in the Conclusion of her book *Barbie's Queer Accessories* that Barbie is a useful pedagogical tool because she "hits a nerve well worth locating and tweaking – in the classroom, in the bedroom, and on the political stage" (1995: 195), we see that we might engage usefully in a process of either "historicizing Barbie" or "contemporizing the past."

In order to illustrate our alternative history of Barbie and the fashion doll, we divide the remainder of this chapter into several sections. First, we juxtapose the standard history of Barbie's birth in 1959 with the more than 200-year-old history of the fashion doll, and of the lady doll in England, Europe, and North America. We provide a critical context for understanding the fashion and lady doll by locating them in relation to the criticism regarding children and toys, of leading pedagogues of the period: Jean-Jacques Rousseau and Maria Edgeworth. Next, we provide a comparative Barbie history by analyzing early fashion dolls and lady dolls, as well as Barbie dolls, as examples of material culture. Our method ventures to examine them as they are represented in doll histories, supplemented by our viewing of some actual nineteenth-century fashion and play dolls. We examine the dolls as objects by themselves or "out of context," for we consider their respective representation in doll histories, both scholarly ones and those targeting a collector's market. Our responses upon viewing numerous nineteenth-century fashion dolls and play dolls held in the vaults of the McCord Museum, Montreal are also included in this chapter.[3] Finally, we approach the material culture of fashion, lady, and Barbie dolls by providing an ethnographic approach to doll play. Here we compare historical research on children and dolls with present-day studies of Barbie play and, in the process, speculate on the wide range of play use of fashion dolls across two centuries.

Contextualizing Barbie History

Origin Stories of Barbie: Contesting Tales

There are two main versions of the Barbie story in circulation and they contest one another for veracity. One is the "official tale" used by Mattel, and the other is a slightly risqué unauthorized one. The authorized story states that Mattel (or Ruth Handler, the co-founder of Mattel) invented Barbie when she noticed how much her daughter Barbara loved playing with paper dolls that were modeled on adult women's bodies. Accordingly, Handler thought of transposing the paper doll to a three-dimensional form 11½ inches in height. That Barbie was originally based on paper dolls is the story distributed by Mattel in their promotional material, as is her birth month of March 1959, when she was launched at the American Toy Fair in New York (Rand 1995: 23–4). Researchers such as Wayne Miller have discovered that it is difficult to obtain more than the "official" details of Barbie's origin since Mattel company officials rarely grant interviews (1998: 308 n.).

At the same time there is a subversive, slightly salacious origin story that circulates, and which is popular among those seeking to undermine Mattel's sanitized version. One source is Cy Schneider who worked closely with Mattel in the 1950s as an advertising executive. In his book *Children's Television* he describes how the Handlers developed the idea for a doll while on a European trip:

> Lili [or Lilli] was a German doll modeled after a German playgirl in cartoon form who regularly graced the pages of *Das Bild*, a German newspaper much like our *Inquirer*. The Lili doll was not designed to appeal to children, but was sold to adult men in tobacconists and bars. Lili came in one of two sexy outfits, and if there was an aura or fantasy at all around this doll, it was an adult males' pet. . . . An emissary was sent to Germany and all the rights to Lili were bought by Mattel. Some doll construction patents were bought from Hauser, the German manufacturer, and the cartoon rights to Lili were bought and put aside (1987: 26).

Significantly, when the doll was tested on mothers and daughters, from the outset mothers disapproved of the doll, considering it too mature, and the clothes too sexy. However, when the girls were shown the doll when by themselves, they loved it (Rand 1995: 32; W. Miller 1998: 68).

As a commentary on this tale, it is interesting to see how this origin story is interpreted in *European Readings of American Popular Culture* (1996). The fact that Barbie is an appropriation of a European popular culture artifact is considered to be part of the critique on Barbie. In her discussion of Barbie, Mariane Debouzy therefore adds plagiarism to Barbie's history as well as seizing on the sexualized progenitor by locating Barbie in the Lolita mentality of the 1950s where the "seductive power of the teenager asserted itself." This power was manifest in adolescent movie stars such as Debbie Reynolds and Sandra Dee, while teenage girls became visible as majorettes, cheerleaders or prom queens (1996: 140). Debouzy stresses the sexy pinup origins as essential to the doll – an origin she considers more valid than another historical view which she mentions and then disregards, namely that dolls exist in a life cycle whereby babies follow from fashion dolls and vice versa (1996: 139). Indeed, it is this rejected historical view that interests us. In our version of Barbie history not only is there evidence of a cyclical pattern of appearance of types of dolls depicting women, children, or infants, but also both versions of the origin story are "true," namely the paper doll version and the woman mannequin version. As we will demonstrate, moreover, there is no innocent version to offset as a comparison to the sexy version: paper dolls, or three-dimensional mannequins are neither innocent nor sexy in themselves, but carry contradictory and multiple meanings according to their use.

A History of Fashion Dolls and Lady Dolls: Dolls for Women and Girls

The Hogarth painting referred to above is not the only evidence that children, primarily girls, owned or borrowed small-scale fashionable dolls in earlier periods. Indeed, as Kerry Taylor, a doll historian notes, there are numerous portraits of girls, daughters of noblemen, posed with elaborately dressed dolls dating from the sixteenth century. Typically, a young child holds a turned wooden doll, usually a lady doll, elaborately dressed in a costume echoing that of the child. To illustrate this in her book, Taylor includes a reproduction of an Elizabethan oil painting of three sisters all identically dressed in sumptuous gowns, with a similarly dressed woman doll attributed to an artist from the circle of Robert Peake *circa* 1598 to 1626 (Taylor 1990: 7–8). Lady dolls were not exclusive to Europe. According to historians of childhood material culture such as Karen Calvert, these dolls were occasionally transported to the American colonies during the seventeenth century. For example, a member of William Penn's family brought a doll to Pennsylvania as a present for a young woman in her late teens in 1699. Calvert notes that these dolls were rare and expensive, and apparently more a woman's keepsake than a girl's plaything, especially when new (1992: 50). This migration would suggest that the global reach of the fashion doll is not a new phenomenon.

James Steward's hypothesis about a new focus on the ideas of a separate state of childhood with distinct material artifacts being associated with it may be seen in the following examples of children with toys. During the last quarter of the eighteenth century more portraits of children and toys, including dolls, began to appear. For example, a family portrait of Don Ferdinando painted by Johann Zoffany in 1778 shows four children with musical instruments, and the smallest girl holding a lady doll in elaborate dress complete with formal headdress (Slier 1994: 36–7). In America, even in middle-class homes, Calvert notes that the toys in portraits of girls of this period include doll furniture, doll dishes, grace hoops, and dominoes, while in portraits of boys the most common toys are balls, rolling hoops, miniature wagons, sleds, toy horses, and tin soldiers (1992: 80). The doll's association with girls as a toy is part of the history of the doll. In this context, the history of the European, particularly English, fashion doll should be understood in terms of an emerging middle-class "consumer society" in which marketing is directed towards the female consumer.[4]

The fashion dolls of the early eighteenth century were connected with French fashion and served an elite, mainly aristocratic clientele, continuing a royal tradition dating back some four hundred years (McKendrick 1982: 46). These hand-carved "wooden Mademoiselles" were shipped periodically (reports vary from once a year to once a month) to the English court. This one-way traffic continued even when England and France were at war as "an act of gallantry . . . for the benefit of the ladies" (Addison, Abbé Prevost, quoted in McKendrick 1982). Once the queen and court ladies had studied these mannequins they would be passed on to the leading London dressmakers. These dolls, also called "pandoras" or "dolls of the Rue St. Honoré," were elaborately coiffed and richly dressed. Some dolls were made half-size; however, many dolls were made life-size so that the clothes could be copied and worn soon after by the women customers (King 1977: 84). These dolls were intended to serve as models for hairstyles, hats, underclothes, and other accessories. The geographical spread of the dolls was quite broad. After they had been seen in England, they would be sent to the colonies and could be viewed at a price, much like a modern-day museum exhibit. For a higher price one could borrow a doll, even if briefly, in order to take it home to copy the fashion (McKendrick 1982: 44–5). These dolls, which were not life-size, but which were of various sizes, had an additional life after their fashion function was complete; there were instances where some mothers would pass on their dolls to their daughters as playthings (Cross 1997: 17).

In the late eighteenth century the English fabricated an inexpensive mass-produced version of the French fashion doll. It was flat, cut out of cardboard, about 8 inches high, with simply arranged hair, and complete with underclothing and corset. These were printed by the thousand, initially (in 1790) costing three shillings, but subsequently costing a few pence. The novelty is described in the German fashion journal *Journal des Luxus und der Moden* (1791) in the following way:

> [It has] six complete sets of tastefully coloured, cut-out dresses and coiffures, which means summer – and winter – clothing, complete dresses and negligees, caracos, chemises, furs, hats, bonnets, poufs etc. Each dress and hat is made in such a way that the doll can easily be dressed in it, giving a fully dressed or *décolleté* effect while the dress fits perfectly in either case. The hat or bonnet can be adjusted freely to be pulled over the face or set back. . . . This dressing and undressing, being able to set up and change again, makes for the uniqueness of the English doll. One might obtain even more changes by having some extra dresses designed and painted. The whole is packed in a neat paper envelope, can easily be carried in portfolio or working bag (quoted in McKendrick 1982: 45).

Because of the ease of manufacturing, soon there were hundreds of different versions of (paper) dolls aimed at different classes and professions, including the wives and daughters of artisans, craftsmen, and laborers. Sometimes these flat paper dolls were modeled in paper to achieve a three-dimensional appearance (Fritzsch and Bachmann 1966: 70). In the American colonies, these cardboard dolls, called "protean figures," were popular among people who considered themselves elegant (Fraser 1966: 92). While some mothers passed the dolls on to their daughters after they had finished with them, the producers also manufactured and marketed the fashion paper doll separately as a toy aimed at girls. Unfortunately, due to their fragile material composition, very few have survived to the present day to provide tangible proof (McKendrick 1982: 46). By the Regency period, historians such as Constance Eileen King cite evidence from children's books as well as scrapbooks to suggest the widespread nature of paper dolls. For instance, in 1810, S. N. J. Fuller published an anonymous account entitled *The History of Little Fanny* which served as a storybook accompanied by a paper doll and an assortment of costumes and accessories to illustrate the tale (1977: 146, 147).

These paper fashion dolls were produced and targeted at a girls' market, as an adjunct to the adult woman market. At the same time, during the late eighteenth century various kinds of three-dimensional dolls proliferated, and they were similarly intended as presents for girls. In England, these dolls, called "babies," could be simple or elaborate, "dressed, jointed, wax or common" and they had wax or earthenware faces, jointed bodies, and elaborate wardrobes (McKendrick 1982: 310). There were also doll houses and accessories to complement the small dolls that were inside the doll houses (Armstrong 1996: 39). In Europe during the same period, toy catalogs also began to appear. Researchers most often refer to two: one French catalog from the Napoleonic period showing fashionable lady dolls and male dolls (Jackson 1908: facing

17), and a German catalog of Hieronymous Bestelmeir of Nuremberg (1800) which listed and depicted 500 toys. These included English fashion dolls of paper, jointed wooden dolls mechanical dolls and a nursemaid and child with a baby cart (King 1977: 138).

Calvert describes a wide range of dolls available in America from the late eighteenth century on. These ranged from simple, inexpensive penny wooden dolls, to sturdy dolls of rubber, to elaborate dolls with heads composed of china, parian, wax, or metal. There were also homemade baby dolls made of rag or wood (1992: 117). She notes how in Philadelphia a store advertised "drest dolls, naked ditto and Lilliputian dolls" for sale, which were carved out of wood and depicted a lady of fashion (ibid.: 81). Calvert observes that these elegant lady dolls dominated the market in store-bought dolls until 1850, when European factories began producing child dolls (and infant dolls) of porcelain and other materials. She states that the lady dolls' function was didactic: young girls were to be introduced to a female world composed of fashion, dressmaking, and entertaining. Playing with the dolls presumably gave young girls the opportunity to learn skills that they would practise in later life (ibid.: 117).

While there has been less research on the production history of eighteenth-century three-dimensional dolls, most researchers consider the wooden dolls to have been individually crafted by skilled carpenters as a sideline. However, Taylor speculates that the similar facial characteristics and features of construction among many eighteenth-century wooden dolls suggests that they were produced in workshops and then distributed by traveling "journeymen" (1990: 13). The nineteenth-century china-headed dolls were obviously mass-produced because their head shape and size and facial features appear identical. This brief history of the fashion doll as an artifact serves to establish a context for Barbie within female consumer society. While we have suggested a connection between dolls and girls as a pedagogical tool, in the next section we present how leading pedagogues of the day viewed girls and dolls.

The Cultural Climate: Equating Dolls, Girls, and Fashion

In the last web page for the art exhibition "The New Child" at <http://www.uampfa.berkeley.edu/exhibits/newchild/arent.html>, James Steward includes a section of problematic images of children entitled "When children aren't children." Some pictures are humorous in that they show children mocking adult behavior through imitation, while others show children in a sexual manner. One picture by Sir Joshua Reynolds, *The Infant Academy* (1782), shows children in both of these ways. The picture depicts four children, two older children who are presumably the stage managers of the scene, and two babies who are naked except for cleverly positioned draperies, their nakedness further hidden by artful posture. They are seated and posed in imitation of a portrait painter and his fashionable subject. While androgynous in shape and size, their respective postures, gestures, and facial expressions clearly indicate a male painter and a female nude model. The props are telling: while the boy holds a paintbrush and is apparently about to apply it to the canvas, the girl wears a large, ornate hat (more than one-third her size) fashionable for the period, made with sumptuous fabrics including lace, elaborately ruched and ruffled, and topped with a tall feather. Significantly, the hat – as well as the girl – has to be held up by one of the older children: it is as if she is a doll. Moreover, while the boy regards her directly in order to paint her, she, with her head partly bent down by the weight of the hat, has a coquettish smile and a gaze that appears to regard the viewer coyly. This gaze completes her transformation into the conventional position of the female nude. As outlined by John Berger, the young female offers up her femininity as the surveyed object. She does not look at the artist but out of the picture towards the (male) viewer – what Berger calls the "spectator-owner" (1972: 55–6).

The elision of girl, doll, and (sexual) object of beauty becomes disturbingly clear when the painting is considered within the context of eighteenth-century views of women and girls. By the time of Reynolds' picture, the equation by moralists of (middle-class) women with fashion and fashion consumption had become a much-derided stereotype (Brewer 1997: 75ff.). On the one hand, moralists considered the lady of fashion to be acting according to her nature "merely fulfilling the will of God" – but on the other hand, they questioned "whether a woman of fashion ought not to be declared a public enemy" (in Kowaleski-Wallace 1997: 7). What is new in Reynolds' period was the inclusion of girls as miniature women of fashion and their representation as fashion dolls. As will be seen below, Reynolds expresses in art ideas that are articulated in their definitive form by Jean-Jacques Rousseau, and subsequently became accepted as "true."

In Book 5 of *Emile* (1762) Rousseau describes what he considers to be the "essential" female and the male in terms of their sex roles. While acknowledging that "in everything that does not relate to sex the woman is as the man: they are alike in organs, needs and capacities," he maintains that "all we know with certainty is that the common features are due to the species and the differences to sex" (1963: 130–1). He isolates three sets of differences. First, in personal relations he conceives men and women to be polar opposites: men are active and strong, women passive and weak. Second, following from this, he deduces that man's role is to be masterful and dominating while woman's role is to please the man by making herself agreeable through the "strength" of her "charms." Third, he encourages uncertainty in sexual relations, whereby the woman controls the man's sexual domination through "guile" as to whether or not her "subjection" has been "willing" (Rousseau 1963: 131). Ultimately, Rousseau subjugates women due to their sex, limiting it to sexuality, proclaiming that while "the male is only a male at times; the female is a female all her life and can never forget her sex" (ibid.: 132).

Based on this binary opposition between women and men, his proposed educational program for girls is extremely limited, especially in contrast to the breadth of his program for boys. Because he conceives of women only within their familial role – dependent on men – he advocates an education totally "directed to their relations with men:" "to give [men] pleasure, to be useful to them, to win their love and esteem, to train them in their childhood, to care for them when they grow up, to give them counsel and consolation, to make life sweet and agreeable for them: these are the tasks of women in all times for which they should be trained from childhood" (Rousseau 1963: 135). Accordingly, in his early education for girls, he emphasizes two traits: love of finery, and a need to be noticed: "not content with being pretty they want notice taken of them." While boys do not care what others think of them, girls "can be controlled by telling them what people think of them" (ibid.).

When Rousseau discusses toys he does so in a fashion parallel to his previous discussion of sex roles, for while he does acknowledge similarities as well as differences, he emphasizes the latter:

> Children of the two sexes have many amusements in common, and that is right since it will be the same when they grow up. But they have also distinctive tastes. Boys like movement and noise: their toys are drums, tops and go-carts. Girls would rather have things that look well and serve for adornment: mirrors, jewels, dress materials and most of all, dolls. The doll is the special plaything of the sex. Here the girl's liking is plainly directed towards her lifework. For her the art of pleasing finds its physical expression in dress. That is all a child can acquire of this art.

Rousseau goes on to describe a fairly elaborate scenario of a young girl playing with her doll:

> Look at the little girl, busy with her doll all day long, changing its trappings, dressing and undressing it hundreds of times, always on the outlook for new ways of decoration whether good or bad. Her fingers are clumsy and her taste unformed, but already her bent is evident. "But," you may say, "she is dressing her doll, not herself." No doubt! The fact is that she sees her doll and not herself. For the time being she herself does not matter. She is absorbed in the doll and her coquetry is expressed through it. But the time will come when she will be her own doll (Rousseau 1963: 137).

This dictum seems to be illustrated literally in Reynolds' painting. Moreover, Reynolds exaggerates Rousseau's logic to create an even more disturbing scenario. By his selection of infants as subjects he collapses the timetable of girls' expected life pattern, becoming their own doll, into an even more compressed time-frame. As Calvert remarks in her gloss of Rousseau's attitude towards dolls and girls in the eighteenth and nineteenth centuries, the focus of society remained on the potential adult the girl would become, and the role dolls played as educational tools that groom girls to become (conventional) women interested in fashion, dressmaking, and entertaining (1992: 117).

The power and longevity of this reductionist logic that declared girls should grow up to become dolls was so widespread by the end of the eighteenth century that this life course was accepted as natural behavior. The comments directed against dolls and doll play by educationalist Maria Edgeworth demonstrate her appreciation of the difficulty of making such a criticism when it was accepted as a truth and had Rousseau as spokesman. In her treatise *Practical Education* which she co-authored with her father Richard Edgeworth, a former disciple of Rousseau, she did not single out girls and dolls for criticism. Rather, she included dolls and doll houses as examples of "fashionable toys" (1798: I: 5) that she disapproved of along with other luxuries such as rocking-horses, baa-lambs, squeaky pigs, cuckoos and all simple action toys. Indeed she opens her discussion, and the book, with a description of a scene of doll destruction amidst the wreckage of other toys, including "disjointed dolls" among "maimed horses, coaches and one-horse chairs without wheels, and a nameless wreck of gilded lumber" (ibid.: I: 1). Most unusually for her period she does not criticize the destruction, for she considers it to be a sensible reaction to "frail and useless" toys: "as long as a child has sense and courage to destroy the toys, there is no great harm done." Rather she criticizes the parents' attitude and influence in placing value on the toys for their price, or for viewing toys as miniature versions of what they themselves represent (ibid.: I: 3).

Edgeworth's general objection was that she considered all these toys to be of no use. For example, she considered the completed construction of a ready-made doll house to impede activity:

> an unfurnished baby-house might be a good toy, as it would employ little carpenters and seamstresses [*sic.*] to fit it up; but a completely furnished baby-house proves as tiresome to a child as a finished seat [country house] is to a young nobleman. After peeping, for in general only a peep can be had into each apartment, after being thoroughly satisfied that nothing is wanting, and that consequently there is nothing to be done, the young lady lays her doll upon the state bed, if the doll be not twice as large as the bed, and falls fast asleep in the midst of her felicity (1798: I: 6, cited in Armstrong 1996: 26).

The elision of girl and doll can be perhaps read as ironic, as will be seen in our subsequent discussion of Edgeworth and Rousseau.

In opposition to such elaborate toys, the kinds of toys that Edgeworth proposes are those which promote "trials of dexterity and activity" such as tops, kites, hoops, balls, battledores, shuttlecock, ninepins, and cup and ball (Edgeworth and Edgeworth 1798: I: 17). While she encourages carpenters' tools and models of machines for older children, for younger children she urges "card, paste board, substantial but not sharp pointed, scissors, wire, gum and wax" (ibid.: I: 23). She especially advocates giving children a pencil and plain paper at an early age, and remarks on the early dexterity of little girls cutting out "camels, and elephants with amazing trunks" (ibid.: I: 13).

When she does criticize dolls, she introduces them in the context of domestic toys which encourage an imitation of adult women's actions. Her discussion of the tea-table, indeed, recalls the Hogarth painting *The Children's Party* (1730) discussed at the beginning of this chapter. Significantly, Edgeworth's objection is not to the toy itself but to the facile social behavior the girl may be learning:

> A little girl, presiding at her baby tea-table, is pleased with the notion that she is like her mamma; and before she can have any idea of the real pleasures of conversation and society, she is confirmed in the persuasion, that tattling and visiting are some of the most enviable privileges of grown people (1798: I: 3).

When Edgeworth criticizes dolls she does so only hesitantly, aware that she is opposing Rousseau: "dolls, beside the prescriptive right of ancient usage, can boast of such an able champion in Rousseau, that it requires no common share of temerity" (ibid.).

She begins by examining what she considers to be the positive aspects of playing with dolls: that they may encourage a taste for "neatness in dress" and spark an interest in learning how to sew for oneself, loosening dependence on milliners. However, her criticism again concerns superficiality:

> a watchful eye should be kept upon the child to mark the first symptoms of a love of finery and fashion. It is a sensible remark of a late female writer [probably Wollstonecraft], that whilst young people work, the mind will follow the hands, the thoughts are occupied with trifles, and the industry is stimulated by vanity (ibid.: I: 4).

Wollstonecraft's language of disease regarding love of fashion that Edgeworth uses here is a revealing indicator of how "naturalized" the logic which equated the female with love of fashion had become by the end of the eighteenth century, so that even as astute a social critic as she would accept it as "truth."

Edgeworth's criticism about toys resonates with contemporary thought (Plumb 1982: 311). It is easy to compare her comments with those made by contemporary experts in childcare. For example, Dr. Spock's famous manual from the 1950s advised parents to purchase simple toys over ornate ones: "the less specific, [the toy] is, the more it stimulates the imagination," for Spock considered the wooden block to be the ideal toy, although he allowed boys to have trucks and girls domestic toys in order to help form conventional social roles (cited in Cross 1997: 161). Revealingly, despite the many revisions in later editions of his manual (for instance, the edition he co-wrote with

Michael Rothenberg in 1985 that is still widely available for sale), this view was maintained (376ff.). Most interesting is that one of the radical revisions concerns boys and dolls, for now doll play is distinguished as "parental" not "effeminate" (Spock and Rothenberg 1985: 47).

Edgeworth's observations about realistic detail hampering play options may also be seen as an interesting precursor to Roland Barthes' structuralist ideas about closed as opposed to open texts. Barthes considered these types of texts to be opposites, whereby closed or realistic texts (or toys) limit the readers' (or players') input, placing them in a passive position, enabling them only to consume meanings, while open texts (or toys) call upon the readers (or users) to actively construct or produce meaning (1970). These utilitarian and rationalist explanations recur throughout the criticism that is leveled today at Barbie, as well as other highly gendered popular culture toys such as G.I. Joe, Strawberry Shortcake dolls, etc. when they are opposed to so-called quality toys such as blocks, Lego, or other construction sets.

When the attitudes of Rousseau and Edgeworth are compared with contemporary beliefs, Rousseau becomes even more disturbing for present-day feminists and critical educationalists. Not only were his views acknowledged by his contemporaries as being reactionary (Misenheimer 1981: 48), but more than two hundred years later, they are still current as part of conventional or "commonsense" knowledge about girls, dolls and fashion. To realize the tenacity of this kind of thinking we have only to compare Rousseau's views with the predominance of pre-school beauty pageants, the ever-moving downward edge of sexualized fashion for girls, and the knowledge that market research has demonstrated: little girls like to comb and adorn long hair (W. Miller 1998: 215). By contrast, Edgeworth seems to prefigure the "progressive" attitude towards gender and childhood play that criticizes certain toys in terms of their design features. Her rationalist critique of dolls can also be seen to forecast the basis of the liberal feminist critique which is based on a concern that girls are rehearsing conventional (and trite) feminine behavior in their play, thereby reinforcing the status quo in gender relations. By casting both Barbie history and critical response into a longer time-frame, it may be seen that just as the 200-year-old dolls Edgeworth criticizes may be the precursors of Barbie, similarly her pedagogical ideas are forerunners of our own.

Material History: Early Fashion Dolls, Lady Dolls and Barbies as Material Artifacts

In this section, we provide a second type of alternative Barbie history by comparing early fashion dolls with Barbie dolls as material artifacts. While our focus is primarily on dolls as physical objects, we are also interested in how they are to be interpreted as social texts. For early dolls, we examine images of dolls in a wide range of books, scholarly publications, and books for collectors, as well as view dolls in museum collections. For Barbie dolls, we examine images from books for collectors and look at Barbies in private collections. Our decision to study images of dolls from books directed at collectors is due partly to expediency and partly in response to criticism of these books by Miriam Formanek-Brunell in *Made to Play House: Dolls and the Commercialization of American Girlhood 1830–1930*. She points out that while most research on dolls has been done by collectors, she dismisses their work because they "isolate cultural artifacts from the larger context of inventors' creativity, producers' mentalities, workers' experience, parents' consumer behavior and children's play" (1993: 1). We agree with some of her criticisms on work done by, and for, collectors, but as a methodological approach we are interested in the value of surveying dolls both as isolated objects and in social contexts. We derive our categories of analysis from the categories the curators and auction-house experts themselves use and so focus on the physical aspects such as the shape, dimensions, and material composition of the unclothed doll and the clothed doll. Our purpose for studying in minute detail these examples of dolls from three different centuries is to isolate features of similarity and difference in the evolution of the fashion doll.

One recent and widely available collectors' book is *The Ultimate Doll Book* by Caroline Goodfellow (1993). Three types of fashion dolls and lady dolls are presented in three sets of double-page layouts: early English wooden dolls from the 1680s to 1820s; fashionable French lady dolls from the 1860s to 1890; and a section entitled "The changing face of Barbie" from 1959 to 1993. The same conventions for representation are utilized in each set of diagrams for the unclothed as well as the clothed figures, with descriptive notes about height, dimensions, composition and so on. The only difference in presentation occurs with the early doll, shown with front and back views. When we compare the three sets of pages – although the figures and dolls are of different sizes – the first thing that strikes the eye is the shapeliness of the four unclothed dolls in terms of the degree of anatomical correctness. The dolls are distinguished by the degree of attention paid to facial detail and to the extremities of hands and feet.

What is most surprising about the photographs of the unclothed dolls is the similarity between the 1700 to 1720 model and the Barbie doll in terms of the slender yet shapely womanly body (Figure 6.1). At the same time, the size of the illustrations is somewhat misleading, for the 1700s doll is 19 inches high, while the Barbie is only 12 inches high. The wooden doll has a sculpted head, a neck and a torso, and is jointed at the hips and knees. The doll is very curved, with voluptuous and pointed breasts, narrow waist, wide hips, and a lower torso shaped at the back to suggest buttocks (Goodfellow 1993: 13). The upper legs have little definition, while the lower legs have shapely calves and ankles. While the hands are carefully detailed to include separate fingers, the feet are carved to enable the doll to stand flat-footed, but they do not have separate toes – the toes are all joined together. The upper arms are composed of linen, while the lower arm is of wood (ibid.). The face bears a mild expression: the bulbous brown-colored glass eyes stare directly ahead,

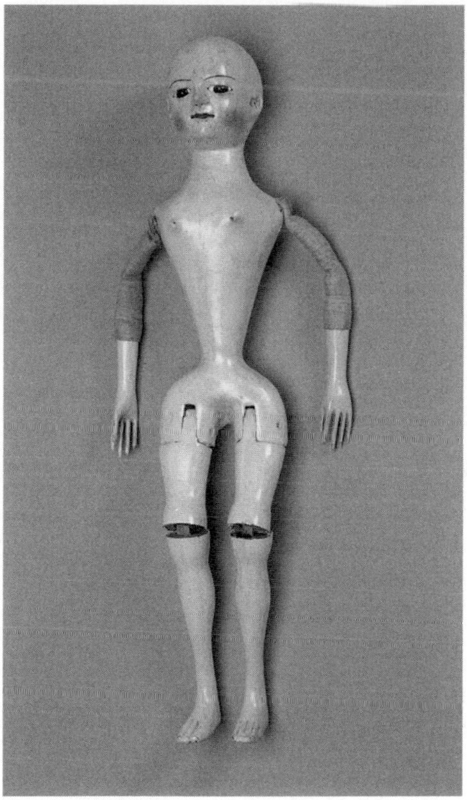

Figure 6.1 Early 1700s doll, Britain (reprinted with the permission of the Victoria and Albert picture library).

while the nose, mouth, and ears are all defined. The lips are red, the cheeks and breast tinged with pink: otherwise the wood is a pale beige. The neck is substantially wider than the waist, the shoulders are narrow in comparison to the hips, and the doll is bald.[5]

In comparison to the 1700s doll – in terms of shape – the unclothed Barbie *circa* 1990 has a longer and thinner neck, broader shoulders, a bigger bust and waist, and narrower hips than the early doll. While the Barbie legs appear proportionally longer, with better definition of the upper leg, the lower leg, ankle, and foot have less definition than the 1700s doll. The upper torso of the Barbie is jointed at the arms and waist, while the rigid legs are jointed only at the hips. The stance places the doll on her toes. The head has large quantities of pale blonde hair, the face has wide turquoise and black eyes staring directly ahead, with red lips and white teeth fixed in a wide smile. The fingers are partly separated with prominent thumbs. The color of the molded vinyl and plastic is a medium beige.

In contrast to both of these slim dolls, the *circa* 1875 dolls, of mixed composition with a bisque head, and stuffed kid arms, torso, and legs, are much broader. The *circa* 1875 doll is 13 inches high, has a curvaceous torso, with wide shoulders, undefined but large bust, comparatively narrow lower torso and waist (although bigger than that of the other two dolls), wide hips and relatively short, stocky legs. The feet appear small but flat. The most attention to detail occurs on the painted china face and head, topped with a long, lavishly dressed strawberry blonde wig. The bisque face is a pale beige color, with full cheeks, inset brown eyes (unusual for the period, since most dolls then had blue eyes) staring straight ahead. The pink mouth is very small in comparison to the large eyes, and the swivel head has a short neck; the full features suggest a young woman (Goodfellow 1993: 54).

According to Goodfellow (1993), the function of each of these three types of doll is that of a fashion mannequin. The physical and anatomical shape of the dolls and the details of construction suggest that their function was to display the respective features of the period fashions. Indeed, doll historians reiterate that early dolls may be seen as microcosmic representations of societal expectations regarding beauty and fashion. For instance, Kerry Taylor, in another book intended for a collectors' market, *The Letts Guide to Collecting Dolls*, contrasts the eighteenth-century wooden doll with its aristocratic severe face, black enameled eyes, long neck, straight, slender torso, and elongated limbs, with the late nineteenth-century doll and its "peaches-and cream" complexion, curly blonde hair, and generous bodily curves. She considers the contrast to indicate how the idea of beauty changes from age to age and what tastes prevail – thin or plump, fair or dark hair, pale or tanned skin, brown or blue eyes, and so on. She considers dolls to possess a kind of truthfulness, and to be three-dimensional representations of social history that exceed the two-dimensional representations of the art medium (1990: 7–8). If we compare her interpretation of the formal features of eighteenth- and nineteenth-century dolls with the extrapolations which present-day commentators make from Barbie's shape to desired images of womanhood, we can perhaps begin to consider Barbie in the context of such a historical "landscape" of fashion artifacts. Then we can usefully reduce Barbie to an object instead of seeing her as a "metasymbol" in a similar way to what Daniel Miller (1998) does in his study of Coca-Cola as an artifact.

In our paragraph on the Barbie doll above, we used only a 1990s doll, not a 1959 doll as our example. But we do need to mention here that Barbie is not a single or unified object, for there have been some changes in the facial construction of Barbie dolls over the years, particularly regarding eye definitions and makeup. Goodfellow highlights this aspect by entitling the relevant section "The changing face" of Barbie. Furthermore, there have been some slight modifications to the torso of Barbie as well, for in 1998 there appeared one line of Barbie dolls with a slightly wider waist and slightly smaller bust (Portanier 1998). These dolls, however, are provided as another "specialized" Barbie line, a gesture in production strategy that recalls "specialized" dolls aimed at other specific markets, such as an African-American Barbie, East Indian Barbie, a Native American Barbie, or other ethnic lines. These are supplements to the main Barbie products, not substitutes. Our interest, however, remains focused on the standard Barbie, and on approaching Barbie history through an analysis of her changing gaze and facial expression, not her changing shape. We compare the illustrations Goodfellow provides of three dolls: 1962 Barbie, 1990 Barbie and the German prototype Lilli supplemented by images of the 1959 doll on the cover of Mattel's *Barbie* magazines issued in 1994. Our contention is that notwithstanding the body shape of the respective dolls, what may be disturbing to Barbie critics is that accepted ideas of childhood innocence are flouted by the facial expressions of early Barbie dolls, for they approximate that of the sex-toy Lilli. Subsequent changes to her eyes have altered the gaze significantly, and changes to the mouth have been in accordance with the changes to the eyes. We speculate that Mattel's changes to facial expressions, especially around the eyes and mouth, may be based on their awareness of this disturbing similarity to Lilli![6]

The following are sets of descriptions of the facial features of the Lilli doll, early Barbies, and a more recent 1991 Barbie, based on our observations and Goodfellow's annotations:

1 *Lilli doll*: The eyes do not have a direct gaze; the doll seems to look out of the corner of her eyes – angled – at an onlooker. The mouth, painted deep red, reminds one of the stereotypical "rosebud" mouth. Goodfellow describes the doll as having "flirtatious, side-glancing eyes, with molded eyelashes," and a "pert mouth" (1993: 117).
2 *1959 Barbie doll*: The eyes again do not have a direct gaze, but are angled in the opposite direction to those of Lilli. The doll appears to look out of the corners of her eyes at an onlooker. The mouth is closed, and is adorned with bright red lipstick. There may be a hint of a "Mona Lisa," knowing smile. Goodfellow describes the smile of the 1962 Barbie as having "pouting red lips drawn into a slight smile" (1993: 117).
3 *1991 Barbie doll*: The eyes are wide-staring, and look directly at a viewer. The mouth has thin lips, painted bright pink, with white teeth, held in a closed mouth but with a wide smile. Goodfellow describes the "full-of-life" Barbie as having "painted eyes look[ing] straight ahead" and an: "open/closed slightly thin-lipped mouth [which] is fixed in a broad smile" (1993: 117).

Earlier, we employed some of the ideas from John Berger's (1972) work in our discussion of Reynolds' painting *The Infant Academy* (1782). In this painting the infant girl appears to occupy the position of a nude not only through her lack of attire but also in her invitation of the male gaze, demonstrated by her sidelong, coy glance and smile.[7] The Lilli doll could be seen as similarly offering herself up for display. Likewise the early Barbie dolls are similar in terms of their gaze, for it seems to be one of ennui, suggesting a worldly young woman. Indeed, her gaze is reminiscent of the indirect, angled gazes of some of the famous nude paintings described by Berger, such as *Venus of Urbino* by Titian (1487–1576), or *Nell Gwynne* by Lely (1618–80) (1972: 63, 52). Berger argues that these paintings present the women as sexualized objects, offering themselves up to display in response to their owners' feelings or demands (ibid.: 52–5). If we expand our description of the facial expression of the 1959 doll with its pensive expression, and closed, slightly smiling mouth, indeed it eerily does recall the expression in the painting Berger uses to open his chapter. Called the *Reclining Bacchanate* by Trutat (1824–48), the painting depicts a nude young women lying full-length on a leopard skin, gazing out resignedly at the onlooker. Unobserved by her, a man's head looms in the window, face turned towards her (ibid.: 45). We argue that the first Barbies (clothed or unclothed) recall images of these female nudes used as sexual, potentially available objects in classic paintings and pornography. By this logic then, the girl who played with an early Barbie doll was placed, however unknowingly, in an invidious double bind. By the very act of looking at the doll, she is placed in the male voyeur's position; she becomes the gendered male, for she assumes automatically the position of what Berger calls the "spectator-owner" (1972: 55–6). There is also the fact that the doll, in a sense, represents the girl. This recalls Rousseau's observations as well as the suggestiveness of the Reynolds' painting, *The Infant Academy*.

Another painting by a contemporary of Reynolds, Thomas Lawrence, illustrates the point Rousseau makes about girls as dolls, although in a different way. While this is not a sexualized painting, playing on gender relations, the sketch nonetheless is disturbing when seen in the context of his *oeuvre* of child paintings. It shows a girl and a fashionably dressed woman doll sitting in bed facing one another as equals. Both, similarly dressed, about the same size, and seated – steadily regarding each other – in a similar upright position, are similarly dressed and regard each other steadily. According to Antonia Fraser who includes the sketch in her *History of Toys*, it is obvious that the doll is a play doll, not a fashion doll; this is based on the implications of its "stilted appearance" and "weird beauty" (1966: 107). Fraser claims that the artist has captured the relationship between girl and doll. Yet the vacuity of the doll's expression also recalls Edgeworth's critique of doll play where she expresses her concerns that girls may be learning only how to perform a social round of vapidity by imitating their mothers' actions. Again the girl is a "living" doll (ibid.: illus. #125).

The fashionable dolls from three centuries, we maintain, may all be said to have emphasized period ideals of womanly proportions, with details in facial construction providing what individual emphasis there is. By contrast, the survey of clothed dolls reveals that the overwhelming abundance of fashion detail ensures that each doll appears distinctive and different. Taylor (1990) believes that dolls encapsulate the style of a period better than any other medium, and this point is reinforced by numerous doll historians (e.g. Fritzsch and Bachmann 1966). Indeed, when one looks at and touches the fabrics of the costumes of numerous dolls from different periods, one can see a different type of "landscape" beginning to emerge. Paradoxically, the specific doll with a certain body shape becomes almost invisible and is seen only as part of the range of dolls, for the focus is on the elaborate costuming and the details of accessories that create a panorama of changing fashion with different colors, fabrics, and textures, and not on the doll itself as a specific example of this range.

Indeed, for the unqualified person, it is almost impossible to ascertain which dolls are fashion dolls or mannequins and which are play dolls. For example, the fashion dolls and lady dolls in the McCord Museum from 1820 onwards demonstrate equally good construction in relation to overall proportioning, facial features, and coloring. In addition, the dresses are all elaborate and fashionable. Experts, however, such as the curator at the McCord Museum, will talk about certain details being significant indicators of the type of doll, such as the presence or absence of pierced ears, earrings, the degree of elaboration of hairdo, detail of undergarments, and so on (Conrad Graham, personal communication, June 1 1999). Similarly, doll historians such as Constance Eileen King talk about key physical features of dolls such as size, density of eyes, and the overall quality of construction (1977) as indicative of the type of doll. Only an expert eye, it seems, can determine intended use.

From our point of view, these early fashion dolls and lady dolls, regardless of their intended use, may be seen to be reinforcing the cultural elision among girls, dolls, women, and fashion, as discussed above, for both kinds of dolls are representations of fashionable women. This period landscape may be compared with a present-day landscape of fashion dolls which includes the Sindy, introduced in the U.K. in 1962 but now produced by Hasbro (Goodfellow 1993: 120), and more topical dolls that come and go, such as Beverly Hills 90210 dolls or Spice Girls dolls. Barbie, however, seems to dominate the market, a fact that is highlighted further if we consider the space devoted to Barbie in department stores. Mattel's statistics on the number of Barbies sold, and owned by American girls are also quite telling. Moreover, in terms of the popular imagination, Barbie appears to have attained category status; by this we mean that she is representative of that process by which, for example, a single product name like Kleenex is understood to refer to a generic type of product (paper tissue), or Hoover to vacuum cleaners, or "Coke" to a certain type of carbonated soft-drink. A "Barbie" nowadays is a fashion doll.

Elsewhere, we have presented the notion of Barbie as a "cumulative cultural text" (Mitchell and Reid-Walsh 1995): the doll, tie-in products, including textual forms such as magazines, comics, and trading cards, as well as artifacts such as clothes, lunch boxes, watches, and so on are all meant to be read inclusively as part of the text of Barbie. Looking at Barbie as a material artifact, we see a similar cumulative process at work. The physical artifact of the Barbie doll is not fixed, as we have seen in the above discussion of changing face and form. Similarly, the hundreds of combinations of wardrobe create a landscape of Western women's fashion from the late 1950s onwards, and the inclusive exploration of this landscape must, we think, include various types of occupation suggested by the clothes and accessories, along with an examination of the changing styles. For example, in different decades Barbie has worn a gymnastics leotard, ballet tutu, airline stewardess uniform, white lab coat with stethoscope, and so on. The attention to detail emphasizes diversity over homogeneity in one extended product. Indeed, in the 1950s and 1960s Barbie was marketed according to a segmentation strategy that emphasized her clothes, not the doll. The strategy, similar to that of selling one razor to ensure the sale of many blades, was not to encourage the purchase of numerous dolls (which were identical) but numerous different costumes and accessories (W. Miller 1998: 214–15). Barbie was intended to be a "hook" to encourage the buying of the clothes. This aspect is reinforced in statements, made by Ruth Handler, that the early Barbies were intended to be stylized representations of young womanhood, and not intended to be differentiated and distinct (Cross 1997: 174). It was only in the 1980s that a range of Barbies was introduced with different themes and activities associated with them (W. Miller 1998), and this trend has continued to the present day.

Toy historians observe that in early periods children were seen to be miniature adults, and were dressed and treated accordingly. As we have discussed, the dolls of these periods were dressed according to the latest fashions, so the history of the doll presents at the same time a history of costume (Fritzsch and Bachman: 1966). We extrapolate from this that perhaps a fashion doll of a certain period could be considered as a microcosm of societal expectations regarding children generally. For instance, if Western doll history is considered in terms of the life cycle of human representations (Debouzy 1996: 139), dolls depicting adult women dominated during the eighteenth century and early nineteenth century. Infant dolls became popular only after 1851 when they were displayed at the Crystal Palace Exhibition (St. George 1948: 169), while fashionable lady dolls lost favor with children after the 1890s (Conrad Graham, personal communication, June 1, 1999). This was during the height of the Victorian era when the ideals of (middle-class) childhood – as a state of idealized purity deserving of a separate world – reached the peak of expression (Cox 1996; Conrad Graham, personal communication, June 1 1999).

In the twentieth century prior to Barbie, infant and child dolls seem to have dominated the market (Formanek-Brunell 1993). Now dolls of every age type proliferate in department stores and mass toy-store aisles, although, if the critics are to be believed, Barbie seems to dominate over all others. If this is valid – and for our purposes the perception that the fashion doll Barbie dominates is just as important as any statistics which may prove or disprove this – we are interested in what this dominance of Barbie suggests about our era. On the one hand, the dominance of women's and sexualized fashions associated with young girls may be read in a (Postman 1982) manner as a major crisis indicating the "disappearance" of childhood. On the other hand, if this change is read against a longer time-frame, not only as a rupture with, or movement away from, Victorian ideals, but as a reapplication and modification of earlier, pre-Victorian ideals, perhaps these changes may be considered in a different manner. For example, Karin Calvert interprets present-day children's fashion –

which is often a miniature reproduction of adult styles – as a kind of return to Georgian and colonial attitudes of the child as (necessarily) a small adult. She considers the present climate to require an early sophistication of attitudes on the part of the child as necessary for survival in a world where "innocence" has become "vulnerability" and the "uninformed child is the child at risk" (1992: 153). Applying Calvert's logic to "Barbie fashion," we can see a cultural shift away from Victorian notions of the isolated, innocent child to a version of childhood that once again sees the sophisticated child entering the adult community at an earlier age; a process which has occurred over the past fifty years. That the age of the ideal child seems to be the stage of an adolescent or young adult is reflective of our youth-obsessed society, but is also noted by Calvert as having occurred with men's fashion during the French and American Revolutionary period of the late eighteenth century (1992: 151).

By contrast with men, the age of the ideal woman has always located her in relation to being nubile – whatever is considered socially appropriately nubile at any period. To present-day observers, this age of nubility in fashion is getting younger and younger, extending even to pre-school age. At the same time, it is somewhat chastening to remember that in seventeenth- and eighteenth-century England the legal age for entering into marriage contracts was twelve years for girls and fourteen years for boys. For example, conduct-book writer Henry Swinburne in his "Treatise of Spousals" (1686) uses analogies to moistness in fruits to substantiate his understanding of differential age of puberty in girls and boys:

> Female Bodies are more tender and moister than the Male: and so Mens Bodies being harder and drier, they are more slow in ripening; and Women's Bodies, because they are softer and moister, are more quickly ripe; like as it is to be seen in Plants and fruits, whereof that which is more soft and moist is sooner ripe, than that which is hard and dry (cited in Vallone 1995: 58–9).

While this reasoning is bizarre to the minds of modern readers, in some ways, the premise of girls' bodies as fruit "ripening" earlier than boys' seems to be enacted in generic popular culture today (not just in those texts targeting children) such as fashion shows, beauty pageants, fashion and beauty ads, and music videos. The nubile early Barbies modeled on the Lilli doll sex-toys are an excellent example of this.

Play Values: The Use and Misuse of Fashion Dolls, Lady Dolls and Barbie Dolls

In this section we provide a third type of alternative Barbie history. We shift our perspective away from consideration of the physical characteristics of early fashion dolls/lady dolls and Barbie dolls, to an examination of ethnographic evidence that reveals how dolls in different periods achieve meaning through play use. We notice a correspondence between the multiple functions of dolls and their contribution to providing multiple meanings to the players. Indeed, in her Introduction, Calvert (1992) makes this point, and cautions readers about the difficulty of working with early dolls. Since dolls' multiple functions and meanings differ according to particular societies at particular times, interpretation becomes difficult. To illustrate her statement, she lists the various uses for dolls, including religious image, magical fetish, fashion mannequin, effigy, educational tool, collectible, as well as *objet d'art* (1992: 6). Calvert's reservation about the interpretation of dolls may be compared with Rand's (1995) caution about the danger of inscribing a unitary meaning onto Barbie dolls. Rand states:

> we need to be very humble about our own ability to inscribe meaning in objects, to discern the meanings that others attribute to them, or to transfer conclusions about resistance, subversion, and hegemony from person to person, object to object, context to context (1995: 195).

As Daniel Miller (1998) wryly observes about working with material culture, the objects are mute, so it is important to obtain ethnographic information about intended use and actual use. Acquiring ethnographic information, however, is always more difficult when studying old – especially commonplace objects – for there is less extant documentary evidence. Although we cannot interview doll players of 200 years ago, there are occasional references to doll play in women's memoirs, journals, and letters, as well as in fiction. The earlier, eighteenth-century references tend to be brief and to the point. For instance, Jane Thackery, a daughter of a prosperous doctor in England, stated that "My playthings were few, a doll that I fondly loved, and who was undressed every night and put into her cradle, and two magnetic fishes with a fishing rod and a green and white skipping rope." Children's writer Mrs. Sherwood (1775–1851) recalls that as a girl she owned a fashionable lady doll with "a paper hoop and hair of real flax" (cited in Fraser 1966: 75). There are also accounts of women "playing" with fashionable dolls, for doll dressing was considered a craft or activity suitable for ladies and their daughters. Notably, the bluestocking Mrs. Delany (1700–88) recorded a tongue-in-cheek comparison between fashionable dolls and women:

> Miss Dolly Mode's box just packed up to go to the carrier next Friday containing imprimis: a lady à la mode in accoutrements but in every other respect tout au contraire, for she can neither rouge nor giggle nor run away, she is nailed down to her good behavior (cited in King 1977: 86).

Notwithstanding the ironic tone, Mrs. Delany was exacting with respect to the high quality of dolls: when a doll was dropped and her nose broken,

Mrs Delany remarked that it would "be some time before I get another doll that will do" (cited in King 1977: 86 and 93). By the late eighteenth century, since the doll had become accepted as being a girl's toy (indeed as an emblem of the girl and woman thanks, in part, to Rousseau), it could be criticized as such. Accordingly, there are occasional fictional references to dolls as objects signaling conventional female behavior, as Jane Austen provides in *Northanger Abbey* (1818), the first draft of which was written in the 1790s. When describing the early childhood of her heroine Catherine Morland who was a tomboy, Austen provides a list of gendered play activities: "She was fond of all boys' plays, and greatly preferred cricket not merely to dolls, but to the more heroic enjoyments of infancy, nursing a dormouse, feeding a canary-bird, or watering a rose-bush" (1948: 13).

References to doll play become more frequent in nineteenth-century women's autobiographical and fictional accounts. Since they also tend to be more extensive, the accounts, moreover, reveal individual activities and complex attitudes on the part of the girls themselves regarding doll play. For example, Jackson, in her *Toys of Other Days*, considers that Jane Carlyle's (1801–66) doll play as a child may prefigure her adult personality:

> She [Jane] had always loved it, but when she got into the first book of Virgil, she thought it a shame to care for it any longer, and, having judged the victim, decided she must die, and die as became the doll of a young lady who read Virgil. With some lead pencils, her four-post bed, her dresses, which were many, a few sticks of cinnamon and a nutmeg to provide the spices for the funeral pile, she poured over it some perfume, then seating the doll on the four-post-bed, she recited the last speech of Dido on behalf of the doll, stabbed it with a penknife, and thus made it perish nobly.
>
> The sequel to this story partakes of the nature of an anti-climax, for the grave student of Virgil had over-rated her callousness, and when the hungry flames licked up the bran stuffing of the second Dido, she would have rescued her doll, and being unable to do so, screamed and danced with anguish of mind, and was presently forcibly carried into the house lest she should disturb the neighbours (cited in Jackson 1908: 25–7).

From this account, it is interesting to note how the dolls appear to inspire complex, contradictory emotions of love and hate, and complex reactions which include both preservation and destruction in the child. Jane Carlyle's dolls have multiple functions, all resulting from how they are played with. She first turns the dolls into victims in a tragedy she is "directing," but then drops her dispassionate role to return to being the passionate girl doll-owner who tries to rescue her possession.

Complex and contradictory attitudes are also noted in occasional later nineteenth-century fictional accounts. For example, in George Eliot's *Mill on the Floss* (1860), Eliot characterizes the heroine as a young girl partly through her treatment of her two dolls. Maggie has a wax doll which she either kisses or neglects. The doll may be the repository of the "occasional fit of fondness" whereby Maggie "neglect[s] its toilette, but lavishes[es] so many warm kisses on it that the waxen cheeks had a wasted unhealthy appearance" (1991, ch. 3: 24). At times, she may forget its presence: she is described as "hold[ing] her doll topsyturvy and crush[ing] its nose against the wood of the chair" (ibid.: 29). However, there is a secret doll which Maggie keeps in her attic hideaway. The doll, in serving as a vehicle through which Maggie has been able to express her own anguish at the hardships of her life, has been reduced to a trunk.

> This was the trunk of a large wooden doll, which once stared with the roundest of eyes above the reddest of cheeks; but was now entirely defaced by a long career of vicarious suffering. Three nails driven into the head commemorated as many crises in Maggie's nine years of earthly struggle . . . if she drove many nails in, she would not be so well able to fancy that the head was hurt when she knocked it against the wall, nor to comfort it and make believe to poultice it when her fury was abated. . . . Since then she had driven no more nails in, but had soothed herself by alternately grinding and beating the wooden head against the rough brick of the great chimneys that made two square pillars supporting the roof (ibid., ch 4: 34).

The contradictory and violent ways in which Maggie treats her first doll may be seen to demonstrate her ambivalence towards it, and by extension herself and female roles. With the second doll, the mutilation may also be interpreted as expressing a complex identification with it.

These autobiographical and fictional descriptions referring to, or describing, doll "play" that range from the decorous to the subversive to the violent, encompass what Bill Brown in "How to do things with things" calls "use value" and "misuse value," or "irregular reobjectification (1998: 954). These lived descriptions of play stand apart from, and indeed in opposition to, the prescriptive literature that emerged during the nineteenth century. Early in the century, the writers followed the lead of educationalists such as Maria Edgeworth who advocated a utilitarian approach towards toys. Girls were encouraged to make dolls and sew dolls' clothes as part of their training in household economy. Later in the century, the doll was considered to be an appropriate repository of affection, but doll play was also presumed to teach girls to enact traditionally feminine rituals such as tea-parties, social visiting, and funeral attendance in a correct fashion (Formanek-Brunell 1993). These adult literary and autobiographical references are also distinct from what is known as "Doll-house fiction" and which emerged as a subgenre of children's literature during the same period (Formanek-Brunell 1993; Armstrong 1996). These stories tend to be didactic in nature, describing how girls should play with dolls according to the mores of the period. Accordingly, while the earlier stories emphasize the development of skills and morals, the later stories focus on interpersonal relationships. In the late 1890s when baby dolls dominated, the stories emphasized maternal attitudes and skills (Formanek-Brunell 1993).

Calvert (1992), Formanek-Brunell (1993) and Armstrong (1996) all appear to agree that girls played with (fashionable) dolls in socially prescribed ways, in unconventional ways, and that at other times they neglected dolls for more active toys. Both Calvert and Formanek-Brunell note that contrary to present-day proscriptions against boys playing with female dolls, during the mid-nineteenth century young American middle-class boys as well as girls played with fashionable lady dolls. Formanek-Brunell further observes that Victorian boys and girls were as likely to play with dolls according to gender norms as well as in attempting to transgress such norms. Calvert uses as her sources photographs of boys with fashionable lady dolls *circa* the 1860s, autobiographical memoirs from the 1860s, and doll fiction from periodicals such as *Babyland* and *Nursery* in the 1880s. She cites the memoirs of E. H. Southern who described his toys of the 1860s to include "many kinds of dolls of both sexes and both black and white, waxen and wooden." Southern is also cited as having a meeting with a poor boy who carried a "dilapidated doll on his lap" (cited in Calvert 1992: 116–17, n. 56). Formenek-Brunell cites an instance of how girls, unlike the female characters in doll stories, were not always attached to their dolls. "When my brother proved my doll had no brains by slicing off her head, I felt I had been deluded; I watched him with stoicism and took no more interest in dolls" (1993: 30–1).

Formanek-Brunell seems primarily interested in what feminist researchers consider subversive or resisting play, for she provides only examples where girls would reject the conventionally beautiful lady doll. For instance, she cites Lucy Larcom in her *New England Girlhood* where she states that she rejected the "London doll that lay in waxen state in an upper drawer at home because she was a "fine lady [that] did not wish to be played with but only to be looked at and admired" (1986: 29, cited in Formenek-Brunell 1993: 14). In the same vein, she cites a girls' advice manual called *The American Girl's Book or Occupations for Play Hours* by Eliza Leslie which asserted that children preferred cloth dolls over the "handsomest wax doll that can be purchased" (1831: 287–8, cited in Formenek-Brunell 1993: 14, n. 12.) Formanek-Brunell also provides examples where Victorian girls would take conventional play patterns such as undertaking doll tea-parties, making afternoon visits, or staging a doll funeral, and turn them into carnivalesque scenes where the code of femininity was turned inside out. She provides examples where girls turned sedate doll parties into "indoor coastings" by sliding down the stairs sitting on tea-trays, or instances where girls staged doll funerals as a way to assuage hostile fantasies. For instance, she quotes George Eliot as stating that she herself "only broke those [dolls] . . . that could not stand the test of being undressed, or that proclaimed their unfleshy substance by falling and breaking their noses" (cited in Formanek-Brunell 1993: 32, n. 45, n. 32).[8]

By contrast, Frances Armstrong (1996) in her article "The doll house as ludic space 1690–1920" provides a carefully nuanced interpretation of early (doll-house) doll play that provides insights into how to avoid interpreting accounts of doll play in terms of binary reversals, whereby a feminist reading becomes simply a revaluation or inversion of conventional evaluations. Her comments also show an interest in what would have been considered conventional play patterns as well as unconventional ones. She begins by offering a sobering proviso about the difficulties of examining and interpreting early children's material culture: "the survivors are often the failures, playthings that were not enjoyed to the point of extinction" (1996: 26). In other words, the "life cycle" of a successful toy probably ends in its complete consumption (destruction) through heavy use. In the section entitled "A space under girls' control," she observes that the most common activity appeared to be acting out daily domestic routines, and that this seems to be consistent in children across time and place. For instance, she quotes an account describing a young French duchess at play in 1630: "The dolls were undressed and put to bed every evening; they were dressed again the next day; they were made to eat; they were made to take their medicine. One day she wished to make them bathe, and had the great sorrow of being forbidden" (Tallemant des Reaux, cited in Armstrong 1996: 37). Armstrong juxtaposes this early account with one from the turn of the twentieth century where children's author Alice Corkan reminisces that in her doll-house events "were the faithful mirror of what happened in ours" (1900, cited in Armstrong 1996: 37). Yet, Armstrong does not see these play patterns as evidence of mindless behaviors: she states that "rather than boring repetition, such exact mirroring could be a kind of journal keeping and could also challenge one's miniaturizing skills."

She also describes other play patterns, especially at doll tea-parties, when decorum would lapse, and the girls would engage in socially subversive antics, citing examples similar to those of Formanek-Brunell (Armstrong 1996: 37, 39). While most of her examples involve wealthy children with elaborate doll-houses, she notes as well that in the eighteenth century the term "baby house" also referred to simple and improvised arrangements of furniture with no enclosing walls. To illustrate, she cites the book *Juvenile Correspondence* (1783) by Eleanor Fenn where the six-year old protagonist says, "I have set my bureau on a window-seat – and that is our baby-house" (ibid.: 38). Armstrong is interested in the possibilities of less affluent and lower-class children engaging in doll-house play. Her presentation of a wide range of doll play, encompassing the conventional and unconventional, shows how ideas of use and misuse value can be understood in complex ways.

Armstrong presents two ideas that are useful in comparing early doll play to present-day doll and Barbie play: she suggests that a doll-house could be seen as a kind of stage where the action is captured at a particular moment, and that the small scale of the doll-house dolls creates emotional distance between the child and doll, not only reducing the degree of identification the child may feel towards the doll but increasing the sense of control. Armstrong notes that staging parties provided a situation where the ability to stage dramas could be connected to achieving a sense of control. While real-life parties may have been stressful to children, doll parties were a "delight," especially in the staging of lapses of decorum (1996: 38–9). Regarding the size differential between child and doll, this was an aspect that could be disregarded at will. Moreover, since most girls also owned large dolls, she speculates that whereas large dolls may be considered a girl's "friend," doll-house dolls are "part of a social entity and are made to interact with one another rather than with a girl. They are kept, literally, at arms' length" (ibid.: 39, 43). Armstrong suggests a therapeutic aspect to the control offered to children by playing with scaled toys, stating that present-day therapists often use dolls and doll-house play for child clients as a way to elicit hidden concerns, citing the work of Dorothy and Jerome Singer (ibid.. 41, n. 15).

Armstrong's points about doll-house play being a kind of drama where the doll-house is the stage, and how there seems to be an emotional distancing when playing with certain smaller dolls, are re-articulated in relation to Barbie dolls in one recent ethnographic study of doll play. Dorothy Washburn's study "Getting ready: doll play and real life in American culture 1900–1980" is a large-scale project for which she interviewed ninety-five women, of which thirty-eight were girls and twenty-seven were mothers. All the subjects are former doll players or are still playing with dolls. Her aims are to educate curators and scholars of material culture about how the participants or "anthropological insiders" understand the definition of a doll, Barbie, and doll play (1997: 107). She is particularly interested in the differences or discrepancies between received notions of doll play and what the players or users report.

Washburn provides direct quotations only from women in her study, not girls: accordingly her generalizations about doll play and Barbie play appear to be based mostly on retrospective accounts, although she provides observations and interpretations based on the girls' actions and speech. She interprets her respondents' comments to indicate that Barbies are considered as a distinct category separate from other kinds of dolls, and indeed are often not considered to be dolls at all. Dolls tend to be imaginary "friends" with feelings, possessing soft bodies, and realistic facial and bodily proportions that can be categorized by a single kind of interaction: baby dolls that are mothered, little-girl dolls that are considered to be peers, and display dolls that are admired. By contrast, Barbies that cannot be "cuddled" because they are too small and made of hard plastic are considered differently. Washburn considers Barbies to have a "multivocalic" status: they appeal to fantasy play, are neither baby nor little-girl dolls but older, and, unlike display dolls, possess numerous changes of dress and can assume multiple roles (1997: 118–24).

To the question "Are Barbies dolls?" Washburn provides the following answers from three women respondents, their lives encompassing three decades of Barbie play:

> No, Barbies are different than baby dolls . . . it's just a different type of doll that you play with differently. Barbies are grown-up dolls, and you can make them be doctors and lawyers. The other dolls were my children. I felt very close to my baby dolls (b. 1957).

> I don't really think we considered Barbie to be a specific age; she could take on the role of mother, daughter, baby. It just didn't seem like we ever set one specific age for Barbie whereas other dolls, if they looked a certain age, they were that age. Baby Victoria looked like a baby, so that's how we would treat her. But Barbie was whatever age fit into the story we happened to be doing . . . because she had a camper and beach house and everything like that. She was just a fun doll. We could make her whatever we wanted to make her (b. 1966).

> Yes, it's a doll but I don't think I saw it as that. I saw it as a Barbie. I think a doll is something larger that you could cuddle (b. 1972).

To the question, "Why do you find Barbies appealing?" Washburn continues the comments of the respondent born in 1966: "Because Barbies had all those great clothes, pets, and neat houses. And they were older so when we got around seven or so Barbie was older and that's the way we wanted to be when we grew up" (1997: 124–6).

Washburn analyzes her respondents' comments by considering the category "doll" to be restricted to "people," whereas Barbies are "possessions." She considers the casual treatment that usually befalls Barbies after a day's use to be indicative of this difference: Barbies end up being stuffed into boxes and/or shoved under the bed, while baby dolls are carefully put to bed. Similarly, after a girl grows up, dolls may be kept while Barbies are thrown away or given away. She considers the separate and ephemeral category of Barbie to be revealed by the fact that when girls were asked to bring their favorite doll to the interview, very few brought Barbies.

To the question "What is doll play?" Washburn finds the strict definition of a doll to be extended into a strict definition of doll play. Doll play was defined only to encompass the "actual pretend involvement of the player with her doll in real-life activities – keeping house, going to school, feeding, bathing, dressing, and rocking the babies." She found that the respondents separated this from preparations for activities, looking at dolls, or directing fantasy dramas with Barbies and/or G.I. Joes. Indeed, "play" may form a minor part of their doll activities (1997: 128–9).

Washburn's final consideration of Barbie focuses on whether they are "fun toys or serious role models." After referring to the heightened critique of Barbie and the rift between Mattel and the critics, she observes how her interviews about present and former Barbies highlight very different aspects of the toy. Whereas critics appear to focus on the implicit sexuality, and Barbie's place within rampant consumerism, she found that girls consider Barbies simply as "fun dolls." The girls found two attributes of Barbie to be significant: the small size which encourages mobility ("they are small enough to hold several in your hand while walking to a friend's house with a plastic bag full of Barbie accessories"), and the low price of clothes which enables multiple ownership of costumes ("they are also inexpensive enough so that your mother will continually buy more outfits"). Body shape was not a concern. Washburn concludes with a "sobering" proviso about the mismatch between what critics, curators, and other adults consider to be dolls and doll play, and what the players consider. She sums up the girls' view which is often opposite to that of the adults: while adults see dolls as pretend props used to enact real activities, girls see dolls as real people that are played with in a variety of pretend scenarios. Similarly, while to adults dolls are a category of toy, to girls some dolls are toys (Barbie), and other dolls are (imaginary) people. She finishes by arguing for others to respect the specificity and ability to make fine distinctions which are inherent in child-constructed categories, based on experiential knowledge (1997: 132–4). Her comments are reminiscent of what Calvert and Rand said about the dangers of ascribing a single meaning to a doll or Barbie discussed at the beginning of this section.

In our own study of women's retrospective accounts of Barbie play (Reid-Walsh and Mitchell 2000) we have similarly found a wide variety of "play use" that encompasses what would be categorized as conventional play and resisting or subversive play. We gathered narratives which described different scenarios that included playing teacher with Barbie, building a Barbie dream house, and constructing an electrical alarm system for a Barbie house. One aspect that interests us is how the narratives reveal girls (located in specific sociohistorical contexts) imaginatively or materially modifying their circumstances through play. We consider this ability to be parallel to David Buckingham's (1993) notion of the "situated audience" in his work on children and television. He argues that children exist in circumstances not of their own choosing; nevertheless, within these limits they have the power to modify what they see on television. He asserts that children are not passive dupes of the media, but have limited agency. For him, the "power" of the media is located in neither the "text" nor the "audience" but in the relationship between them. We see parallels between Buckingham's ideas and those put forward by Thomas Schlerth (1985) in an article about the difficulties of studying historical children's material culture. Schlerth observes that what he considers "significant" toys are those whose material changes reveal how modified or transformed the artifact has become through use. Whereas Schlerth is referring to evidence of physical transformation wrought on the toy, we consider that modification through play use can be equally important, although it is imperceptible to onlookers, since it occurs imaginatively as well as literally. By consulting ethnographic accounts, past and present, we can obtain information on how a fashion doll, a play doll or a Barbie may be altered in this way.

We have seen how a notion of correspondence between multiple functions of dolls creating multiple meanings for the players has been a feature of the studies discussed in this section.

Although we sympathize with the point of view articulated by a long line of pre-feminist and feminist commentators who seem to rate toy destruction (Edgeworth) or doll destruction (Eliot, Formanek-Brunell) or Barbie destruction (Rand) as a more assertive or "feminist" reaction, we consider this focus on (literal) transformation or modification ultimately to be too restrictive an avenue of investigation, for we end up valuing only subversive, or resisting behavior. It is almost as if a mathematically inverted value relationship is established whereby the greater the misuse or destructive behavior, the higher the feminist value. We are more interested in the possibilities offered in trying to move beyond restrictive binary logic and in trusting girls' "play-power" through story-making or play-making. Again, while sympathetic to the feminist interpretation by Washburn on Barbie play, we find her distinctions somewhat limiting. While she distinguishes, indeed opposes, "story-making" to "stage direction" on account of the assumed difference of degree of emotional distance between the child and toy-doll, we are interested in how both abilities reveal the power of fantasy to mentally transform objects in play. If the child is imaginatively "empowered" through the actual or fantasy manipulation of miniature objects, and if the small size of Barbie tends to cause a sense of emotional distance between player and doll – as Washburn (1997) suggests in her summary of the girls' comments – then perhaps Barbie play possesses features similar to play behavior addressed by Armstrong in her discussion of early doll-house play where she considers the small scale to be an advantage because it limits the degree of identification between child and doll (1996: 39). Furthermore, we consider that in addition to her size, other key physical characteristics of Barbie such as her facial appearance, her bodily dimensions, her clothing, and her play-set accessories all reinforce the distance between the girl player and her doll. If this is the case, then, in Barbie play as in early doll-house play, girls can, at will, either disregard the size differential (and other differences) between themselves and their dolls and enter the play realm as equals, or preside over a play environment of their own construction where they make all the rules! This can be seen to create a high play value for the doll because of the numerous possibilities for use, function, and meaning.

Retro-Barbie: On Dolls and Girls

> "The past haunts the present; but the latter denies it with good reason"
> (Walter Benjamin)

In this chapter we have presented an alternative history of Barbie in three ways, we provide a critical history of the fashion doll from the eighteenth century to the present, we analyze examples of the fashion doll and Barbie doll as material artifacts, and we provide an ethnographic survey of doll play from historical accounts and contemporary studies. In our approach to Barbie history and fashion-doll history we are struck by how some of Walter

Benjamin's observations about history, about fashion, and about children may be applied to our discussion. In his "Theses on the philosophy of history" he argues that since "cultural treasures" are the spoils of the victor, the historian's task is to "brush history against the grain" (1969: 257 # vii). He later identifies fashion, specifically that of the French Revolution, as being an accurate historical indicator of dominant societal attitudes: "Fashion has a flair for the topical, no matter where it stirs in the thickets of long ago; it is a tiger's leap into the past" (ibid.: 261 # xiv). Elsewhere in his writing, in the *Arcades Project* and in an article "Toys and games," he presents toys and other children's artifacts as contraries to cultural treasures: he considers them significant because they are more like the "waste products" of a society, and therefore not routinely valued (cited in Buck-Morss 1989: 262). Ultimately, he considers the value of toys to be significant on an individual and collective level: if a toy survives, it provides a sinking away of the world itself, and it remains forever linked to the disruptive potential of the unconscious (cited in Mehlman 1993: 5). With dolls, specifically automans, or walking dolls, however, he – without referring to Rousseau – echoes the latter's insight but in reference to European society some 150 years later: "Ironically, if playing with dolls was originally the way children learned the nurturing behavior of adult social relations, it has become a training ground for learning reified ones. The goal of little girls now is to become a doll" (Cited in Buck-Morss 1989: 365).

Coda

In "Barbie looks back," we have taken the challenge presented by Erica Rand (1995) at the conclusion of *Barbie's Queer Accessories,* to use Barbie as a "pedagogical tool" by "tweaking" a socio-political-historical "nerve." We do this through proposing an alternative Barbie history. By presenting a "history of beginnings," not only from 1959, but which stretches back over 200 years, we hope to have succeeded in presenting an approach to Barbie as a fashion doll in such a way as to disturb the orthodoxy of much current Barbie discourse. Our point is both substantive and rhetorical. By offering a view of Barbie from the perspective of a longer time-frame, we hope to defend our position that children's popular culture needs to be considered within a similarly broader perspective so as to lead to a more thoughtful and nuanced critique. A historical approach situating girls, women and fashion doll play as part of the European Enlightenment understanding of women, girls and the concept of childhood may help critics to learn to respect the complexity and tenacity of certain orthodox assumptions and may also help us to reconsider the observations of early commentators. We conclude with reference to the pedagogical point of our juxtaposing the epigraphs, eliding girls, women and fashion dolls, from the eighteenth century. The limitations of the necessary equation of girls and dolls in contemporary evaluations of the Barbie game with its supposedly feminist impetus can then perhaps be fully appreciated. Moreover, if the equation is, in some ways, valid, perhaps (fashion) doll play and Barbie play has an unintended pedagogical value. Perhaps the act of handling the commodified emblems of conventional, Western femininity in a leisure activity has provided, and continues to provide, girls with a way to literally and conceptually manipulate the concept of commodified homogenous womanhood.

In this book as a whole, we have similarly attempted to "tweak" a research nerve in the area of children's popular culture. One way we have sought to do this is by creating a decolonizing space for doing research on children's culture through employing methods that respect children and children's knowledge. We have done this in two ways. First, we have sought to include children's voices and perspectives in our project as experts, researchers, and creators of popular culture. Children are present as experts of Nancy Drew and Hardy Boys mysteries, as researchers and co-researchers employing certain methods such as photography, and as creators of popular culture forms themselves such as in website construction. Children's insights are also present within a historical perspective, both in the short range of living memory – for we include the retrospective voices of adults discussing their childhood involvement with popular culture – and in a longer range of historical documentation where we include comments on doll play culled from diaries and observers' accounts. Children can also be considered present in a theoretical way when we seek to incorporate child-centered approaches into our textual and image analysis of film, magazines, and websites. In this way we have sought not only to heed Ann Oakley's comment about doing research on children but to implement and extend her points about the need to widen the range of involvement with children in doing research in a sensitive manner. She has observed that the prepositions associated with studying children and childhood have been "about" and "on" but rarely "for" (1994). We have sought to broaden the involvement with children in popular culture research by widening the use of prepositions to include "with" and "by" children.

A second way we have sought to decolonize research on children and children's popular culture has been to take heed of James et al.'s comments about the need to be more "adventurous" and "critical" in the choice of research methods and methodology (1998). We have sought to achieve this by employing several strategies. Through using a constellation of different "spaces" we have moved into different realms of popular culture to include the physical realm of the child's room as a repository of collections of popular culture, and to include the immaterial realm of the Internet. We have sought to widen the perspective on popular culture from being an exclusive focus on the present or recent past to include the long-range view accessible through historical approaches. We have also consciously sought to blur the boundaries that separate disciplines, and to create hierarchies in research. For example, we have sought to make less distinct the lines between high and low culture, academic and kitchen research, and the roles of adults and children in relation to who may and can produce, consume, or research popular culture. Two aspects of children's engagement with popular culture have served as controlling images. One is the method of child photographers who blithely blur the genres of photography by mixing popular-culture artifacts with quality toys in their photography sessions. Another is the "spilling over" of material culture from designated children's spaces into communal or living areas. The vitality and endurance of both the presence of popular culture and children's engagement with it has impelled us to examine in a self-conscious way, as researchers and as parents, the pleasures and challenges of doing research in this area.

Notes

Introduction

1 As a visit to a Gap field site in Montreal revealed, each floor of the three-level Gap megastore has a different genre/type of music filtering in through the speakers. All the music is clean-cut, conservative, popular, and within the boundaries of what is socially acceptable. Never will the Gap play punk, hard-hard rock, traditional, or too culturally "out there" (world) music. In addition, the volume seems to be very carefully balanced at a subtle sound level. Most downtown clothing stores that cater only to youth (unlike the Gap) often make bad marketing mistakes by aggressively blaring out dance club electronic/techno music or hard core "gangsta" hip-hop. Often these stores end up sounding/feeling more like social hang-outs than clothing stores. The first floor/men's section at the Gap usually plays heavy bass/dance clubby beats (similar to what we would hear at a local gym). The second (kids' and baby floor) plays teeny-bopperish, top-forty radio tunes and R'n'B. On the women's floor one can hear everything from Simon and Garfunkel to Madonna's remake of the classic song "Bye, Bye, Miss American Pie" (which speaks to the baby-boomer generation as much as it does to Gen X and younger kids). Occasionally some Canadian content is thrown in to the whole mix to prevent the sound from becoming too Corporate America: for example, a song from Sarah MacLachlan's first album (very late 1980s/early 1990s). The lingerie corner of the third floor will usually feature its own "soundscape" (Schafer 1980), the music ranging from very serene and calming nondescript New Age ambient to hipper and more seductive acid jazz/muzak, all reminiscent, however, of elevator music.

1 Political Spaces: Contexts for Researching Children's Popular Culture

1 Here we refer the reader to a lengthy discussion on the "culturated" reading where the reader has extensive knowledge of popular culture genres such

as series fiction, *The Simpsons* episodes, and so on, that is not typically recognized as literary knowledge.

2 Here we are grateful to Anne Greenberg of Simon & Schuster for participating in an interview in February 1994 about her work on the Nancy Drew and Hardy Boys series.

3 For a more extensive discussion of the role of parents in academic research, we refer the reader to an unpublished monograph by Heather Leedham-Enros (1993) "The Other Side: A Teacher's Personal and Professional Reflections" (Department of Curriculum and Instruction, McGill University).

2 Memory Spaces: Exploring the Afterlife of Children's Popular Culture

1 We do note, as well, the significance of what might be described as "cowgirl chic" fashion since the late 1990s in North America. This includes billboards plastered with pictures of Gucci-clad models in fringed leather pants, brightly colored or white stetsons, snake or crocodile cowboy boots and big buckled belts. It also includes Britney Spears posing at awards shows in cowgirl apparel, Madonna marketing her latest album dressed as a cowgirl, and the rapper Lil Kim – at one point – donning cowgirl hat and gear (personal communication, Farah Malik, April 2001).

3 Visual Spaces: The Gaze of the Child

1 We also refer the reader to the catalog which accompanied the *Open Ends* exhibition at the Museum of Modern Art under the banner MoMA 2000. In the catalog there is a segment from Boltanski's Favourite Objects installation (Varnedoe Siegel, *Modern Contemporary Art at MoMA since 1980*, New York: The Museum of Modern Art, 2000).

2 Here we acknowledge the participation of young people from each of the school districts in the Free State in this project as part of the Canada–South Africa Education Management Program (CSAEMP), a partnership between the Government of South Africa, the Canadian International Development Agency, and McGill University (1996–2001). The work from this project was presented at the Education Management Association of South Africa conference held in Durban, March 2001 (Matsenang).

3 Here we acknowledge the work of teacher Darlene Miller and the students of the Untitled Collective of Villa Maria High School in Montreal who held an installation of their work in Duggan House, McGill University, on March 31, 2001.

4 See Image and Identity Research Collective website at <http://www.iirc.mcgill.ca>

4 Physical Spaces: Children's Bedrooms as Cultural Texts

1 See, for example the twenty-seven page exclusive to *7 Jours, Edition Speciale*, March 17, 2001, vol. 12, no. 20, 11–42.

5 Virtual Spaces: Children on the Cyber Frontier

1 See David Buckingham's insightful discussion of technological determinism in Chapter 3 of *After the Death of Childhood: Growing Up in the Age of Electronic Media* (2000).

2 Both the dangers to children and the role of adults as regulators are beginning to be addressed by new lobbying organizations. For example, in the United States the American Center for Media Education seeks to bring academics, policy-makers, and educators together to make the Internet safer for children. As a result of a growing awareness of dangers to children, advice about how to use the Internet safely is included on most "How-to" guides intended for children available on the Web, whether they are written by adults or by children themselves.

3 These concerns are beginning to be addressed by non-governmental organizations such as the British National Children's Bureau in their volume *Electronic Children: How Children are Responding to the Information Revolution* (1996) edited by Tim Gill. These issues also provided one main focus of an international conference, the 3rd World Summit on Media for Children, held in Thessalonki, Greece, March 23–26, 2001 and co-sponsored by UNESCO, UNICEF, and the Media Programme of the Economic Union.

4 It is important to note that because all Internet sites are in flux, our description of each pertains only to the period of access: November 17 to December 9, 2001. The Warner Brothers site is defunct as of October 5, 2001, but many of the features have been transferred to another commercial site at the new network site with the same URL.

5 Here we are grateful to the anonymous reviewer of this book who first alerted us to the possibilities for engaging in a reading of homepages using Foucault's work on heterotopias.

6 Historical Spaces: Barbie Looks Back

1 Here, for example, we are thinking of such full-length works on Barbie as Erica Rand's *Barbie's Queer Accessories*; Mary Lord's *Forever Barbie*; and Mary F. Rogers' book *Barbie Culture* (1999), along with Lynn Spigel's chapter "Barbies without Ken: femininity, feminism, and the art-culture system" in her *Welcome to the Dreamhouse: Popular Media and Postwar Suburbs* (2001). We are also interested in popular Barbie accounts such as Richard

Peabody and Lucinda Abersole's (eds) *Mondo Barbie: An Anthology of Fiction and Poetry* (1993), and Yona Zeldis McDonough's (ed.) *The Barbie Chronicles: A Living Doll Turns Forty* (1999).

2 A 1995 interview with James Steward, curator of the New Child Exhibition, is located at the following website: <http://www.uampfa.berkeley.edu/exhibits/newchild/ncinterview.html>

3 It should be clarified that the range of objects covered by the term "fashion doll" is quite wide, for it encompasses full-size mannequins, miniature "lady" dolls, three-dimensional models of various sizes, and paper cut-outs, although the occasional historian uses the term strictly to refer to dressmakers' models (Cross 1997; King 1977).

4 The curators who kindly aided us in our research are Conrad Graham and Suzanne Morin.

5 To see an image of the 1700 doll at the virtual image archive of the Victoria and Albert museum go to <http://www.vam.ac.uk/Explorer/Virtual/images/image_records/CT6968A>

6 In light of the following discussion on the gaze and the nude, it is ironic that it may be the gaze of the Lilli/early Barbie that is sultry – not the body shape.

7 For a different discussion of Barbie as artist's model please refer to the discussion of the work of Dean Brown's "Olympia" in *Forever Barbie* (Lord 1994: 15, 262).

8 Perhaps due to her interest in only "resisting" or "subversive" play Formenek-Brunell cites only the instances of Maggie Tulliver's doll destruction from *Mill on the Floss.* Quoting only these instances ignores the complex relationship with (conventionally pretty) dolls that the conventionally (plain) Maggie (and Eliot) had with these toys.

Bibliography

Abbott, C. (1998) "Making connections: young people and the Internet," in J. Sefton-Green (ed.) *Digital Diversions: Youth Culture in the Age of Multimedia*, London: UCL Press.

Adler, P. and Adler, P. (1998) *Peer Power: Preadolescent Culture and Identity*, New Brunswick, NJ: Rutgers University Press.

Aitken, S. (1998) *Family Fantasies and Community Space*, New Brunswick, NJ: Rutgers University Press.

Arendt, H. (ed.) (1969) *Walter Benjamin Illuminations*, trans. H. Zohn, New York: Schocken.

Armstrong, F. (1996) "The doll house as ludic space 1690–1920," *Children's Literature* 24:23–54.

Armstrong, N. and Tennenhouse, L. (eds) (1987) *The Ideology of Conduct: Essays on Literature and the History of Sexuality*, New York: Methuen.

Austen, J. (1984) *Northanger Abbey*, in R.W. Chapman (ed.) *The Novels of Jane Austen*, Vol. 5, 3rd edn, Oxford: Clarendon Press. First published 1818.

Bachelard, G. (1964) *The Poetics of Space*, Boston, MA: Beacon Press.

Bailey, K. (1993) *The Girls are the Ones With the Pointy Nails: An Exploration of Children's Conceptions of Gender*, London, Ontario: Althouse Press.

Barone, T. (2000) *Aesthetics, Politics, and Educational Inquiry: Essays and Examples*, New York: Peter Lang.

Barthes, R. (1970) *S/Z*, trans. R. Miller (1974), New York: Hill and Wang.

—— (1972) *Mythologies*, trans. A. Lavers, London: Jonathan Cape.

Benjamin, W. (1969) *Illuminations*, ed. H. Arendt, trans. H. Zohn, New York: Schocken.

Berger, J. (1972) *Ways of Seeing*, Harmondsworth: Penguin.

Bird, L. (1994) "Creating the capable body: discourses about ability and effort in primary and secondary school studies," in B. Mayall (ed.) *Children's Childhoods: Observed and Experienced*, London: Falmer Press.

Birnbaum, C. (2000) "Your bedroom decor – decoded," *YM*, spring: 18–21.

Blackman, S. J. (1998) "The school: 'Poxy Cupid!' an ethnographic and feminist account of a resistant female youth culture: the New Wave Girls," in T. Skelton and G. Valentine (eds) *Cool Places: Geographies of Youth Cultures*, London: Routledge.

Blain, V., Grundy, I. and Clements, P. (1990) *The Feminist Companion to Literature in English: Women Writers from the Middle Ages to the Present*, New Haven, CT: Yale University Press.

Brewer, J. (1997) *The Pleasures of the Imagination: English Culture in the Eighteenth Century*, London: HarperCollins.

Brill, A. (1995) "Barbie, my liberator," in F. Howe et al. (eds) *Re-visioning Feminism Around the World*, New York: Feminist Press.

Brown, B. (1998) "How to do things with things," *Critical Inquiry*, 24: 935–64.

Brown, J. D., White, A. B., and Nikopoulou, L. (1993) "Distinterest, intrigue, resistance: early adolescent girls' use of sexual media content," in B. S. Greenberg, J. D. Brown, and N. L. Buerkel-Rothfussand (eds) *Media, Sex and the Adolescent*, Creskill, NJ: Hampton Press.

Brown, J. D., Dykers, C. R., Steele, J. R., and White, A. B. (1994) "Teenage room culture: where media and identities intersect," *Communication Research*, 21(6): 813–27.

Bryson, M. and de Castell, S. (1995) "So we've got a chip on our shoulder! Sexing the texts of educational technology," in J. Gaskell and J. Willinisky (eds) *Gender Informs Curriculum*, Toronto: OISE Press.

—— (1998) "Retooling play: dystopia, dysphoria, and difference," in J. Cassell and H. Jenkins (eds) *From Barbie to Mortal Kombat: Gender and Computer Games*, Cambridge, MA: MIT Press.

Buchli, V. and Lucas, G. (2000) "Children, gender and the material culture of domestic abandonment in the late twentieth century," in J. S. Derevenski (ed.) *Children and Material Culture*, London: Routledge.

Buck-Morss, S. (1989) *The Dialectics of Seeing: Walter Benjamin and the Arcades Project,* Cambridge, MA: MIT Press.

Buckingham, D. (1991) "What are the words worth? Interpreting children's talk about television," *Cultural Studies*, 5(2): 228–45.

—— (1993) *Reading Audiences: Young People and the Media,* Manchester: Manchester University Press.

—— (1996) *Moving Images: Understanding Children's Emotional Responses to Television*, Manchester: Manchester University Press.

—— (1997) "Dissin' Disney: critical perspectives on children's media culture," *Media, Culture & Society*, 19: 285–93.

—— (2000) *After the Death of Childhood: Growing Up in the Age of the Electronic Media*, Cambridge: Polity Press.

Buckingham, D. and Sefton-Green, J. (1994) *Cultural Studies Goes to School*, London: Taylor & Francis.

Buckley, C. (1996) "Children's clothes: design and promotion," in P. Kirkham (ed.) *The Gendered Object,* Manchester: Manchester University Press.

Burney, F. (1997) *Evelina*, ed. S. Cooke, New York: W.W. Norton. First published 1778.

Calcutt, A. (1999) *White Noise: An A–Z of the Contradictions in Cyberculture*, New York: St. Martin's Press.

Calvert, K. (1992) *Children in the House: The Material Culture of Early Childhood 1600–1900*, Boston, MA: Northeastern University Press.

Carlsson-Paige, N. (1987) *The War Play Dilemma: Balancing Needs and Values in the Early Childhood Classroom*, New York: Teachers College Press.

Cassell, J. and Jenkins, H. (eds) (1998) *From Barbie to Mortal Kombat: Gender and Computer Games,* Cambridge, MA: MIT Press.

Chalfen, R. (1987) *Snapshot Versions of Life,* Bowling Green, OH: Bowling Green State University Popular Press.

—— (1991) *Turning Leaves: The Photograph Collections of Two Japanese American Families*, Albuquerque, NM: University of New Mexico Press.

Charron, H. (2000) "Your room: messing up," *Seventeen*, January: 60.

Christian-Smith, L. (1990) *Becoming a Woman Through Romance*, New York: Routledge.

Cohen, S. (1972) *Folk Devils and Moral Panics: The Creation of the Mods and Rockers*, Oxford: Blackwell.

Cox, R. (1996) *Shaping Childhood: Themes of Uncertainty in the History of Adult–Child Relationships*, London: Routledge.

Crawford, J., Kippax, S., Onyx, J., Gault, U., and Benton, P. (eds) (1992) *Emotion and Gender: Constructing Meaning from Memory,* London: Sage.

Cristofovici, A. (1999) "Touching surfaces: photography, aging, and an aesthetics of change," in K. Woodward (ed.) *Figuring Age: Women, Bodies, Generations*, Bloomington: Indiana University Press.

Cross, G. (1997) *Kids' Stuff: Toys and the Changing World of American Childhood*, Cambridge, MA: Harvard University Press.

Currie, D. (1999) *GirlTalk: Adolescent Magazines and Their Readers*, Toronto: University of Toronto Press.

Daigon, A. (1964) "The strange case of Nancy Drew," *The English Journal*, 53(9): 669.

Daly, M. (2001) "Your room: lofty surroundings," *Seventeen*, April: 154.

Davies, B. (1989) *Frogs and Snails and Feminist Tales*, Sydney: Allen & Unwin.

Davies, L. (1984) *Pupil Power: Deviance and Gender in School,* London: Falmer Press.

Debouzy, M. (1996) "The Barbie doll," in J. Dean and J. P. Gabilliet (eds) *European Readings of American Popular Culture*, Westport, CT: Greenwood Press.

Dewdney, A. and Lister, M. (1986) "Photography, school and youth culture: The Cockpit Arts Project," in S. Bezencenet, and P. Corrigan (eds) *Photographic Practices: Towards a Different Image*, London: Comedia.

Donmeyer, R. and Raylene, K. (1993) *At Risk Students: Portraits, Programs and Practices*, Albany, NY: SUNY Press.

Drotner, K. (1992) "Maternity and mediapanics," in M. Skovmand and K. Christian Schroder (eds) *Media Cultures: Reappraising Transnational Media,* London: Routledge.

Dwyer, C. (1998) "Contested identities: challenging dominant representations of young British Muslim women", in T. Skelton and G. Valentine (eds) *Cool Places: Geographies of Youth Culture,* London: Routledge.

Edgeworth, M. and Edgeworth, R. L. (1974) *Practical Education*, 2 vols ed. G. Luria, New York: Garland. First published 1798.

Eliot, G. (1991) *The Mill on the Floss*, ed. S. Shuttleworth, London: Routledge. First published 1860.

Elkind, D. (1982) *The Hurried Child: Growing Up too Fast too Soon*, Reading, MA: Addison Wesley.

Ennew, J. (1994) *Street and Working Children: A Guide to Planning,* London: Save the Children Fund.

Entz, G. and Galarza, S. L. (2000) *Picture This: Digital and Instant Photography Activities for Early Childhood Learning,* Thousand Oaks, CA: Corwin.

Environics Research Group (2001) Media Awareness Network Study, Funded by Industry Canada in Partnership with Health Canada and Human Resources Development Canada. Available at: <http://www.media-awareness.ca/eng/webaware/netsurrey/ parents/finalreport.htm> (accessed September 7, 2001).

Ewald, W. (1985) *Portraits and Dreams: Photographs and Stories by Children of the Appalachiana*, London: Writers and Readers Publishing Cooperative Society.

—— (1996) *I Dreamed I Had a Girl in My Pocket*, London: W. W. Norton.

—— (2000) *Secret Games: Collaborative Works with Children, 1969–99*, Zurich: Scalo.

Farber, P., Provenzo, E. Jr., and Holm, G. (eds) (1994) *Schooling in the Light of Popular Culture,* Albany, NY: SUNY Press.

Fehily, C., Fletcher, J., and Newton, K. (eds) (2000) *I Spy: Representations of Childhood,* London: I. B. Tauris.

Fine, M. (1994) "Distance and other stances: negotiations of power inside feminist research," in A. Gitlin (ed.) *Power and Method: Political Activism and Educational Research*, New York: Routledge.

Fiske, J, (1987) "British cultural studies television," in R. Allen (ed.) *Channels of Discourse*, London: Methuen; repr. in R. Allen (ed.) *Channels of Discourse Reassembled: Television in Contemporary Criticism*, 2nd edn (1992), Chapel Hill: University of North Carolina Press.

—— (1993) *Power Plays Power Works,* London: Verso.

Fitzmorris, M. (1997) "What does your room say about you?," *YM*, spring: 8–9.

—— (1997) "How to 'snoop-proof' your space," *YM*, spring: 10.

—— (1997) "Does your room need a serious makeover?," *YM*, spring: 10.

—— (1997) "The hidden meaning of your stuff," *YM*, spring: 11.

Flax, J. (1987) "Remembering the selves: is the repressed gendered?," *Michigan Quarterly Review*, 26(1): 92–110.

Fleming, D. (1996) *Powerplay: Toys as Popular Culture*, Manchester: Manchester University Press.

Flick Filosopher (1999) "Toying with the past," available at <http://www.flickfilosopher.com/flickfilos/archive/4q99/toystory2.html> (accessed March 29, 2001).

Formanek-Brunell, M. (1993) *Made to Play House: Dolls and the Commercialization of American Girlhood 1830–1930,* New Haven, CT: Yale University Press.

Foucault, M. (1986) "Of other spaces," trans. J. Miskowiec, *Diacritics*, spring: 22–7.

Fraser, A. (1966) *A History of Toys*, London: Delacourte Press.

Friedman, S. J. (1995) "Making sense of software: computer games and interactive textuality," in S. Jones (ed.) *Cybersociety,* Thousand Oaks, CA: Sage.

—— (2000) *Children and the World Wide Web: Tool or Trap?*, Lanham, ML: University Press of America.

Frith, S. (1983) *Sound Effects: Youth, Leisure and the Politics of Rock*, London: Constable.

Fritzsch, K. E. and Bachmann, M. (1966) *An Illustrated History of Toys*, trans. R. Michaelis-Jena and P. Murray, London: Abbey Library.

Fuchs, C. J. (1999) "Girling Popular Culture: Proving What I've Got to Prove: Pop Culture, Sex, and the New Girl Power," paper presented at the Modern Language Association Conference, Chicago, December.

Garvey, E. G. (1996) *The Adman in the Parlor: Magazines and the Gendering of Consumer Culture, 1880s to 1910s*, New York: Oxford University Press.

Gill, T. (ed.) (1996) *Electronic Children: How Children are Responding to the Information Revolution*, London: British National Children's Bureau.

Gillespie, N. (1999) "Does kids' TV have to be edifying?," *New York Times*, July 6, editorial desk section.

Giroux, H. (1997) "Are Disney movies good for your kids?," in J. L Kincheloe and S. R. Steinberg (eds) *Kinderculture: The Corporate Construction of Childhood*, Boulder, CO: Westview.

—— (1998) "Stealing innocence: the politics of child beauty pageants," in H. Jenkins (ed.) *The Children's Culture Reader*, New York: New York University Press.

—— (1999) *The Mouse that Roared. Disney and the End of Innocence*, Lanham, ML: Rowman & Littlefield.

Gitlin, A. (1994) *Power and Method: Political Activism and Educational Research*, New York: Routledge.

Glassman, S. (1999) "Your room: Tara's flower bed," *Seventeen*, February: 70.

Goodfellow, C. (1993) *The Ultimate Doll Book*, Montreal: Reader's Digest.

Griffin, S. (1999) "Kings of the wild backyard: Davy Crockett and children's space," in M. Kinder, (ed.) *Kids' Media Culture*, Durham, NC: Duke University Press.

Griffiths, V. (1995) *Adolescent Girls and their Friends: A Feminist Ethnography*, Aldershot: Avebury.

Hallam, J. and Marshment, M. (1995) "Questioning the 'ordinary' woman: *Oranges are not the Only Fruit*, text and viewer," in B. Skeggs (ed.) *Feminist Cultural Theory Process and Production*, Manchester: Manchester University Press.

Hampl, P. (1996) "Memory and imagination," in J. McConkey (ed.) *The Anatomy of Memory: An Anthology*, New York: Oxford University Press.

Hartley, J. (1999) *Uses of Television*, London: Routledge.

Macnamee, K. (1998) "The home: youth, gender and video games: power and control in the home," in T. Skelton and G. Valentine (eds) *Cool Places: Geographies of Youth Cultures*, London: Routledge.

Macnamee, K. (2000) "Heterotopia and children's everyday lives," *Childhood*, 7(4): 479–92.

McRobbie, A. (1991) *Feminism and Youth Culture: From "Jackie" to "Just Seventeen,"* Cambridge, MA: Unwin Hyman.

—— (1999) "More! New sexualities in girls' and women's magazines," in *In the Culture Society: Art, Fashion and Popular Music*, London and New York: Routledge.

McRobbie, A. and Garber, J. (1991) "Girls and subcultures," in A. McRobbie *Feminism and Youth Culture: From "Jackie" to "Just Seventeen,"* Cambridge, MA: Unwin Hyman; originally printed in S. Hall and T. Jefferson (eds) (1978) *Resistance Through Rituals: Youth Subcultures in Post War Britain*, London: Hutchison.

Maingard, J. (1994) "New South African cinema: Mapantsula and Sarafina," *Screen*, 35(3): 235–43.

Mandell, N. (1988) "The least-adult role in studying children," *Journal of Contemporary Ethnography*, 16: 433–467.

Martin, M. A. (1991) *Claudia and the Middle School Mystery*, The Baby-sitters Club series, No. 40, New York: Scholastic Press.

Massey, D. (1998) "The spatial construction of youth cultures," in T. Skelton and G. Valentine (eds) *Cool Places: Geographies of Youth Cultures*, London: Routledge.

Matsaneng, J. (2001) "Youth Leadership and Photography: Putting Ourselves in the Picture," a paper presented at the Education Management Association of South Africa conference, Durban, March.

Mavor, C. (1999) *Becoming: The Photographs of Clementina Viscountess Hawarden*, Durham, NC: Duke University Press.

Mayall, B. (ed.) (1994) *Children's Childhoods Observed and Experienced*, London: Falmer Press.

—— (1999) "Children and childhood," in S. Hood, B. Mayall, and S. Oliver (eds) *Critical Issues in Social Research: Power and Prejudice*, Buckingham: Open University Press.

Mehlman, J. (1993) *Walter Benjamin for Children: An Essay on his Radio Years*, Chicago, IL: University of Chicago Press.

Michlig, J. (1998) *G.I. Joe: The Complete Story of America's Favorite Man of Action*, San Francisco, CA: Chronicle Books.

Miller, D. (ed.) (1998) *Material Cultures: Why Some Things Matter,* London: UCL Press.

Miller, W. (1998) *Toy Wars: The Epic Struggle between G.I. Joe, Barbie and the Companies that Make Them*, New York: Times Book and Random House.

Misenheimer, H.E. (1981) *Rousseau on the Education of Women*, Washington, DC: University Press of America.

Mitchell, C. (1991) "Seventeen, Soap Operas, and Swett Valley High: Isolating Girls in Their Reading of Popular Culture," paper presented at CRIAW Conference, Edmonton, November.

Mitchell, C. and Reid-Walsh, J. (1993) "And I Want to Thank-you Barbie: Barbie as a Site of Cultural Interrogation," paper presented at the Canadian Women's Studies Association Conference, Ottawa, June.

—— (1995) "And I want to thank-you Barbie: Barbie as a site of cultural interrogation," *The Review of Education/Pedagogy/Cultural Studies*, 17(2): 143–56.

—— (1996) "Reading on the edge: serious series readers of *Nancy Drew* and *Hardy Boys* mysteries," *Changing English*, 3(1): 45–55.

—— (1998) "Mail-order memory work: towards a methodology of uncovering the experiences of covering over," *Review of Education/Pedagogy/Cultural Studies*, 20(1): 57–75.

—— (1999) "Nine Going on Seventeen: Boundary Crises in the Cultural Map of Childhood/Adolescence," paper presented at the American Educational Research Association Conference, Montreal, April.

Mitchell, C. and Weber. S. (1999) *Reinventing Ourselves as Teachers: Beyond Nostalgia*, London: Falmer Press.

Mitchell, C. Weber, S., and Cloutier, S. (2000) Image and Identity Research Collective website. Available at: <http://www.cel.mcgill.ca/iirc>.

Morrison, T. (1996) "Memory, creation, and writing," in J. McConkey (ed.) *The Anatomy of Memory: An Anthology*, New York: Oxford University Press.

Nava, M. (1992) *Changing Cultures: Feminism, Youth and Consumerism*, London: Sage.

Nelson, M. and Steinberg, S. (1997) "Dealing from the bottom of the deck: the business of trading cards, past to present," in J. L. Kincheloe and S. R. Steinberg (eds) *Kinderculture: The Corporate Construction of Childhood*, Boulder, CO: Westview Press.

Nodelman, P. (1996) *The Pleasures of Children's Literature*, 2nd edn, White Plains, NY: Longman.

Norquay, N. (1993) "The other side of difference: memory-work in the mainstream," *Qualitative Studies of Education*, 6(3): 241–51.

Oakley, A. (1994) "Women and children first and last: parallels and differences between children's and women's studies," in B. Mayall (ed.) *Children's Childhoods Observed and Experienced*, London: Falmer Press.

Opie, I. and Opie, P. (1969) *Children's Games in Street and Playground*, Oxford: Oxford University Press.

Paley, N. (1995) *Finding Art's Place: Experiments in Contemporary Education and Culture,* New York: Routledge.

—— (2000) *Questions of You and the Struggle of Collaborative Life*, New York: Peter Lang.

Paley, N. and Jipson, J. A. (eds) (1997) *Daredevil Research: Re-creating Analytic Practice*, New York: Peter Lang.

Paley, V. (1984) *Boys and Girls: Superheroes in the Doll Corner*, Chicago, IL: University of Chicago Press.

Paulson, R. (1971) *Hogarth: His Life, Art and Times*, 2 vols, London: Yale University Press.

Peabody, R. and Ebersole, L. (eds) (1993) "Introduction," *Mondo Barbie: An Anthology of Fiction and Poetry*, New York: St. Martin's Press.

Penn, H. (1999) "Children in the majority world: is Outer Mognolia really so far away?," in S. Hood, B. Mayall, and S. Oliver (eds) *Critical Issues in Social Research: Power and Prejudice*, Buckingham and Philadelphia: Ohio University Press.

Perry, R. (1997) "Review of T. G. A. Nelson. Children, parents, and the rise of the novel," *Eighteenth-Century Fiction*, 9(1): 107–9.

Plumb, J.H. (1982) "Commercialization and society: the new world of children," in N. McKindrick, J. Brewer, and J. H. Plumb *The Birth of a Consumer Society: The Commercialization of Eighteenth-Century England*, Bloomington: Indiana University Press.

Plunkett-Powell, K. (1993) *The Nancy Drew Scrapbook: 60 Years of America's Favorite Teenage Sleuth,* New York: St. Martin's Press.

Portanier, S. (1998) "Flatter Barbie" in "Postmodern Barbie," available at <http://www.alphalink.com.au/~pfs/Postmod.htm> (accessed May 28, 2001).

Poster, M. (1995) *The Second Media Age,* Cambridge: Polity Press.

Postman, N. (1982) *The Disappearance of Childhood,* New York: Delacorte.

Radstone, S. (1995) "Remembering ourselves: Memory, writing, and the female self," in P. Florence and D. Reynolds (eds) *Feminist Subjects, Multi-media, Cultural Methodologies*, Manchester: Manchester University Press.

Rand, E. (1995) *Barbie's Queer Accessories*, Durham, NC: Duke University Press.

Reid-Walsh, J. (1993) "'Adolescent girls' romance fiction: contemporary conduct books?," in D. Martens (ed.) *Weaving Alliances. Selected Papers Presented for the Canadian Women's Studies Association*, Ottawa: CWSA.

Reid-Walsh, J. and Mitchell, C. (2000) "'Just a doll?': Some 'Liberating' accounts of Barbie play," *Review of Education/Pedagogy/Cultural Studies*, 22(2): 175–90.

Reynolds, P. (1996) *Traditional Healers and Childhood in Zimbabwe*, Athens: Ohio University Press.

Rheingold, H. (1993) *The Virtual Community: Homesteading on the Electronic Frontier*, Reading, MA: Addison-Wesley.

Rich, A. (1978) *The Dream of a Common Language: Poems 1974–1977*, New York: W. W. Norton.

Richards, C. (1998) *Teen Spirits: Music and Identity in Media Education*, London: UCL Press.

Riggins, S. H. (1994) "Fieldwork in the living room: an autoethnographic essay," in *The Socialness of Things: Essays on the Socio-Semiotics of Objects*, Berlin: Mouton de Gruyter.

Rogers, M. F. (1999) *Barbie Culture*, London: Sage.

Rohde, R. (1998) "How we see each other: subjectivity, photography and ethnographic re/vision," in W. Hartman, J. Silvester and P. Hayes (eds) *The Colonising Camera: Photographs in the Making of Namibian History*, Athens: Ohio University Press.

Rousseau, J. J. (1963) *The Emile: Selections Jean Jacques Rousseau*, ed. and trans. W. Boyd, New York: Teachers College, Columbia University. Originally published 1762.

Ruby, J. (2000) *Picturing Culture: Explorations of Film and Anthropology*, Chicago, IL: University of Chicago Press.

Rupp, R. A. (1996) *Treasury of Barbie Doll Accessories, 1961–1995*, Grantsville, MD: Hobby House.

St. George, E. (1948) *The Dolls of Yesterday*, London: Scribner.

Salinger, A. (1995) *In My Room: Teenagers in their Bedrooms*, San Francisco, CA: Chronicle Books.

Schafer, R.M (1980) *The Tuning of the World*, Toronto: McClelland and Steward.

Schlerth, T. (1985) "The material culture of childhood: problems and potential in historical exploration," *Material History Bulletin*, spring, 21: 1–14.

Schneider, C. (1987) *Children's Television*, Chicago, IL: NTC Business Books.

Scott, K (1997) "Karin Geiger: plush toys and poster boys," (*Plug In*). Available at <http://www.plugin.org/geiger/intro.htm> (accessed February 20, 2001).

Sefton-Green, J. (ed.) (1998) *Digital Diversions: Youth Culture in the Age of Multimedia*, London: UCL Press.

Sefton-Green, J. and Buckingham, D. (1998) "Digital visions: children's 'creative uses' of multimedia technologies," in J. Sefton-Green (ed.) *Digital Diversions: Youth Culture in the Age of Multimedia*, London: UCL Press.

Seiter, E. (1993) *Sold Separately: Parents and Children in Consumer Culture*, New Brunswick, NJ: Rutgers University Press.

Semin, D., Garb, T., and Kuspit, D. (1997) *Christian Boltanski*, London: Phaedon Press.

Sendak, M. (1983) *Where the Wild Things Are*, New York: Scholastic Press.

Skelton, T. and Valentine, G. (eds) (1998) *Cool Places: Geographies of Youth Cultures*, London and New York: Routledge.

Slier, D. (1994) *Good Manners*, New York: Modern Publishing.

Smith, L. (1999) *Decolonizing Methodologies: Research and Indigenous Peoples*, London: Zed Books.

Spence, J. (1995) *Cultural Sniping: The Art of Transgression*, London: Routledge.

Spence, J. and Solomon, J. (eds) (1995) *What Can a Woman Do With a Camera?*, London: Scarlet Press.

Spencer, J. (1986) *The Rise of the Woman Novelist: From Aphra Behn to Jane Austen*, Oxford: Blackwell.

Spender, D. (1989) *The Writing or the Sex?, or Why You Don't Have to Read Women's Writing to Know it's no Good*, New York: Pergamon.

Spigel, L. (2001) *Welcome to the Dreamhouse: Popular Media and Postwar Suburbs*, Durham, NC: Duke University Press.

Spivak, G. (1988) "Can the subaltern speak?," in C. Nelson and L. Grossberg (eds) *Marxism and the Interpretation of Culture*, London: Macmillan.

Spock, B. and Rothenberg, M. (1985) *Baby and Child Care*, New York: Simon & Schuster.

Stearns, P. N., Perrin, R., and Giarnella, L. (1996) "Children's sleep: sketching historical change," *Journal of Social History*, 30(2): 345–66.

Steele, J. R. and Brown, J. D. (1995) "Adolescent room culture: studying media in the context of everyday life," *Journal of Youth and Adolescence*, 24(5): 551–76.

Steinberg, S. R. (1997) "The bitch who has everything," in S. R. Steinberg and J. L. Kincheloe (eds) *Kinderculture: The Corporate Construction of Childhood*, Boulder, CO: Westview Press.

Steinberg, S. R. and Kincheloe, J. L. (eds) (1997) *Kinderculture: The Corporate Construction of Childhood*, Boulder, CO: Westview Press.

Stern, S. L. and Schoenhaus, T. (1990) *Toyland: The High-Stakes Game of the Toy Industry,* Chicago, IL: Contemporary Books.

Steward, J. (1995) "The new child: British art & the origins of modern childhood, 1730–1830," online at <http://www.uampfa.berkeley.edu/exhibits/newchild.html> (accessed May 17, 2001).

Sutherland, N. (1992) "When you listen to the winds of childhood, how much can you believe?," *Curriculum Inquiry*, 22(3): 235–56.

Sutton-Smith, B. (1986) *Toys as Culture*, New York: Gardner.

Tapscott, D. (1998) *Growing Up Digital: The Rise of the Net Generation*, New York: McGraw-Hill.

Tasker, Y. (1998) "Cowgirl tales," in *Working Girls: Gender and Sexuality in Popular Cinema*, London: Routledge.

Taylor, K. (1990) *The Letts Guide to Collecting Dolls*, London: Charles Letts.

Thompson, G. (1999) "Review, *Toy Story 2*," *Philadelphia Daily News*, November 24.

Tobin, J. (1998) "An American Otaku (or a boy's virtual life on the net)," in J. Sefton-Green (ed.) *Digital Diversions: Youth Culture in the Age of Multimedia*, London: UCL Press.

Tsakalis, G. (1998) "Memory Work and Gender Socialization," unpublished M. Ed. monograph, McGill University.

Turkle, S. (1995) *Life on the Screen: Identity in the Age of the Internet*, New York: Simon & Schuster.

Valentine, G. (1997) "'My son's a bit dizzy.' 'My wife's a bit soft': gender, children, and cultures of parenting," *Gender, Place and Culture*, 4(1): 37–62.

Vallone, L. (1995) *Disciplines of Virtue: Girls' Culture in the Eighteenth and Nineteenth Centuries,* New Haven, CT: Yale University Press.

Varnedoe, A. P. and Siegel, J. (eds) (2000) *Modern Contemporary Art at MOMA since 1980*, New York: The Museum of Modern Art.

Waksler, F. C. (1996) *The Little Trials of Childhood and Children's Strategies for Dealing with Them*, London: Falmer Press.

Walkerdine, V. (1985) "Video replay," in V. Burgin, J. Donald, and C. Kaplan (eds) *Formations of Fantasy*, London: Routledge.

—— (1997) *Daddy's Girl: Young Girls and Popular Culture*, Cambridge, MA: Harvard University Press.

—— (1998a) "Children in cyberspace: a new frontier," in K. Lesnik-Oberstein (ed.) *Children in Culture: Approaches to Childhood*, Basingstoke: Macmillan.

—— (1998b) "Popular culture and the eroticization of little girls," in H. Jenkins (ed.) *The Children's Culture Reader*, New York: New York University Press.

Walton, K. (1995) "Creating positive images: working with primary school girls," in J. Spence and J. Solomon (eds) *What Can a Woman do With a Camera?*, London: Scarlet Press.

Washburn, D. (1997) "Getting ready: doll play and real life in American culture, 1900–1980," in A. N. Martin and J. R. Garrison, (eds) *American Material Culture: The Shape of the Field*, Winterthur, DE: Winterthur Museum.

Weber, S. and Mitchell, C. (1995) *That's Funny, You don't Look Like a Teacher: Interrogating Images of Identity in Popular Culture*, London, Falmer Press.

Weiser, J. (1999) *Photo Therapy Techniques: Exploring the Secrets of Personal Snapshots and Family Albums*, Vancouver: Photo Therapy Centre.

West, N. M. (2000) *Kodak and the Lens of Nostalgia*, Charlottesville, VA: The University Press of Virginia.

White, M.(1993) *The Material Child: Coming of Age in Japan and America*, New York: The Free Press.

Williams, M. (1998) "Remembering Barbie," unpublished M.Ed. monograph, McGill University.

Willis, P. (1990) *Common Culture: Symbolic Work at Play in the Everyday Cultures of the Young,* Milton Keynes: Open University Press.

Willis, S. (1991) *A Primer for Daily Life*, London: Routledge.

Winship, J. (1987) *Inside Women's Magazines*, London: Pandora Press.

Wojcik-Andrews, I. (2000) *Children's Films: History, Ideology, Pedagogy, Theory*, New York: Garland Press.

Wong, L. (ed.) (1999) *Shootback: Photos by Kids from the Nairobi Slums*, London: Booth-Clibborn.

Woodward, K. (1991) *Aging and Its Discontents: Freud and Other Fictions*, Bloomington: Indiana University Press.

—— (1999) Introduction in K. Woodward (ed.) *Figuring Age: Women, Bodies, Generations,* Bloomington: Indiana University Press.

Wuest, P. (2001) *Beloved,* Munich: Kechayoff.

Yoe, C. (ed.) (1994) *The Art of Barbie: Artists Celebrate the World's Favorite Doll*, New York: Workman.

Zandy, J. (ed.) (1995) *Liberating Memory: Our Work and Our Working-class Consciousness,* New Brunswick, NJ: Rutgers University Press.

Zipes, J. (2001) *Sticks and Stones: The Troublesome Success of Children's Literature from Slovenly Peter to Harry Potter*, New York: Routledge.

Index